From Big Sky to the Badlands

Two Decades of Trailin' Sheep

JOHN STONE

outskirts
press

Dedication

*This work is dedicated to my Father and Mother,
Tom and Mary Stone with all my admiration for the life
they lived and all my love for the gifts they gave.*

*John Danley Stone
Harrisonburg, Virginia
2019*

Table of Contents

Author's Introduction

WHILE IT MAY sound like a given, I must begin by saying "I knew my Dad." I began to know him in the West River area of South Dakota when he "taught me to drive a tractor" when I was not yet 5 years old. I can still hear his instructions as he rode horseback alongside the little Farmall C as we tried to get back to the ranch site (He said the horse would have spooked if he had tied it to the tractor to lead). I knew him as we sat in our little "loaned" Jeep in front of the Red Owl (grocery store) in Pierre, South Dakota every other Friday night while Mama shopped for groceries before she drove us back to the ranch—in the cold and after dark. It was a time for Rosalie and me to listen to Daddy talk about "town" and some of the people we saw in downtown Pierre. We could not have imagined that within two years we would be living within 2 ½ blocks of that very parking spot.

I knew him when I walked with him and proudly carried his large (to me) black lunch bucket to the Federal Housing project in north Pierre (residences being built to house the Oahe Dam Federal workers). It was a trip that seemed like miles for my short legs, but gave me a chance to ask countless questions—most of which he answered in his own inimitable manner. I would stay at the project all day, have lunch with him and then walk back home to 112 Rear West Pleasant Drive (our tarpaper duplex in an alley in town).

I knew him when I tried to get him to come to PTA so my room could compete for the parent's attendance prize and didn't understand why he would be embarrassed because he could not "sign in."

It was shortly thereafter that I taught him to write his name—a memorable experience as he was totally left-handed, but I wouldn't allow that. He did it as I instructed him—with his right hand, in cursive but with all small letters. He was not insulted nor did he seem appreciative but used his new skill the rest of his life.

I knew him when he came to live with me when I taught both high school and college in the Black Hills of South Dakota. We would spend hours sitting on the wooden steps of my rented duplex and hours riding in my car through the grasslands of northwest South Dakota—country that he was revisiting for the first time in over a quarter century. This was the country around Belle Fourche, Sturgis and Newell—and he could see the 5200-foot Bear Butte (Mato Paha) rising in the distance. It was revisiting a life of the past but a life that was truly loved.

We saw miles of rolling grassland where he and my Mother built their lives and their family together. I could sense the affection (perhaps not as strong as love) he had for this country. *It was a place where he could survive*—on his own, not dependent on anyone else. That was his way. As he described his memories and told me of some of the bad times he had lived in "this country"—the long cold winter nights and the hot, dry summers—yet how he loved those days of what must have been personal freedom and accomplishment. He talked of the times when he literally risked his life to care for a herd of sheep—and the long winter when he buried his 18—month old baby girl just outside Elm Springs (SD). He still had his bearings as he gestured due east.

Our early days and weeks in Pierre were taken getting adjusted to "city life." For all of us, this was a real change. None of the kids had ever lived in a town and Tom and Mary hadn't lived this close to others for over 25 years. This was new for all of us. We had to get used to neighbors, the kids were going to start school and Tom and Mary had to find a way to make a living.

While we lived in Pierre, he worked "away from home" much of the time with the Army Corps of Engineers as a "contract laborer."

It was not until my Mother and Father bought a small restaurant in downtown Pierre (SD) that I was around them every day—as the entire family worked in Stone's Café. My older sister and I did everything except the major cooking. We waited on tables, cut up French fries, served meals, bused and washed dishes, cleaned counters and booths, took cash, swept floors, cleaned the bathroom and scrubbed the entire café each night. I can vividly remember coming down from Junior High school every noon to help by waiting tables and cleaning. My pay was the knowledge that my Mom and Dad appreciated it. At that time in my life, that was enough.

I would not deny that the Dad I "knew" was quite likely not the same man that my older brother and sisters remember. Such is the case in many families with multiple children. The relationships—at least the *perceived* relationships—are unavoidably different. To me, that is not surprising. For while my Dad did not change very much in the years I knew him, the circumstances in which he and our family lived were quite different for the *older three kids and the younger three* (remembering that Dorothy Jean died at 18 months of age).

To me, my Dad was always concerned about two major things: first, it was important to him that my sisters and I got *enough* to eat—pretty basic; but that's who he was. And second, he wanted us to go to school—and when we did, to get something out of it and behave ourselves. I'm convinced that was one of the ways he said "I love you and care about your future." The older I get, the better I understand that my Dad did not have a "good" father model—he only had his own father. I'm also convinced that he had little idea about *what* our futures might entail—he seemed willing to leave that up to us—not unlike the way he had built his own life.

My Dad quite likely lived his life from day-to-day with little concern for/control of the future—at least in the long-term. He probably had no idea "what was out there for young people" as he would so often say: "That's your business."

After the café in Pierre burned down, he started a small café on his own in Ft. Pierre—a town that seemed to "fit" him better. In Ft.

Pierre, he and I were together nearly every day as I worked at a high-way gas station starting my high school years. In his first small café (seating 20), he did not have a waitress (my Mom did not join him in this venture) so he did all the cooking, cleaning and "managing the business." And, as always, he spent the time he was closed to do the shopping. And while we didn't talk much during my short lunch breaks, just be being together we showed a concern for each other in our own way. He seemed proud that I worked "hard" every day. There was no doubt we were quite different in many ways. And, while we didn't show our feelings in the same ways, we had a mutual sense—mostly respect for hard work, and some not-so-obvious love for each other. He wasn't one to openly show love for anyone and would have been embarrassed if I had openly shown my love for him. It was obvious that "Stone men" did not do that.

Driving was a bit of a problem as he did not have a driver's license. Since he still lived in Pierre, he had to get across the river each day to his café. He had convinced the Chief of Police in Pierre to write him a personal note that he carried in his billfold giving him permission to drive. As I now look back on this predicament, it was just short of amazing.

He left the smaller café and rented a larger restaurant in Ft. Pierre that he planned to run with my second-oldest sister Jody. She was a great manager and a good restauranteur with a considerable amount of experience in food service.

She eventually moved into an apartment in the back of the restaurant with her family of three children and her husband. Relations between the three adults were sometimes strained but the business did well. She and her husband took good care of my Dad. Still, he seemed restless and wanted to move on again. After about 6 months of the "new partnership," my Dad started feeling "closed in" and wanted to do "his thing"—whatever that might have been. It was about time for him to walk away—again.

Soon, my Dad was doing work as a "private contractor" (he wouldn't have called himself that). He got a group of customers through word-of-mouth and took care of their lawns, shrubberies and flower gardens as though they were his own—and he did it for a very reasonable price. His financial needs were quite minimal.

He had some problems. He needed to drive and haul his own equipment, so he got an old pickup truck and, after a manner, learned to drive it. The note in his billfold was evidence he "could" drive. This actually worked fairly well until he had his first accident. ("Why the hell would I need insurance?") A second problem was that he worked his own schedule. My dad always believed that he should "get up and work when the sun came up" and "you oughta go to bed when the sun goes down." The former works fine until you start mowing lawns between 4 and 5 AM in some of the nicer neighborhoods where he worked. This was work he continued until he finally left Pierre "for good" after a small, unsettled traffic accident. He went to Phoenix, Arizona and would never return to South Dakota. He didn't want to. He loved the sun and the fact that there were few "weather restrictions" in Phoenix.

My mother most often excused my Dad's attitudes of intolerance, closed-mindedness and prejudice with "you just can't blame him for the way he was raised." In later years, as I spent considerable time in his native north Georgia, I saw some of "how he was raised." My father practiced an either-or orientation about most things: "If you ain't with me, you're agin' me." You were either "right or you were wrong." And, in most cases, if you disagreed with him, he wanted little to do with you. People surely learn their values, beliefs, language habits and attitudes early in life. While these fundamental systems may change *some* as we grow older, it often takes a major event (or series of events) to modify them significantly—they are very deep-seated. My Dad changed some, but not very much—not that I expected him to change. First impressions stayed with him a long time. If you ever lied to him or were disloyal to him, *he would not forgive you.* He believed every person, unless badly physically or mentally disabled, should "stand on their own two feet."

Tom Stone's thoughts of the *future* were most likely about

tomorrow and perhaps stretched to early next week. While his life was somewhat under his control, the circumstances that surrounded his life were certainly outside his very limited sphere of influence. He didn't like that. He could not do much about it. Long-term plans were not something he had ever made—it had been the next watering hole and feeding area for the sheep. It was about café supplies for the next couple of days. He had little or no idea where he, Mary and the kids would be a year from now. He could, for the most part, control the *immediate* circumstances of his life and that of his family. Quite frankly, not much else seemed to matter.

He was a "person of the moment." Looking back, my Mom and Dad actually had few options except to live this way. Momma thought pretty much the same as Dad. Perhaps she had to do so.

Because of the pressing needs of *today*, she couldn't afford to think about much past next week. This type of short-term thinking was their shaky foundation for never owning a house—not even a car for many years and moving from one rental unit to another on a regular basis for many years. Deep down, this type of truncated, nomadic thinking was actually counter to Mary Stone's fundamental nature. Their circumstances, however, did not really allow her to do otherwise.

Although my Mom had lost her parents while still very young, she had known stability. She had known loving and caring fundamental family units. She had known roots. But, she loved Tom Stone and was loyal, often blindly, to him. She would, and did, follow him almost anywhere as a willing helper—giving up almost everything in their meager quests.

I rarely saw my Dad hug or kiss my Mom although I'm sure he did. As a matter of fact, I never saw him hug or kiss anyone—an overt show of affection was not a part of who he had learned to be and still was. I never heard him say "I love you" to anyone except a little dog he had in later life, though, I'm sure he told my Mom that, albeit not often. I believe he showed his love by providing for us *the best he could*—enough to eat and a place to sleep. My Mom showed her love for him through her never-wavering loyalty—even though she must have questioned him at times. Our Mom was very special. She told us more than often that she loved us and was a truly affectionate person. Her attempts to show affection to my Dad, were met with "oh, go on with that damned stuff." Unusual circumstances brought them together. An apparently deep, abiding love kept them together, in some manner, for over 52 years.

John D. Stone

CHAPTER 1

From Big Sky to the Badlands: Setting

FROM BIG SKY to the Badlands is about the life of George Thomas Dewey Stone. Tom Stone was born outside Dalton, Georgia on May 29, 1900 (though the 1900 census says he was born in 1898). He left this earth on February 12, 1978 in Phoenix, Arizona. His life was a menagerie of resurfacing familial scars, exasperating independence, intense personal and "professional" loyalties and the apparent belief for most of his life that showing love was a sign of weakness.

The Stone family had emigrated from the Roxburgh (sp. also Roxburghshire) district in Scotland. Roxburgh was one of the border areas that stood between England (Cumbria and Northumberland) on the south and the "counties of Dumfries, Selkirk and Berwick (Scotland) to the north. The people who lived in these areas were called Borderers. And, they lived in 6 distinct sections (counties) or Marches. 3 were controlled by the English and 3 by the Scots.

> Ask a Scotsman where 'the Borders' are and he will indicate the counties of Roxburgh, Selkirk, Peebles and Berwick. . . . Ask an Englishman where 'the Borders' are and he may well not know, but he will recognise

the singular 'Border'. To him it means the frontier with Scotland and nothing else (Fraser, 2008, 33).

At their "peak," it is estimated that some 45,000 Scots lived in the Borders while the English population is judged to have been about 117, 000. While there is some question as to the precise population of the 6 Marches, there is little issue about the kind of people they were:

> Visiting contemporaries as well as local sources are emphatic. Barbarous, crafty, vengeful, crooked, quarrelsome, tough, perverse, active, and deceitful. . . . In general, it is conceded that the Borderers, English and Scottish were much alike, that they made excellent soldiers if disciplined, but that the raw material was hard, wild, and ill to tame. (Fraser, 2008, 42)

This was the heritage of the Stones who lived in the Marches of Scotland. They were tough and they were mean. They feuded with each other, they stole from each other and many with whom they associated *disappeared* from their communities. In many ways, this heritage was unavoidably a major part of what the Stones brought to America.

In the middle ages, the Roxburgh District had at least as much importance and population as did Edinburgh to the northwest but it was gradually torn apart by constant battles among the inhabitants (the Scots against the English, the Scots against the Scots and the English against the English). Without "profiling" the clans, they were thrust into a role of defending their homeland against almost constant threats from the south—the hated English. Such behaviors became an attitude that still lives today in some corners of Scotland.

Having booked passages to America, (c. 1740) the early members of the Stone family settled in Schenectady, NY. Shortly thereafter, they moved near the city of Spartanburg, SC (northwest section of South Carolina). William Stone (b. 1730) was the paternal head of the clan who married Victoria James (b. 1733). They had one child—a son named John Stone who was born in Spartanburg, SC in 1754.

John Stone married Irene Winegar (b. 1755) and they moved to Pickens, South Carolina (80 miles east of Spartanburg near Greenville, SC). They would have 5 children. Their first-born, James Stone, was born in Pickens County, SC (1805) and the family soon moved again to Walton County, Georgia (just east of Atlanta)—a trip of some 240 miles. It was in Walton County that James Stone (sometimes inaccurately referred to in historical records as James, Jr.) married Rachel Ellison (b. March 6, 1811—d. August 11, 1885) on February 8, 1829.

James Joel Stone, Jr. was their eldest son (August 1, 1836—September 10, 1918). James Joel was born in Walton County, Georgia on August 1, 1836. He married Mary Roberts (May 23, 1843—June 6, 1914) at Tilton , Georgia on January 19, 1860, moved to Carbondale Community in south Whitfield County where they raised 10 children: Robert E. Lee, Eliza Ann, James Buchanan, Dollie, M.A. (Mug), Margaret Emma, Sally, John W., Lulu, and Grover Cleveland.

James Joel Stone enlisted in the Army of the Confederacy on March 10, 1862 for three years or the duration of the Civil War. He was assigned to Company C, 39th Georgia Volunteer Infantry. Early in the War Between the States, James Stone served at Missionary Ridge (Chattanooga, TN) and Vicksburg, MS (Baker's Creek/Champion Hill). After the Confederate surrender at Vicksburg, he became a prisoner for a period of only 4 days and was able to rejoin his company by the fall of 1863, and was initially stationed at Lookout Mountain (Chattanooga, TN) under the command of Major General Carter C. Stevenson. Their goal was to intercept the Union forces led by Major General "Fightin'" Joe Hooker. His company was soon moved to the Wauhatchie Valley just north of Chattanooga to serve under General Braxton Bragg.

As Confederate troops again moved to occupy Missionary Ridge,

James Joel Stone, Jr. [1836-1918] married Mary Roberts in 1860 after his service in the Civil War. He had lost part of his right leg. At home in Whitfield County, GA Parents of Robert E. Lee Stone

General William Tecumseh Sherman's troops attacked but were re-pelled by counterattacking Confederate forces. The Army of the CSA wintered near Dalton (GA) during 1863-64 in preparation for Sher-man's inevitable march on Atlanta. In a series of battles, Stone's di-vision fought at Rocky Face Ridge, Resaca, Cassville, New Hope Church, Kolb Farm, Kennesaw Mountain and Ezra Church.

General John Bell Hood assumed command of the Confederate forces and learned that the Union army was moving toward Jones-borough, GA (Jonesboro current spelling). On the afternoon of Au-gust 31, 1864, the 39th (Stone's volunteer regiment) was engaged at Jonesboro. James Stone suffered a serious wound (mini-ball) and was told that his right leg would have to be amputated. After battlefield surgery, he was sent to the Ocmulgee Hospital (Macon, GA) to recu-perate. He was in the hospital at the time of the surrender of the Army of the Confederacy in April, 1865. A few weeks later, "Colonel" James Joel Stone returned to Whitfield County to resume farming. His wife (Mary Roberts) passed on June 6, 1914 and James Joel Stone died on September 10, 1918.

Within two generations, the Stone family had propagated and moved into the northwest corner of Georgia—near what is now Dal-ton. Northwest Georgia would be home to most of the Stones for the next century and beyond. There would be very limited "defec-tions" from the family and those that did so [left the family] were duly chastised for "turning on" their kin. While they were, and still are, clannish,[1] they seem to quickly find fault with each other, fight with each other and have even been known to even shoot a relative in one

---

1   The first 3 Georgia generations of the Stone family are buried in one of two cemeteries southwest of Dalton, Georgia. With the exception of R.L. (Robert Lee) and Lizzie (Mary Elizabeth Harper) Stone and their offspring, who are buried at the Swamp Creek Methodist Church Cemetery, the Stones are buried at the Swamp Creek Baptist Church Cemetery—located within a short distance of each other.

of their family squabbles.[2]

The oldest child of James Joel Stone and Mary Roberts Stone was Robert Edward Lee Stone (October 2, 1864-September 2, 1945). Robert Edward Lee Stone (R.L.) married Mary Elizabeth Harper (December 1, 1866—February 27, 1939). They had 6 children and raised a seventh (discussed later).

George Thomas Dewey Stone (Tom) was born on May 29, 1900 and passed on February 12, 1978.[3] This is a story of a good part of Tom Stone's life as he lived through some good times—and some he described as "just about as tough as hell."

---

2 Tom Stone was actually shot by his younger brother Paul during a fight involving R.L. and demands for money by Paul. Tom nearly died and was a day away from losing a leg when he surprisingly recovered. Tom never ceased to express disdain for Paul and vowed never to return to the Georgia "home place." At the urging of the author, Tom reluctantly returned in 1972.

3 This is the date Tom Stone always used as his birthdate. Census records for 1900 lists him as two years old when the census was taken in June,1900. This would indicate that Tom Stone was more likely born in 1898.

Robert Edward Lee Stone [1864-1945] and wife Mary Elizabeth Harper Stone [1866-1939] at home in Whitfield County, GA. Parents of Thomas D. Stone

CHAPTER 2

Tom Stone: Whitfield County Georgia

THE U.S. CENSUS reported that some 14,500 people lived in Whitfield County Georgia on the day George Thomas Dewey Stone was born, May 29, 1900 (see footnote 3 on page 6). Of course, even if Tom Stone could have known that, such data would not have impacted him.

Tom was the third child of Robert Edward Lee (R.L.) and Lizzie (Mary Elizabeth Harper) Stone. In order of their birth, Fred Brown, Mary, George Thomas Dewey (Tom), Robert Paul (Paul), Jessie Mae, Minnie Lee and James ("Little Jim") were the children of R.L. and Lizzie Stone. ("Little Jim," whose given name was Grover--ostensibly the son of Mary Townshend Stone their oldest daughter—was born from a relationship in Dalton. He was raised by R.L. and Lizzie as one of their own and referred to by many as a "catch colt").

Tom was born into a family that was, thanks to the business acumen of R.L. Stone, fairly well off. At one time, R.L. Stone was said to have owned 7 "farms" and made considerable income off such ventures as huckleberry harvesting. R.L. and his family picked the huckleberries from local hillsides (free), packaged them and shipped them to market for a nearly 100% profit. "Huckleberry Bob," as he was known, was reported to have made thousands of dollars from such harvests over the years. At the "home place," they raised their own meat (hogs) and maintained a large garden under Lizzie's direction. R.L. was also a salaried officer of the law, working in the areas of revenue collections and process serving. As one who knew nearly everyone in the Whitfield County area, he was known as a "realistic enforcer" of the laws.

Although not for sale, R.L. produced moonshine from at least two stills he operated (regularly producing "good whiskey") in the hills surrounding the home place. [4]

Profiling family members from disparate and mixed reports is not an easy task. Fred, the oldest of the Stone children, was, according to his younger brother Tom, "the laziest person ever to set foot on earth." While Fred married and had children, his wife divorced him and Fred lived alone for most of his life, spending his days "walking the railroad tracks into town" (Carbondale), then immediately turning around to walk back home.

The oldest daughter in the family, Mary, lived in nearby Dalton most of her life. According to an email of February 16, 2003, "Mary Stone Townshend was a well-known prostitute in the area. Mary Townshend was always in some sort of trouble and Robert Lee cut her out of his will because of her scandalous activities." Her only known child was nicknamed "Little Jim" in honor of his great-grandfather, James Joel Stone. R.L. and Lizzie "raised" Little Jim.

Robert Paul (Paul) lived his entire life in and around the Dalton area. As the youngest of the children, he was considered his mother's "favorite." Tom remembers Paul as never working, even around the farm and constantly pestering R.L. for money. Paul, in his younger days, always had plenty of girlfriends—apparently a practice he continued as he was married multiple times during his life. While Tom

---

[4] It was a most common practice for the people of this area to operate a still to make whiskey (moonshine) for their own consumption and that of friends. The rationale for not collecting taxes was that the whiskey was *not being sold*. While R.L. Stone's sworn duty as a deputy sheriff was to "destroy" such installations, it was widely known that only those making "bad whiskey" would be torn down. The making of "good" whiskey was acceptable and not taxed in most instances.

never cared much for his younger brother, he would eventually develop a deep "hatred" for him as Paul shot him with a pistol during an argument with R.L.—over money.

Jessie Mae was the fifth of the Stone children. She early on developed a "reputation" around Dalton and moved north to Chattanooga, Tennessee. When asked about a rumor of being married more than once in Chattanooga, she responded with a chuckle, "I had a couple of 'em." Later in her life, she would develop diabetes and was a double amputee (both legs). She still dipped snuff (and enjoyed it), ate anything she wanted in spite of her illness and unavoidable reactions went regularly to "rasslin" matches and seemed to enjoy her life until the early 2000's. Until her death, she was cared for by her extremely loyal and devoted husband Ernest Davis—who passed away in 2003.

Very little is known about Tom's sister Minnie as records of her life are scant at best. The same seems true of Grover ("Little Jim"). He was never a healthy child and passed away at an early age. Grover Stone is buried in the Swamp Creek Methodist Church Cemetery outside Dalton. It's notable that in talking with members of the family, you could "convince" them to remember and talk *some* about others that had passed. Still, they said very little and if they did not like the person in question, the conversation would be quite brief.

This was a family Tom Stone seemed to know little about. Sadly, he seemed to prefer it that way. He had little or no desire to be in contact with them and resisted efforts by others to do so. When asked about his family in Georgia, his typical cautioning response was: "You don't know what they's like. I can tell you one thing, you'll be damned sorry if you have anything to do with any of 'em." The feelings were obviously deep and had been built up over many years. Even with the 1973 visit, such feelings changed little--if at all.

When the opportunity arose to visit the Georgia family in 1973, Mary strongly encouraged her husband to make the trip. She went so far as to suggest that "people change over time—that they would have mellowed." Tom's response was terse:

> Hell no. I don't want nothin' to do with any of 'em. They wasn't any good then and they ain't changed. And I'll tell you somthin' else: if you ever knew 'um, you'd know what I meant and feel just like me. My brothers were so damned lazy they stunk; my sisters didn't know right from wrong and when it came to my Dad. . . well, he was about the meanest man I ever seen.

Tom Stone was raised on a "farm" near Carbondale, Georgia by his parents, R.L. and Lizzie Stone. He went to school—some—but never learned to read or write much. While he had a seemingly oblig-atory *respect* for his parents, he had little use for his 6 brothers and sisters—family was not much more than a biological state of being. The concept of *love* seemed totally foreign—and unspeakable. Until much later in his life, Tom Stone seemed to regard "loving someone" as a sign of weakness.

R.L. (as he was known in Whitfield County) and Lizzie (the name R.L. used most of the time to address his wife when he didn't refer to her as "old woman") raised their family much like others in the area. The children were supposed to do chores, feed stock (pigs, chickens and mules), and help their mother in her garden. R.L. had built a good-sized house outside Carbondale with an upstairs loft for sleep-ing and a large open fireplace that served for both heat and cooking.

It was a good house. It was solid and well-built. It served the basic needs of the Stone family—even when some of them moved back home for a time—with or without *their own* family members. In that sense, it seemed that family, no matter what the conditions, were always welcome at the home place. And while there were no open "displays of affection" or "expressions of sentiment," members of the family could come and go as they wished

The fireplace served two coffee pots. R.L.'s pot was *his* and *his alone.* Each morning he merely added more coffee and water before boiling. He did not empty the pot until it got so full of grounds he could add no more water or coffee. The second pot was for the remainder of the family.

Lizzie also had 3 frypans (cast-iron skillets) that she used for baking biscuits each morning. These were "flat top" biscuits and did not rise.[5] These three pans of biscuits were to last all day—they were eaten with each meal. After biscuit service, the pans were used for frying meat (virtually all the meat the Stones ate was fried) on the open fireplace or cooking those vegetables that needed preparation (i.e., okra). The Stones lived a simple life. But, they had all they "needed" right on the home place.

R.L. Stone had two stills (moonshine) up in the hills near his home where he made "good" whiskey. Obviously, this was a value he instilled in his boys as they would eventually set up their own stills. The small still was 5 gallons and the larger was slightly over twice that size. This was not whiskey to sell—it was whiskey for personal/family/guest consumption and to be used as a gift for special friends. R.L. checked his stills nearly every day—assessing the final "product" with a small test tube. He dipped the test tube in the batch and took a drink. A skilled "whiskey man" could tell if it was good and when it was ready.

While they raised some chickens and hogs on the farm, they were only for food (not for sale) "We had a couple a mules but old Jack and the other one just hung around the house. Dad did use them to pull the wagon into town ever' so offen—otherwise, they didn't do much a' nothin.'" The house was big enough for R.L.'s family and even an occasional "guest" now and then—if you didn't

---

5   When Tom and Mary Stone came to live with R.L .and Lizzie at the home place outside Dalton in late 1932, Mary "took over" the house—*her first real house* as a wife and mother. She did the cooking and caregiving. Mary made what R.L. called "high top" biscuits. He enjoyed them immensely. To the normal ingredients of flour, water and lard, Mary also added baking soda so her biscuits were fluffy and light. Her biscuits actually rose so they had "high tops."

need much privacy. It was apparent that Lizzie ran the kitchen and the garden. R.L. ran everything else and nobody ever questioned him—about anything.

> I 'magine my mother was like mothers were sposed to be in Georgie.' Tom would say, almost lamenting. 'Women had as many kids as they could and their husband wanted them to have. She stayed home except when we went to church and they were quiet— women did not speak their opinions about nothin' in those days. Mother was very quiet and just tended her garden out back—with our help whenever Dad told us she needed it. I guess Dad treated her like you're sposed to treat your wife. He could be pretty damned mean to her—he even brought women home from town. Mother never said anything about that.

And so, this was the model of a family and a husband and wife that Tom Stone knew. He had seen the way his Uncle John and Aunt Mat lived—and it was very different from the relationship his mother and father had. Still, the example set by his "blood" would seem to become a part of who he was. Sadly, this example would often surface in his relationships with his own family in the years to come.

While the Stone's house may have been considered somewhat primitive by modern standards, it was typical for that part of the country in the early 1900's. It was well built and did not leak during the frequent rains. It kept most of the cold out during the damp Georgia winters and had two out-buildings (one for animals and one for storage of feed and cobs used for heat). R.L. also had a shelter with sides and back but no front door where he kept his wagon. Near the wagon shelter was a 5-foot pit into which R.L. lowered a hog at least twice a year. After continuous feeding the hog got so fat it couldn't stand up any longer. Then the hog was raised up with the ropes tied around him/her and butchered. Tom remembers "only keepin' the hams, roasts and some side meat for seasonin'." They didn't keep things like ribs or bacon except for use in cooking with greens or pinto beans. "We ate good. My mother had plenty of chickens and her big garden. There was always plenty to eat. In life, you don't ask for much more than that-- enough to eat and a dry place to sleep."

Tom Stone's own family would hear that same philosophy expressed many times in their lives—especially if they complained about not having "the finer things of life."

R.L. Stone grew some cotton and each of the kids got a bale a year to sell for spending money. Whatever else he was, Bob Lee was a good businessman. His huckleberry business was nearly 100% profit—the berries, the labor and even the shipping were provided at no charge to him. After each shipment, R.L. arrived at home with the front pocket of his bib overalls full of cash money—even though he had shared some of his earnings on the way home while passing certain houses of "personal acquaintances." Everyone knew—but again, nobody said a word.

Tom often remarked: "We lived pretty good."

The family was close. *Not* in the sense of affection but in the ways they stayed together. Tom Harper (Lizzie's parents) and the rest of his family lived over near Ugly Girls Holler and they visited on occasion. Nobody strayed very far from their basic roots—that was not acceptable. At least in the first two Georgia generations of Stones, it was unheard of. *You did not leave your kin*—the family took care of each other.

"My grandmother and grandfather lived within two miles of the home place so we visited them reglur. And even though they were my father's parents, they seemed quite different from him. They were happy and seemed to care about each other."

> I remember my grandmother pretty good. She wasn't 5 feet tall and stood under my grandfather's arm (he was 6'8" tall). She wore a number 2 shoe, played the fiddle and liked to dance. Like many of the women in the area (and likely the south), she dipped snuff, smoked a

pipe and took a drink ever' now and agin.' She wasn't like my mother—she almost always seemed happy.

"James Joel Stone (my grandfather) looked rough and tough. He was tall and pretty thin and had some health issues since he lost his leg in the war." Eventually, he would have to have his other leg amputated as well. Still, he got around with some help on a small wagon and moved around the house on a small cart with wheels.

"After my grandmother (his wife Rachel) died, he lived with each of his children for about a month at a time during the year. Colonel Stone, as everyone called him, seemed content to make his brief visits and spend the remainder of the year in an 'old soldier's home.'" Even as disabled as he was, he was still fiercely independent:

> I'll tell ya: He always paid his own way and before he left at the end of the month, he gave my Dad a couple of gold coins that he kep' in a little box on his cart for his month's keep. 'Payin' your own way was how it was sposed to be.'

"When I think about my grandmother and grandfather-and I knew them real good—I can't see how my Dad turned out the way he did. They was both decent people."

In those days "people stayed to themselves and didn't bother each other much." Most everybody got along OK because you knew enough to mind your own business. It wasn't that people didn't know what other people were doing but they didn't talk about it. It wasn't that people didn't know that some men messed around with women who weren't their wives, but they didn't talk about it. It wasn't that people didn't know where most everybody's still was, but they didn't talk about it. People just kept to their own.

The third generation of the Georgia Stones was not like the first two. When they found themselves unhappy with their lives, some of them rebelled. Some of them had multiple marriages. Some of them moved away from the home place and built lives of their own. For whatever reasons, this third generation did not hold fast to their roots.

Tom Stone left home twice. The first time he was in his late teens. This late summer venture was to "Ugly Girls Holler" near where his mother had been raised. It was just east of Dalton and near his Grandfather (Tom) Harper's general store. He stayed there for "the better part of a year" but the code of the valley betrayed him. R.L. was visiting Tom Harper's store one day late the next spring when grandfather Harper remarked that "I see your boy Tom is stayin' down in the holler." By the end of the day, R.L. Stone had found Tom and brought him back to the home place—leaving Tom with reminders he would never forget. Later, Tom would admit that his Dad "beat me so bad that he damn' near killed me." It was then that Tom Stone swore to himself that "If I ever get outta here agin, I'll get so damned far away he'll never find me. If I don't, he'll beat me to death."

If one recognizes that "we learn what we live," it would be accurate to conclude that offspring develop their personalities (in large measure) from those who raise them and from the specific environment in which they are reared. And, such exposure can "teach" in both positive and negative senses. Tom Stone would seem to have been a good example of both influences. Knowing this, he often vowed to "never be like they was."

During the early part of World War I, Tom Stone was too young to serve in the military. Even so, he found a way to work for his country and get away from home at the same time when he joined the efforts to build a storage and munitions plant for the Construction Division of the U.S. Army in Muscle Shoals, Alabama (not far from the home place). He worked there for over a year, saved some of his pay and made plans (secretly) for his future—plans that did *not* include any of the Stones and would be void of life in Whitfield County, Georgia. True to his character as well, Tom never talked to anybody about his strategies. First, he "didn't trust any of 'em" and didn't think his plans "was anybody's else's business." Besides, he knew that if his Dad found out, there would be hell to pay—he'd paid that before.

16

CHAPTER 3

Walking to Montana: Toward a New Life

NEARLY 3 YEARS later, Tom Stone set out again taking what he needed for the *rest of his life* in a rucksack over his shoulder. With the "clothes on his back" and his small pack, he left home early one spring morning—never intending to return to his family. He had not said a word to anyone. Tom Stone did not know "eezackly" where he was going, but he did know that he would be getting out of the reach of his Dad. That day in the early months of 1920, Tom Stone would begin his walk—to Montana.

He did not know it yet, but ahead of him was a 1650 mile trip to a place he had never even heard of. For a young man on foot with all his worldly possessions in a gunney sack over his shoulder, the task before him now sounds surreal. Tom caught the train in Dalton (GA). With the help of his uncle Mug (his Dad's brother Marion who had also "left" the family) who worked for the Southern Railroad (which controlled most of the rail lines across the south). Tom rode to the end of the line near Ft. Worth in north Texas.

In his tote, he had packed a clean pair of "long-handled under-wear, 2 pairs a socks, a half-dozen biscuits, some salt pork, a bag a coffee, a fryin' pan, a can for boilin' coffee, a light coat and my own little still." He didn't want anything else from what was never going to be home again—and he didn't want to take anything that "wasn't his'n." He got off the train and started walking north and "kep' the sun on his right side in the mornin' and on his other side at night." And, he never looked back. He didn't know where he was going—but that it was north and "none of them was gonna be around."

Neither did Tom Stone think about how far he was going—only that he was "gonna git a helluva of a long ways away." To his family in north Georgia, Tom Stone had now committed the unforgiveable sin—he had left them. And while they did actually "invite" him back some 10 years later, they never forgot—and they never completely forgave him. In that part of the country, it seemed that nobody ever completely forgave anybody.

Tom Stone was a nomad—in the literal sense. While he and Mary Ellen Danley would be married for over 50 years, they lived separately much of the time and never owned a place to live—always renting or living in housing (including the sheep wagons while herding) provided by their employer. And, they moved often.

During the early years of their marriage, "home" was a sheep wagon—an all-purpose unit built for both cooking and sleeping on the prairies of eastern Montana and western South Dakota. (For a thorough discussion of the traditional sheep wagon, see Chapter 9)

Later, as their family grew, their employer supplied them with two wagons—one for cooking and supplies and the second for sleeping. During the worst parts of the winter, Mary and the children moved to various small cabin courts (a one-room unit) in towns closest to the location where Tom was wintering the herd. *They never did own the wagons nor any of the sheep.* As Tom often remarked, "I owned my horse and the saddle I rode on." In addition, virtually all those who lived in that part of the country owned their own firearms (usually a Winchester 30.30 and a sidearm of choice).

Tom and Mary had little income and lived "close to the land." Yet, while they didn't have much of anything except each other, that seemed enough for the time being. And, for all intents and purposes, "we didn't have anybody around to tell us what we could and couldn't do."

Mean? At times. Tough? As tough as he needed to be to survive. Proud? Very—often to a fault. Did he have a strong set of principles? After some consideration you would likely conclude that he did. Prejudiced? He learned it early and it never left. A bitter grudge-holder? For sure. A survivor? Without a doubt! In the final analysis, this was Tom Stone. He was a pretty simple north Georgia man who transplanted himself in a brand-new world. All these traits were part of who he was. Most of the times he acted *proud* of who he was. And he spent most of his life looking for a place where he could "be who he needed to be."

Tom Stone had most likely never heard of Ekalaka, Montana where he would eventually wind up—Tom Stone most likely had never even heard of the state of Montana. Quite likely, all he knew about what was north or west of Tennessee was what he had heard from others while working on the Muscle Shoals project. But as he would later remark, "I'd heerd enough to think it was a place he wanted to go." He had "heerd" that it was big, there was work to be had there if you "was willin" and he heard that people there left you alone. The older Tom got, the more important this became to him. It was likely he didn't know much about the states he would have to go through to get to Montana either—that was likely something he had missed in Geography class.

He knew nothing about Texas to the west except what his Uncle Mug told him after the train was well under way. He had probably never heard of Oklahoma, Kansas, Nebraska, Wyoming and South Dakota either. And as he walked through them on his way north, he may not have been aware of where he was at the time. Anyway, it didn't matter much—he was going to Montana.

He had little idea of how he was going to eat or where he was going to sleep on his trip, little idea how far it was or how long it would take him to get there. He was young enough, angry enough—and a little bit scared of getting caught—that he had little fear of these unknown things. What he did know was that there were places a "long ways from Corbindale" and all his family. Tom Stone had decided that even a life about which he knew very little, had to be better than the life he had known at home. He knew wherever he was, he could make a new life for himself, and most importantly, be left alone to do what he wanted to do.

Thanks to his uncle Mug (R.L.'s estranged brother Marion), Tom was able to ride the train from Carbondale, Georgia to the end of the line in north Texas—a trip of nearly a thousand miles. Mug, who worked for the railroad, wasn't the least bit hesitant to help his nephew get away from the rest of the family—that *he* knew fairly well. For he was a Stone himself and 14 years before had done just what Tom was doing—"he had gotten the hell outta there." He knew them well and had a personal sense of what Tom had to deal with at the home place.

Heading north, Tom walked—and he walked. By the end of his journey to Ekalaka, Montana, Tom Stone, now in his early twenties, had ridden the train and walked close to 1650 miles—it had taken him weeks as he frequently stopped at places where he could work for food and "lodging." This young man on a mission willingly traded "pickin' rocks in the field" or "fixin' fence around the corral" for some pitched hay to sleep on in the barn, a hot meal and some extra food to take along for the next couple days on the "trail." While rare, some along the trail were hesitant to help Tom Stone—a perfect stranger. When he could not find someone to help, he bedded down under the best shelter he could find. He wasn't in any hurry. He wasn't really going any specific place in particular. It was just important to keep going "away" from a "specific place" he knew too well.

He came north through the panhandle of Oklahoma and touched the southwest corner of Kansas before spending the bulk of his time moving north through Colorado. For the first time in his life, he saw the Rocky Mountains in the clear distance. He didn't know what to call anything he saw but thought "this is the biggest place I ever seen." He touched the southwestern edge of Nebraska and moved into Wyoming. As he moved along the Wyoming/South Dakota Border he could see the Black Hills to the East—and stayed on a path to avoid getting up into high country. Tom stayed as straight north as he could and unknown to him, crossed into Montana.

While he made sure he avoided the Black Hills to his east,[6] He crossed into Montana. There were no "Welcome to Montana" signs and no road signs—in fact, there were *no roads*. He didn't see any houses, any fences or any people—but he did see hundreds of cattle and countless white woolies. He was in sheep and cattle country.

Something said this would be home—at least for a while. It was wide-open and it was big. This land that spread out before him like a big rug was more than just acres of open range. It was a chance for more—much more. For Tom Stone it meant no boundaries and a chance to move as he pleased. To him, this looked like a place that was going to be friendly to the nomad in his spirit. He kept heading north and entered what he soon learned was Carter County and came to the small town of Ekalaka. Looking north he could see a small range of mountains he would later learn was called Rim Rock. Since it looked like the end of the flat grass land (his comfort zone), he decided this was as far as he wanted to go. He decided to look for work and settle for at least "a month or two."

He saw what people would come to call "Big Sky Country" and on a clear day a person could see for a 100 miles or more—which is a bit misleading because it didn't seem nearly that far. Most of the land was still fairly flat (in the eastern part of the state) though Tom could see mountains to the southeast [Black Hills of South Dakota] and what he would learn were the Rocky Mountains to the west. There was grassland as far as his eyes would take him and what appeared to

---

6   The Black Hills of South Dakota were named *Paha Sapa* by the Lakota Sioux. *Paha* meaning "anything of height" and *Sapa* meaning black. They are the oldest mountain range in the U.S. at some 60 million years of age. From north to south, the Black Hills reaches some 100 miles (Spearfish to Edgemont) and extends some 40 miles from east to west (Rapid City to the Wyoming border). Harney Peak is the highest "hill" in the range at 7,242 feet. Griffith called the Black Hills "an oasis in a sea of grass" as the Hills are surrounded by vast grass-lands on all sides—areas with Tom Stone would become very familiar in the next 25 years.

be at least one sheep for every square foot of green.[7] At the time Tom arrived in his "new home," sheep were a major, revenue-producing industry.

Although the winter of 1919-1920 had taken its toll on all live-stock herds, the dedicated herders from all over the country (Wyoming, Idaho, Oregon, California, Utah and Texas had brought their herds to the grasslands of Eastern Montana and western South Dakota. By 1925, it is estimated there were some 6 million sheep being raised in the state (Montana) making it the largest sheep producing state in the nation at that time (Montana still remains the 6th largest sheep-producing state in the nation with a sheep population of approximately 360,000).[8] Although he didn't know much about sheep at the time [actually nothing], he was soon to discover an opportunity for a pretty good job. Even more, he would find a job that translated into a "way a' livin'" that would truly fit him and his needs.

Where Tom Stone had landed was impressive. The name "Big Sky Country" comes from the Latin and Spanish words for mountainous. It is the 4th largest state in land mass (145, 415 square miles) in the United States though 44th in actual population (2014 est. 1,023,579) with over 48% of the population living in rural areas (national average is 25%). It just seemed "big."

And, Montana, he found, has "weather." While there are summers with very little rain making grass a premium at these times, the winters have considerable moisture in the form of snow. The average snowfall in the state varies from 20-300 inches during the year at different altitudes, with the highest recorded annual snowfall reported

---

7   It is important to note that sheepherding in this part of the country was somewhat different from sheepherding in other parts of the country (i.e., California, Utah,Idaho). While most physical features of the sheep were the same in the San Joaquin, for instance, sheep were held in smaller herds and most often lambed earlier due to warmer weather (earlier grass to eat which stimulated the birthing process following impregnation).

8   The *open range boom* peak in Montana was reached in 1886 when there were some 700,000 cattle and a million sheep in the state. The future for stock owners looked great. Then came the winter of 1886-87 that decimated nearly half the cattle and an innumerable number of sheep—many of them starved to death.

in Cooke City in the winter of 1977-78 at 418.1 inches. The accompanying temperature range is in excess of 70 degrees below zero to a high of 117 above (Fahrenheit measures). Residents take careful note that at 70 degrees below zero, it takes less than one minute for a human face to freeze.

One other thing Tom noticed almost immediately was that "the damned wind blew all the time." (The *average* daily wind speed of 12.7 mph is second in the nation only to Wyoming's 12.9 mph.) It wasn't the cold wind out of the north--it was a "strange" warm wind that came out of the west (the *schnook*: a wind that blew over the mountains was actually warm enough to melt some of the ice and snow on the mountainsides).

The weatherman tells us that the sun shines only about 51% of the time in Montana. The wind, married to nature's bitter winter temperatures, made Montana a place where only a few very tough people would even *choose* to live. Still, early on, this north Georgia native decided this was the place for him.

Tom Stone set about "learning the land" and the weather that was an integral part of it. He would eventually [necessarily] forge a "working partnership" with the lands of eastern Montana and western South Dakota. This was to be his home for the next quarter-century of his life. His personal demeanor fit well into what he sensed in his surroundings. He "figgered" early on that this country wasn't going to adapt to him—because this country wasn't going to change for anyone. It was stronger than any one man or group of men.

He admired the land: it was strong and forceful and no man controlled it. This land exerted itself when it felt like it. This vast, new country would likely not be "tamed" by men. He soon learned that to survive, he would need to become like those he rarely saw in the small towns. They were a special breed. He would need to become a west river (Missouri River) person. He would soon find that such people were known for their "fierce independence, rugged individualism, distrust of outsiders and conservative outlook." (McLaird, 1989, 491). Strangely, this profile fit the young, north Georgia nomad.

Lucky for him that it did.

Ekalaka, Montana (meaning "swift one" in Oglala Sioux) was a small town in east central Montana (south of Baker) very near the western North Dakota border. While it was the county seat of Carter County, even today it has only 1202 inhabitants. It was named for Sitting Bull's niece, Ijkalaka, who had married a settler near the town site. Ekalaka was established by Claude Carter whose wagon broke down there so he decided to build a saloon on the site and settle for good—or bad. Even if Tom Stone had known any of this, it would not have mattered. Here was a place where nobody knew him—and that was good. It was a place where he felt he could start a new life—a totally different kind of life—and that was good as well. Inside himself he cautiously began to develop some "peace a' mind."

CHAPTER 4

Mary Ellen Danley: Mrs. Tom Stone

MARY ELLEN DANLEY was just starting her junior year in high school in Ekalaka when Tom Stone came to town—most likely she had no idea he had arrived. It was not so unlikely, however, that in this small town (less than 1,000 at the time) that they would meet at some time. Mary had been born in Nauvoo, Illinois on July 23, 1907. Nauvoo was at one time the "Mormon capital" of the United States with an estimated population in the late 19th century rivaling that of Chicago with a population in excess of 12,000.

Although the data (records) are unclear, Mary Danley [July 23, 1907-March 24, 1999] was the seventh child of Henry H. Danley (1869-1918) and Edith Lizetti (some records suggest Lissetta) Riggins (1868-1915). Mary had three older sisters Grace Danley Nims (1895-1977), Loma (1898-1899), Louise (1899-1899),[9] two older brothers, Edwin (1901-1904), Louis Henry (1904-1985)[10] and one younger

---

9 While certain ancestry-tracing firms have suggested there were two girls that were born to Henry and Edith Danley in 1898, no birth certificates have been found and only a brief notice in the local paper reporting "the infant daughter of Mr. and Mrs. Henry Danley died Sunday at the age of 15 months." [May 1899]

10 At the time of Louis' birth, Lee County records showed that LIzetti Riggens Danley had "5 previous children." As Louis was born prior to Mary Ellen, the last of the children born to Henry and Edith Danley, this would suggest a total of 7 children were born to the couple. The US Census of 1900 listed 4 children for the couple.

brother, William J. (1921-1986). Mary never mentioned, perhaps because she did not know, three of her siblings had passed *before* she was born—Loma, Louise and Edwin.[11] She *did know* her other siblings (Grace, Louie and Bill) and spent *considerable* time with her sister Grace and older brother Louie while living in South Dakota. She located her younger brother Bill and visited him and his wife Winnie in Arkansas shortly before his passing in 1986.

Edith Lizetti Riggins, Mary's Mother, was described as a "slightly-built" person and not very healthy. It was, of course, commonly accepted that childbirth was often quite physically difficult for a mother. Edith was the daughter of Lafayette [once recorded in "Illinois County Marriages, 1810-1834" as Lafeter Riggins] Riggins and Catherine E. Evans.

Catherine Emaline Evans, Edith's mother and Mary's grandmother was born in 1845 in Illinois as was Edith's father, Lafayette Riggins. They had four children—all born in Illinois: Mary E. [born 1862], Edith Lizetti [born 1868], Balis R. [born 1871] and James A. [born 1878]. Information concerning Edith Lizetti Riggins' siblings was not available.

Edith Lizetti Riggins was born in Pontoosuc, IL on April 1, 1868. Records that are available list Edith Lizetti Riggins Danley as a "housewife" and note her cause of death as "acute cerebro (sic) spinal meningitis." She died at her home in Fort Madison, IA on June 15, 1915. She was 46 years old. She and Henry Danley were married on July 20, 1893, in Hancock County, Illinois. They were married some 22 years and had 7 children—only 4 of whom lived

---

11   Records in Nauvoo and Carthage, IL in Hancock County and Keokuk, IA [one of *two county seats in Lee County* that existed until 2014] and Fort Madison, IA [the permanent county seat of Lee County} are somewhat limited. While the records that exist do attest to the birth and death of family members details (names/dates/cause of death, etc.) are very limited as are newspaper obituaries. One of the most surprising discoveries in my research on the Danley family was that nobody had ever talked about the births/deaths of these infant children. Grace, as the oldest, surely knew of them as one brother lived to be 3 years old. I believe my Mother was never told of them.

*Henry H. Danley [1869-1918] and wife Edith Lizetti
Riggins [1868-1915] and their oldest child Grace.
Date 1895. Parents of Mary Ellen Danley Stone.*

to adulthood.

Lafayette Riggins [also listed elsewhere with the full name of Marquis de Lafayette Riggins] was Edith Lizetti Riggins father and Mary Stone's grandfather. As previously noted, he was born in Illinois in 1830. He was reported by a local newspaper to have passed away on November 24, 1893:

> Friday morning last Lafayette Riggins of Nauvoo, was found dead in bed at the home of George Ellison Appanoose township, where he was working. He had taken a load of wood to Nauvoo and appeared in his

usual health. He was 53 years of age, and for some time has had trouble with his heart, and that evidently was the cause of his death.

While this date of death does not correspond to other reported dates of his passing, Lafayette Riggins apparently died some years before his wife.

Upon the death of their mother, Grace, Mary and the two Danley boys, Louie and Bill, moved to Ft. Madison [IA] to be cared for by their two living aunts and a nurturing maternal grandmother. At that time [1910 Census] Ft. Madison was a town of nearly 9,000 inhabitants.

Henry Danley, Mary's father, had come to Nauvoo, IL from Council Grove, [Morris] Kansas when he was 6 years old. Henry was the son of Edwin Johnstone Danley [1835-1900] and Allena Frances Lane [1848-1915].

Alena Frances Lane Danley, Henry Danley's mother was born in Illinois in 1848 and died on April 26, 1915 of general septicema following abdominal abcesses. She was buried in Bevier, MO on April 29, 1915, just four months before her daughter-in- law, Edith Lizetti Riggins passed away in Ft. Madison, Ia.

While data suggests Henry Danley had three brothers and a sister, little evidence is available concerning his father's [Edwin J. Danley] life or death. Historical records and burial "patterns" indicate that Henry H. Danley had some family connections in the state of Missouri. Census reports show that he worked some time as a bartender in Nauvoo and later took a job with the Illinois Central Railroad as a brakeman. While working for the railroad he was injured on the job and died after a short illness on April 13, 1918 while living in Milwaukee, WI.

Evidence suggests such railroad accidents were not unusual in the "early days" of railroads. Sadly, within three years of the death of their mother, the four Danley children lost their father as well. Mary Danley was not yet 11 years old.

Mary's sister Grace [who was then nearly 20 years old] married

Edwin Johnstone Danley [1835-1900] and wife Allena Frances Lane Danley [1848-1915]. Parents of Louis H. Danley and grandparents of Mary Ellen Danley Stone. Council Grove, KS. [circa 1890]

Gilbert W. Nims, a local horse "dealer," on June 6, 1914 in Lee, IA. As the oldest of the Danley children, Grace took charge of the family and moved Mary and the two boys, Louie and Bill with her and her husband from Ft. Madison, IA to Ekalaka, Montana. Ekalaka was a small town on the eastern border between Montana and South Dakota. There, Grace and Gilbert (Gib), as he was called, would attempt to raise a blended family.[12] It was there that Mary learned to break range (wild) horses to help her brother-in-law (Gib Nims) fulfill a contract with the Army for riding mounts.[13]

Mary Ellen Danley loved every horse she ever worked with and understood them as "more than animals." She also knew there was more to life than coming home from school every day and breaking Gib's wild horses to help her sister's husband honor his contract with the U.S. Army. For she also loved to read, play the piano (for the silent movies at the local theater) write poetry and sing. Frustratingly, she found there was little time for such things when you're a full-time "horse breaker" beginning at age 13.

In her early years in Ekalaka, Mary didn't think much about a past life she could barely remember. She remembered her mother but talked very little about her. And, she sorely missed the nurturing of her grandmother and her two maternal aunts. She knew from her extensive reading that the world was much bigger than the main street of Ekalaka, Montana which she could see from the front window of

---

12 Mary's brothers, Louie and Bill were soon separated. Louie went off on his own to work on ranches and would later move to South Dakota where he and Mary would reunite—some years later. Bill eventually joined a circus and was not reunited with Mary until shortly before his death in 1986. Grace and Gib (Gilbert) had two sons. The older, Buck, disappeared in Montana and was never heard from. Conrad (Connie) located in Portland, OR and raised a family of his own. Still, he kept in close contact with his mother back in Montana.

13 There were hundreds—perhaps thousands—of wild mustangs on the plains of Montana, South Dakota and Wyoming at the time. And the price was right. All you needed were the "hands" to locate the herds and then round them up and corral them—then they had to be broken to the bridled and the saddle. That was Gib Nim's contract and Mary Danley was his "hired hand." One should not be mistaken. This was time-consuming and labor intensive. It just did not take much upfront monetary investment.

the little white cottage just a half-block from downtown—the place where she lived with her sister Grace and brother-in-law Gib.[14] She was convinced there were more interesting places in the world than the corral where she fought to saddle and bridle wild mustangs and then attempt to ride them in an effort to break them to a place where they could be ridden by cavalry soldiers without being thrown. She dreamed of finding a way—perhaps any way—to see more of the world she had only read about.

She first saw Tom Stone in the U.S. Post Office in Ekalaka during her lunch break at school. She had no idea who he was and never even thought about what he might be doing there. One thing she did notice was that he *dressed* quite a bit differently than any of the other men in town. He wore blue bib overalls, a flannel shirt with the sleeves rolled up so that the arms of his long underwear showed. He did not wear cowboy boots like all the other men (and most of the women) in town. And, he always wore a cap—not a cowboy hat like the other men, but a small, round cap [a "driving" cap].

While that seemed a bit strange, it was not strange enough to demand that she talk to him. At first, as she recalls, "I didn't pay much attention to him. He was shorter than most of the men in town, had very dark hair and was sort of handsome." Actually, she later admitted she thought he was "very handsome." Not knowing who he was actually piqued her interest as she thought she knew most everybody in town—a town of less than a thousand people inside the city limits.

Mary was in the Post Office nearly every day during her lunch break from high school (which was less than a block away) and she never stayed there more than ten minutes. It was by "mutual design" that she saw Tom Stone a couple more times but had never talked to him. This day he was staring at her. When she "caught him," he

---

14 This house still stands and is occupied. It is ½ block from downtown Ekalaka and 2 short blocks from the rodeo grounds where Mary spent many hours breaking wild horses and watching weekend rodeos—a major part of the summer entertainment in small western towns for many generations. Rodeos (mostly professional) are still held in many areas of the "west" as well as Canada and even such venues as Madison Square Garden.

didn't turn away. So she finally and bluntly asked him: "Where do you work?" "In the country," he quickly answered in a dialect that she and never heard the likes of. He didn't want to tell her he was a sheepherder—sheepherders were generally regarded quite lowly as a profession—even up here.

Sixteen-year-old Mary Danley had never met someone from the "deep south" before. His response really didn't tell her much but was enough to get the conversation started—which was really the goal for both of them. Tom Stone didn't like anybody asking him questions, but he had seen her enough to be interested. And he liked girls.[15] Besides, he didn't have a real friend in town. He was a long way from anybody that he knew and, while he never would have admitted it, he needed someone to at least talk with. After he got into a conversation with her, he liked her even more "cuz she was the only person in this part of the country that didn't make fun of the way I talked." Tom Stone didn't even know Mary's age—in Montana she was a girl—in Georgia she would have been a woman. When she was in school, Mary felt like a girl. When she was at home with Gib and Grace, she felt like a girl. When she came over to the Post Office during her lunch break, she felt like a girl. When she started to talk with Tom Stone, all of a sudden, she felt like a *woman*.

"Where do you live?" Tom asked her directly.

"In town." Mary replied. Since it was such a small town, she thought that would be all the information he would need—*need for what* she had no idea. She surely wasn't going to tell him exactly where she lived for fear that he might come to visit her and her brother-in-law would have none of that. It was enough information for Tom too—there would be enough time to find out more later--but not much later.

"What are you doing around here?" Tom queried somewhat clumsily to keep the conversation going as best he could. He was *interested*.

"I come here to get the mail," she answered matter-of-factly. She

---

15   As Mary would find out some years later, by his own admission, Tom Stone had actually been married two times before he left Tennessee and Georgia.

didn't really want to tell him she was at the Post Office every day the last few days hoping she would run into him. She sure wasn't going to tell him she was in high school. In all likelihood, that wouldn't have mattered to him anyway.

While both Tom and Mary had their own agenda for these meetings, *it is quite likely that much more was unsaid than was said.*

"My name is Tom Stone," he finally told her—thinking that bit of information would keep the conversation going and hoping she would tell him her name as well. She obliged.

"Mine's Mary Danley," she replied in kind and without hesitation.

"It's a good name," Tom volunteered, not knowing what else to say. His thoughts dashed back to his mother—her full name was Mary Elizabeth Harper Stone. He didn't say so because nobody needed to know that—and it was pretty personal. And Tom Stone did not want to get personal just yet.

Mary added, "I've got family here," as if to let him know that she was settled—and not some wayward girl out on her own.

Mary felt the conversation had gone as far as *she* wanted to carry it for right now—but only for now. It was important for Tom Stone to know that they had made real contact but this was as far as things *could* go at this time. Since she had to get back to school, she didn't really want to explore "new areas" until they had more time. Besides that, the last thing Mary wanted Tom to know was that she was a junior in high school!

She didn't know when they would meet again, but something told her it wouldn't be long—at least she hoped so. She was already planning for the next time they met. By then, she would have some "good" questions.

Mary wanted to see Tom again but didn't really know how to tell him so she just smiled and raised her hand in a half-wave and said "I've got to go." Maybe he knew she was a student—maybe he didn't—maybe it didn't matter. She knew that she wasn't going to tell him and risk not seeing him again because "she was just too young or just a school kid." The truth was, he didn't care much how old she was or what she did—he still lived in his "home culture." His home culture was one where anybody who looked like Mary Danley was a *woman*. Mary liked him and he liked her. They were going to see each other even if it was only at the Ekalaka Post Office.

Neither of them wanted to leave before the other because *she* didn't want him to see where she was going (to the high school) and *he* didn't want her to see that he didn't have any place to go until he went back to Blackford's ranch that evening. And, there was only one door out so they "brushed" a bit as they moved through the double doors-quite unintentionally . . . . of course.

"You gonna be back here tommorra?" Tom asked in an unmistakably serious tone as he got to the street.

"I don't really . . . " Mary paused and then almost blurted, "Yes! How about you?"

"Can't make it for a coupla days—I hafta work ya know." He responded, hoping she would give him a specific time when she would be back—to meet him.

"I come over here quite a lot—to get the mail," she hastened to add. She wanted him to know that she didn't just hang around the Post Office with her friends every day—just talking with strangers—especially strange men. Talking with him now was OK since "she knew his name and where he worked." So, Tom Stone wasn't really a stranger at all.

As Mary walked down the street—in the opposite direction of the high school—she half-yelled: "I could be here every day." She slipped into an alleyway by Scooter's Bar and started to run so she wouldn't be late for school. She was excited!

Tom didn't know if he would (could) get back to town in the next "coupla" days but would certainly try to. Liking this girl and taking a day to come into town were two things that didn't work well together. His first priority was his job—especially since he knew he was getting a new herd and would be with the sheep (day and night) most of the time in the next couple of months. If he got to town, his first stop would surely be the Post Office. If he didn't get into town in the next few days. . . . Well, things would be what they would be.

They started to meet at the Post Office once every week. One day they met after school (she finally told him she was at the high school and it didn't matter to him). Both of them were "interested" in building some kind of "relationship." It may have been that neither of them knew what that really meant but they were developing a *genuine attraction* for one another. Tom didn't care if anybody else knew what he was doing [as he had no family in Ekalaka so 'what he was doin'' was nobody else's business]. Not so with Mary Danley. Mary knew that if her sister Grace found out that she was "meeting" a man in town, she would tell her husband Gib. And if Gib Nims found out, there would be "hell to pay" and that would be the end of it. It was unlikely that Gib knew Tom Stone, but you can be sure he was not about to lose his only "hired hand" to some "sheepherdin' drifter."

Though Mary Ellen Danley liked school and was a very good student, when it came down to a choice between being around Tom Stone and school, it was no contest.[16] It is doubtful that it was a "full-blown love" at this stage. But it was much more than just the way high school girls spent their lunchtime in a small town in Eastern Montana.

Most likely, Mary saw this as a *potential* opportunity to get away from her controlling brother-in-law Gib Nims. Or she saw a chance to get out of this confining small town—it may have been a combination of these things and more. Whatever else Mary Danley saw in Tom Stone, she saw a chance—no matter how remote—for freedom

---

16 Mary already had enough credits to graduate. Besides that, a high school diploma was not something that was revered at this time, in this part of the country and for a girl. Montana's school system was not dissimilar to most on the frontier. It was very difficult to find a qualified teacher and even more difficult to keep one (salary, quality of life, prospects for marriage/family, working conditions, community support, etc.) for very long. In 1880, students attended school *(both* elementary and secondary school) an average of 4 years—totally. By 1900, that average had risen to 5 years. Mary Danley (at this time) had completed 10 years of school and was nearing completion of her junior year in high school and already had enough credits to graduate. On many occasions, the better students served as teachers for the younger grades. Mary Danley had already served in this capacity for three years.

from those things that shackled her to this small Eastern Montana community and her drudging way of life. Mary Danley was intelligent. She knew what her options were and weren't in Ekalaka, Montana. For her, this developing relationship was more about *getting away* from some things and some places than *getting to* something or someplace else. Besides that, she was a "full-grown" woman at 16 and had "every right to make her own decisions." And there was this thing she was feeling for this stranger from the south. She was almost ready to call it "love."

So, Tom and Mary "sneaked" around—but not much. Mainly because in a town the size of Ekalaka there aren't many places to sneak. Whenever she played the piano at the movie theater (for the silent movies), Tom tried to be there. After the movies they would spend a few minutes "talking" as Gib and Grace knew what time the movie was over, and they expected her home. Tom and Mary both knew it was only a matter of time before Mary's brother-in-law Gib found out. Tom had asked around town enough to know that when Gib found out, there would be "big trouble."

Still, Tom Stone wanted a mate and Mary Ellen Danley was the mate he wanted. Mary was "falling in love" . . . at least with an idea and would have done almost anything to get out from "under the heel" of her sister's husband. Neither Mary nor Tom thought much about what was ahead for them. Even if they had, they could not have imagined what might have been down "their road." Inevitably, they talked about marriage. At this time, Mary was 16. She had certainly read some about marriage and married people. And, for the last few weeks had thought about being married almost constantly. It may have seemed romantic at first impulse. Still, this sixteen-year old was probably beginning to look at the practical side of their future(s). Tom Stone, probably not.

Mary Danley loved her sister Grace. She did not love Gib Nims, her brother-in-law. Neither did she respect him. Mary didn't feel that she owed Gib anything and she felt she owed her sister only an account of *what* she was going to do—not an explanation *why*.

Someplace, sometime, perhaps in the Post Office, Tom and Mary decided to get married. If you are wondering how that developed, you are in the majority. When you consider a 16-year-old high school junior and a 23-year-old southern man who had little more than a job, it's a wonder Tom Stone and Mary Danley got that far, that fast. But they did. And some how they knew they couldn't waste any time getting it done—it was only a matter of time before Gib and Grace would find out.

They talked about someone they could find to perform the ceremony and who they would invite to the actual wedding. They talked about a "celebration" with a small group of friends (mostly Mary's) and how they would leave town to get out to the herd with which Tom was working. In the back of their minds, they were both thinking about Gib and Grace Nims but chose not to talk about them. For reasons that became apparent, neither wanted the Nims to know about their dating much less their upcoming marriage.

Short courtships were not uncommon in this part of the country—neither had they been in Whitfield County, Georgia. Tom couldn't "figger out any reason for all that stuff" anyway. Back where Tom Stone was raised people seemed to make their minds up pretty fast—and then they acted on the decisions they had made. And "the sooner the better." Not unlike many other young couples who got married just a short time after a relatively limited courtship, Tom and Mary had little idea what was ahead of them. That really didn't seem to matter anyway. If you had told them what was "ahead," they would not have believed it—but they wouldn't have changed their minds. They both agreed *this was what they wanted to do*. And, at the moment, they hadn't really thought about the negative consequences of their decisions—they were more concerned with *what they wanted to do* than *how somebody else felt about it*.

It would be difficult to argue that Mary Ellen Danley did or did not know what she was doing. She was giving up a life in town—the only life she had known for a decade. She was giving up her piano, going to and "teaching" school and her family. The trade was for a

primitive existence—full of daily dangers and constant shortages—
of everything except extreme weather, cramped quarters and plenty
of prairie varmints. Little could she have known she was moving
to a life where she would raise a family of 7, lose one as an infant
and risk the lives of her family on almost a daily basis—little did she
know.

CHAPTER 5

Tom and Mary Stone: A Match Made . . . in the Post Office

THOMAS DEWEY STONE and Mary Ellen Danley were married on March 22, 1925 in the Carter County Court House in Ekalaka Montana (See Appendix A). Tom Stone spent his wedding night in the Carter County Jail (See: Appendix B). After an auspicious wedding day, Tom and Mary Stone would spend the next 20 years of their lives raising 7 children and herding thousands of head of sheep on the grassy and sometimes semi-arid plains and Badlands of eastern Montana and western South Dakota. Mary Stone was his partner in good times—and there were some—and bad times—and there were plenty of those as well.

It would be difficult to assess the nature of the newlyweds at the time of their wedding. Tom Stone was fiercely independent and regularly claimed "he didn't *really need* nobody!" To that his new bride would admonish him that "everybody needs somebody" else in their lives—as she intimated, she was that "somebody" in his life. She very likely believed that too, although it may have been her way of attempting to *convince her new spouse*. To suggest that Tom and Mary Stone were quite different from each other at the time they got married would be an understatement. Quite frankly, for whatever reasons, they had similar goals—get out of Ekalaka and build their lives—which may or may not have included a spouse and children and surely didn't consider spending the next 50+ years "together."

Mary Stone was different in so many ways from Tom. While she developed a spirit as tough as "wang leather," she also displayed both a soft human side and a noticeable aesthetic side. If Tom Stone had either of the latter two, he hid them both nearly all his life. He was quite brash and outspoken in his general demeanor. He was tough.

He didn't read and he didn't write. While dealing with people, he was virtually always quite direct and probably had not learned the "the proper way to interact socially." Quite the opposite, Mary Ellen was quite well-mannered and virtually never used a "cuss word" even when one or two might have seemed warranted.

Truly they were raised in very different cultures and environments and had built basic value systems that were significantly different as well—at least in most cases. Mary seemed one innately given to compromise—she wanted to "make things work." Tom Stone had apparently never been exposed to the concept of "give some—get some." So, at most any cost, he was going to have it *his* way, and, if Mary wanted things to "work well," *she was going to have things his way* as well. Early on, Mary recognized this—and accepted it for most of their lives.

From the time they decided to marry, however, they concentrated on more pressing and immediate goals and set any differences on the "back burner." While many things seemed to line up against them--both in the immediate future and "down the road,"--they seemed to find the strength together to weather what to others may have appeared insurmountable obstacles. And, for the first 3 decades of their married life, they seemed of common purpose—they were in step with each other.

In all, Tom and Mary Stone were married for 52 years, had seven children, buried their 4th (Dorothy Jean) in a small cemetery near Elm Springs in west-central South Dakota [north of Wasta] and survived some extremely difficult times to live their middle years in Pierre, South Dakota and their later, perhaps happiest, years in small, rental properties in Phoenix, Arizona where they are buried next to each other.

Back to the wedding. According to the Ekalaka Eagle (the local paper in Mary's hometown), "Tom Stone and Ellen Danley were married at early candlelight on Sunday evening, at the residence of Mr. and Mrs. W. A. Hedrick, the nuptial knot being tied by Justice W. H. Peck." The wedding party moved their celebration to the Old Stand where they were soon interrupted by Carter County Sheriff McLean and an angry Gilbert W. Nims (the bride's brother-in-law). Wisely, the Sheriff took Tom home with him to spend the night. Marshal Fiske and "a few picked men" brought the new bride safely to the home of Justice Peck where she would spend her wedding night.

From the day of her marriage, Mary must have been aware that her life was going to be different—quite different. Having found out about the "wedding," Gib Nims got the Sheriff and made sure that Tom Stone was not allowed to "marry a minor."[17] So, Tom spent his wedding night with the Sheriff of Carter County. What Mary expected and even desired, turned out to be much more than even she had imagined. For now, it was the newlyweds, Mr. and Mrs. Tom Stone against all odds. At least they knew that if anybody told them they couldn't be together, *they* would fight for *their* right to do what they had committed to. Their logic was very straight-forward and their reasoning was "plain as day." -

At the time of their marriage, Tom was working for Mr. A.E. Blackford at a ranch on the Upper Boxelder Creek. According to the Ekalaka Eagle, "the young lady has been attending the Carter County High School, now being a member of the junior class. . .." By most standards, Mary Danley should have been planning for her junior prom. Somehow, the two newlyweds struggled through the next two days.

---

17 Mary Ellen Danley would not have been the first 16-year old to be married in Montana. There were quite likely a large number of young ladies who did so as they were asked to "grow up" much faster than under conditions in later times. One author (Baumber, 2010) writes of Mary Gibson who was married the first time by her 16th birthday in 1914 an even had a child before she was 17. Gibson would enter her second marriage before the age of 19.

Finally, Sheriff McLean convinced Gib Nims to "let her be." Tom and Mary reunited at the Carter County Jail and proceeded with haste to leave the little town of their nuptials. Their feelings were understandably mixed. Mary Ellen Danley Stone had been afforded no blessings from the only family she had. And even though she knew very little about her future, she now had a new husband and they were going to somehow be together no matter what anybody else thought.

They packed what few things Mary could get from the Nims' house and headed "out." Tom knew what was out there—Mary had no idea. But, he soon "figgered out" that his new bride was at least as much of a survivor as he was. "We'll do this . . ." she would resolutely say any time there was trouble or they were faced with any kind of issue. She might just as well have said "We have to do this," since now there was no turning back. While Tom had learned a great deal about sheep in his short time on the Job—from lambing in the spring to shearing and shipping in the fall—Mary knew close to nothing about those several hundreds of woolies from which they would make their living—and determine their nomadic lifestyle for the next two decades.

Mary did know a great deal about horses, and now she would gladly learn about lambing, and shearing, and helping little lambs get their start, and bottle-feeding runts and abandoned babies, and . . . . Much to her dismay, she would also learn about coyotes, and rattlesnakes, and cold and intense heat, and going without—almost everything—and she would learn even more about surviving. They would have 7 children virtually without prenatal care, doctors or hospitals.

Thomas Robert (named after his father and his paternal grandfather) was born in Alzada, Montana (May 14, 1927). Bob, (or Tommy Bob) as he was called by his parents, was the only one of the Stone children born in Montana. The other six of Tom and Mary's offspring were born on the western and central plains of South Dakota.

Phyllis Jean (Sissy) was born in Belle Fourche (December 31, 1929), Joanne Elizabeth (Jody) arrived (January 22, 1932) in New Underwood, Dorothy Jean (August 27, 1936) near Elm Springs, Rosalie Laverne (called Lindy Lou by her sisters) was born On December 4,

1940, in Mount Vernon, John Danley (named After Tom's Uncle John) was born near Philip on May 18, 1943, and Mary Kathleen [Mary Kay] was born on November 9, 1946 in Mitchell [SD], some distance to the east [where Tom had been working with Leif Hansen's livestock sales barns).

Family life was new for both Tom and Mary. While both of them had siblings, neither had much experience being around child-rearing activities—much less newborn children. And while both understood the nature of responsibility in caring for other living things, only Mary had experienced what she knew as *familial love*.

For Tom Stone, love was truly a foreign emotion—an emotion with which he was less than comfortable. His capacity to love, and accept the love of others, would be an issue for the rest of his natural life. Tom Stone had no trouble with many desirable traits: dedication, no! hard work, no! loyalty, no! stubbornness, no! love, not impossible, but still difficult! Remember his models. . . .

Tom Stone spent his early married life with large herds of sheep (sometimes nearing 4,000 head) feeding on the flat grasslands of eastern Montana and western South Dakota, using both Boxelder Creek and Little Beaver Creek as well as the Belle Fourche River. "If you knew what you was doin,' you could hannel that many with two good dogs and a horse." His two dogs, of whom he spoke often and with a good deal of respect were named Nigger and Dog—good sheep dogs warrant a full chapter of their own. He knew that herding sheep was a 365-day a year job. He didn't mind because he was his own boss and didn't have to deal with other people—Tom Stone was happy working by himself. He had developed an overwhelming sense of responsibility. Whether he was protecting the herd from predators or staying with them on horseback during the most brutal winter nights, he took his job seriously—that was "his way." There were few sheep "rustlers" around, but sheep were basically helpless when confronted with the numerous predators (some mountain lions, wolves and countless coyotes). A herder soon learned that both mountain lions and coyotes generally hunted at sunrise and sunset. Wolves, easily the strongest, most vicious and potentially damaging of this group, hunted anytime.

Most predators easily took the docile sheep by surprise as they pounced on their prey at the most opportune times. Knowing this, Tom, always with his dogs, spent nearly all his time by himself, with the sheep.

When Tom and Mary started to raise a family (near Alzada, Montana in 1927) she often stayed in one of the two wagons (sleep and cook) at the base camp or in a small cabin in the local community close to the location of the herd. She, like her husband, became very self-sufficient. The development of such independence would see her through the rest of her life. In the late fall, Tom took the sheep nearer the Black Hills so they could winter where it was typically warmer than on the "flat country." At least at the base of the Black Hills, there was some protection from the brutal winter winds. Tom would often comment that "they wintered pretty good at the foot of the Hills and the cabin was a safe place for Mother and the kids."

During the early spring and summer, he often moved the herd further east in South Dakota where there were thousands of acres of unencumbered (by fences) free grazing and it was relatively easy (and advisable) to avoid another herd—of either sheep or cattle. Just east of the Hills were thousands of acres of rolling grasslands. And by May, this grass was good for lambing. While it was unbearably hot in the summer and freezing cold in the winter, South Dakota was delightfully mild in the spring and the fall.

Tom and Mary soon learned the town names of Belle Fourche, Spearfish, Sturgis, Vale, Newell, Wasta and others. This was not unlike the country from which they'd come in the eastern part of Montana—it was real sheep country. And, this open country was actually a better location for spring lambing than in the thick trees of the Black Hills except that you couldn't get much help from the faraway homeplace (owner's ranch) with the new arrivals if you needed it.

Most anyone in the "sheep business" would argue that this was "no place for a woman." Whether it was the language you had to learn (and endure), the cramped quarters in which you had to live, the dramatically changing weather or the seemingly constant moving, Gilfillan was of the opinion "that in many respects they [women] are unsuited to the work" (Gilfillan, 1929). Mary Ellen Stone was most surely an exception to this opinion. She learned the rules of the range and more than carried her own weight. She had 6 children on the ranges of eastern Montana and western South Dakota [one in eastern SD]. She learned to be a survivor.

When Mary Stone wasn't having a child or taking close care of them, she helped in any way she could. She was one of the "team" who helped with the lambing, riding herd at night and cooking for her family and the shearing crew when they came just after lambing season in the spring. In the midst of all this, the young mother dealt with the heartbreak of losing her 4th child, Dorothy Jean, as an infant. She still never even thought about saying "quit." Tom Stone admired his new bride's grit. He likely never told her so, but she knew.

As Mr. Blackford early on watched his herd grow under very good "management," he awarded the Stones with two wagons—one for cooking and one for sleeping,[18] two horses,[19] and something that was almost unheard of, a raise in monthly wages.[20] Still, they were

---

18 Most herders had one wagon at their base camp or on the trail as they moved from place to place. When Tom and Mary Stone *started their family,* they got a *sleep* wagon and a *cook* wagon. The sleep wagon had both a front and back door and windows with some storage containers built into the walls. Otherwise, it had four beds that joined in the middle when you pulled them down and were propped up on the floor. At one end, there was the standard-sized sheep wagon stove (in which you burned whatever you could find to burn.

19 The second horse was for emergencies at the base camp though Tom and Mary already had horses of their own as well as the tack they needed. Bob was learning to "sit" a horse and would soon do a full-days (or nights) work—just like his folks. .

20 By current standards, such wages were quite low. Still, sheepherders were most often paid *more* than cowboys—especially during the winter months when cowboys stayed close to the ranch most of the time while sheepherders were out in the open country with their herds. In addition, many cowboys did *not* work all year—they were most often seasonally employed. Sheepherders were needed 365 days a year. Seasoned and successful herders earned as much as $45 per month (and remember, the herder had virtually no expenses) if the herd was quite large and the herder did a good job "maintaining" the herd through tough winters and keeping losses (from weather and predators) to a minimum. Tom Stone handled his responsibilities well—many a night was spent in the saddle, with his dogs and his 30-30, keeping "his herd" safe from harm—an all "bunched up."

poor. They owned very little except "the clothes on their backs," a couple of horses and saddles and their carbines. Still, Tom Stone would be heard to remark in later years about those times: "I seen people with a lot less—we didn't have it so bad." For her part, Mary was the one who would pull the "ends together" in the "house" and make things work—and all with a thankful spirit. She learned early on to guard each of her provisions very carefully and never waste.[21] Keeping food safe and clean (for some months, cold was obviously out of the question) was always an issue. It was especially difficult as bugs, weevils, mice, crickets and rats were all over on the prairie and it was mandatory to sift everything—you removed the invader *but did not throw things away!*

If supplies seemed beyond reclamation, the dogs would likely eat them. On the prairie, Mary Stone learned lessons that would serve her the rest of her life.

As long as she had lids and jars (Ball/Mason type), Mary would can things that were left over from their small garden set up at base camp (tomatoes, beets, potatoes). Oftentimes, she preserved berries that she and the kids picked when they got near some bushes or around the base of mountains where a variety of small berries grew different times of the year. With their main provisions supplied by the "owner" and her creativity, they rarely *bought* groceries.

Though it was almost unheard of, Mary Stone had a washing machine—in the middle of nowhere. It was a small metal (many of the earliest machines were wooden) Maytag that ran on white gas. She had ordered it from a Montgomery Ward catalog at the "amazing" price of $27.99 (no S&H charges). The kick-start 2-cycle engine made a considerable racket when it was running and luckily the noxious exhaust rapidly dissipated in the open prairie air. When

---

21 To this day every time I see a real "old clothespin" I think of her winding every little strand of thread or cloth around it—she saved it all. Food leftovers—she "threw nothing out" and by the end of the week, all food was used in some way. She was amazing but not a hoarder as she had little or nothing to hoard.

Typical Western Sheepwagon of the times. About 11.5 feet long and 6.5 feet wide. Tom and Mary Stone lived in one for years and when they started a family they got a second wagon.

they moved the base camp, Tom loaded the Maytag in one of the wagons and it went to the next "stop." The next "stop" was nearly always near fresh water (i.e., the Belle Fourche River) as all clothes were washed in the "cold/cold cycle." When they established base camp, the Maytag stayed outside and Mary put up two clotheslines between the wagons on which she hung the laundry. It must have been quite a site. Quite frankly, appearances weren't really an issue with either Tom or Mary as there were no neighbors and few, if any, people rode or drove by.

Mary had learned to sew when she was a youngster living with her aunts and Grandmother in Iowa and her sister Grace. Because she had such skills, the Stones made a second *unique* purchase for a family living in two sheep wagons on the plains of western

South Dakota—they bought a sewing machine.[22] It was a pedal-driven Singer in a wooden cabinet with two small drawers on the right-hand side. The large pedal on the bottom (plenty of room for both feet) drove the needle mechanism after you had started the machine by rotating the wheel on the top left by hand. Thread and needles were fairly cheap and material for sewing was "around." A spool of thread lasted a long time and Mary wasted none of it. Her "sewing stash" consisted of clothespins wrapped with thread, small pieces of any type of cloth and the almost-magical silver thimble.

Just as it was with food provisions, no piece of cloth was discarded. Flour sacks of that time were designed by the manufacturer (Gold Medal, Pillsbury, Occident, etc.) in colorful flower designs knowing that money-conscious homemakers would make good use of them. In similar fashion, they got their "dishes" in boxes of oatmeal—about two pieces each month.

Mary made more than aprons and curtains (to cover drafty doors and windows and make the small sheep wagons a bit more homey) as she crafted work shirts for Tom and dresses for herself. Later, as she started to raise a family, she would not only make clothes for the kids (except Tom and Bob's overalls) but would teach the girls both how to save and how to sew. Mary Stone wasted nothing—not food, water nor a piece of cloth. Her children "learned" her frugality well—at times to a fault. There was no such thing in her "home on wheels" one could call waste. To Mary Stone, throwing something "out" was wasting—and wasting was unacceptable-she and her husband had very limited needs, but they used what

---

22 It is worth noting that Tom and Mary Stone had some "money." They worked every day of the year and were paid for every day they worked. And, while they didn't make a great deal, they had to spend almost nothing (a new pair of boots, a new pair of bib overalls, some replacement underwear, cartridges for their rifles, etc.). They paid no rent or house payments, had no car (early on), no insurance, no food bills, etc. They did not have an IRA, a stock portfolio and did not take vacations. And, the things they did buy were not that expensive. The exception was the purchase of a new Ford car for $599.00—for Mary since Tom did not know how to drive. Money—they saved nearly all that they earned.

they had to meet those needs as best they could—as both of them would so often say: "We made do."

Later in their first year "on the flatlands" of eastern Montana, Mary convinced Tom to get her some chickens. She had helped raise chickens in Iowa [in town] and when she lived with Gib and Grace in Ekalaka. She knew how to build a chicken coop for them [for nesting and protection] and provided them with the wheat straw they would use for nesting [and laying eggs].[23] She also knew what it took for feed and water as well as how to "wring their necks, pluck em,' singe the pin feathers off and cut them up for frying." For them, the chickens would mean fresh eggs every day [and sometimes for supper as well] and pan-fried chicken on a regular basis. They knew this would be a project *only* for the warmer months [late April into mid-October] but decided to give it a try. Tom built a small roosting area out of some canvas and woven wire so the free rangers had a place to sleep that was relatively safe at night [the dogs would help with that]. With good nests of hay, the hens would be warm and "productive." The dogs didn't bother the chickens, but they still lost one or two a month to coyotes and an occasional fox. It was fairly easy to replenish their numbers every couple of months so they kept over a dozen hens around the wagon and had plenty of eggs and fried chicken for their efforts.

The early years that Tom and Mary Stone spent in eastern Montana and western South Dakota were also the early years of the

---

23 Mary would continue this practice of raising chickens for "Sunday dinner" as well as for fresh eggs through their early years in Pierre where she had as many as 100 hens in the garage [they had no car].

Great Depression and great droughts in America.[24] The first condition didn't really affect them much. For poverty in their profession and in that part of the country was a *relative concern*. Since there were so few people around them, and they "had plenty to eat and a place to sleep," they were content [and somewhat insulated] from the nation's extensive economic woes. As to the great drought, they knew very little about the "natural disasters" [dust bowl] that were wreaking havoc on much of the Great Plains from Texas to Colorado and from Oklahoma and Nebraska into eastern South Dakota. Though they had other trials, they had each other—they felt that was plenty. Tom and Mary were fast developing a most *unusual devotion* to each other and a *deep resignation* to their new life together. In the days, months and years to come, that commitment would be sorely tested.

Tom and Mary could sense the land. They knew the continual drought was a serious matter. And even though the unusually harsh winter of 1886-87 had destroyed nearly half the stock in both Montana and South Dakota, the ranchers had spent the next 3 decades fighting back. Many ranchers rebuilt and maintained large herds—at least large herds of sheep, while many cattle ranchers [in some cases

---

24 The Great Depression in America started in 1929 and eventually affected the entire world. By 1932, 13 million people we unemployed in the US and 34 million people were members of families with NO fulltime wage earner. By 1933, over 11,000 US banks had failed and 37% of all *nonfarm workers* were without jobs. Over one million families lost their farms during the worst years [1930-34] of the Depression as income was reduced by over 40% and there were few banks to loan money for seed or replenishing of stock let alone wages.

"South Dakota could not escape the consequences, both good and evil, of these developments. People living in the state's West River [west of the Missouri] were especially hard hit by the latter decade's droughts and dust storms, which made people wonder about their very ability to survive on the land (Nelson, summary, 1996). Still, much of the native grassland further west [where Tom grazed his sheep] was spared from the disastrous erosion. Because of the poor planting pro-cedures followed for a number of years, these dust storms blew away topsoil that had taken years to accumulate. For example, one such storm is reported to have deposited some 12 million tons of Midwestern topsoil in the city of Chicago.

the same rancher] broke their large cattle herds down into smaller bunches—making it easier to move them when the need arose.

Large herds of livestock, of course, require a good deal of land that supplies both food and water when needed. To move a large herd [1000 head and up] was nigh onto impossible on foot [the *modus operandi* for many sheepherders]—you needed a horse.[25] Tom's favorite was a large gray gelding (15hh) while Mary preferred to ride a smaller chestnut mare to whom she had become very attached within the first few weeks on the trail. Her attachment was short-lived, however. The broad grasslands of eastern Montana and western South Dakota had hundreds of wild horses. While they traveled in "established" herds, they frequently enticed a "working horse" to join their entourage—especially a mare. Some wild stallion apparently had more "pull" on Mary's chestnut mare than she did—and one morning the mare was gone.

Tom's gray was important to them because there weren't that many horses that color in Montana so Mary could identify Tom from a distance when he was approaching the base camp. As they were often miles from any ranch or town, this was a safety issue. When the moon was full, Mary could even see the gray from a good distance. While most people on the plains were friendly and would not harm you [some even avoided contact], there were always some who could not be trusted. Mary kept a loaded 30-30 close just in case—and she knew how to use it if the need arose.

A big, strong horse was important as well because of the tough

---

25 To the sheepherder, a horse was somewhat of a mixed blessing. Especially with larger herds, you needed a horse to keep up with the sheep if they decided to scatter [which they did infrequently but once was enough] as sheep can scatter faster than any man can "gather." A herder with a horse and a couple of good dogs could more readily "recircle" a herd and get them settled into a feeding or bedding ground. Still, two issues arose with a herder having a horse. First, a horse needs special attention during bad weather. Second, having a horse in camp requires the herder to carry a considerable amount of extra feed [oats]. These were both con-cerns as there was no separate shelter for a horse [the dogs *could* stay in the wagon] during bad weather [which was inevitable] and there was little space to carry 2-4 weeks supply of oats used for the supplemental feeding.

terrain [some of the draws and summer grazing in the hills] and the weather [winters were brutally cold, and summers were scorching]. Notably the days for the herder's horse were long—they were sometimes 24 hours straight depending on weather and local predators [coyotes were a nearly constant concern].

Their horses were furnished by the main ranch [Bob and Jody also had their own mounts when they began riding]. While Tom was new to sitting a saddle, he learned fast out of necessity. Mary, on the other hand was a skilled horseperson from her years "working for" her brother-in-law as a "bronc buster." Mary's stories of being thrown [and even stomped on] had been told. That had made her "tough." That toughness was ingrained in her. And whether it was being thrown while saddle breaking a wild horse or raising a family in the "middle of nowhere," Mary Ellen Danley Stone was strong---no one denied her toughness. And, though difficult, she would remark later in life that she "loved her years on the prairie."

Herders had to keep moving. They kept moving because the sheep kept moving in search of a "usable" source of water [one that was not claimed by a "protective" rancher] and grazing [grass]. Herders found out early on that sheep "think with their stomachs" and eat almost continuously.[26] And, if there was no rain, there was precious little grass to be had. It was easy to imagine that especially during the "dry years," grass was guarded as a precious commodity--for it was.

Moving with "their" sheep kept herders out on the plains for long periods of time—weeks, even months—without seeing other

---

26 Not only was this a problem as the grass was cropped so close to the ground by the sheep that the cattle *could not eat*, but large sections of land that could have been used for making hay to help get cattle through the winter were often depleted by large herds of sheep feeding on a regular basis. Therefore, when mowing time[s] came, there was often little hay to mow and stack. Some cattle ranchers argued that cattle *would not eat* where sheep had been and *would not drink* from the same "watering holes."

people. They ate on the prairie and slept on the prairie [literally][27] And spent 24 hours each day with their charges—often up to 2000 head of sheep. Most herders were accompanied only by their dogs and a horse if they had one—very few were married couples. Of those, rarely did the wife live out In the country with her mate and the herd. This solitary life was indeed a very unusual existence.

---

27   Sleeping "under the stars" was not an uncommon practice when a herder could not get back to the base camp [and the wagon]. On "decent" nights, they slept most often on a bedroll covered by a long coat or slicker. During colder nights, herders often dug a hole about 2 feet deep, burned a number of logs in the hole before covering the smoldering logs with dirt. This makeshift "furnace" provided the herder with a warm bed throughout the cooler evenings. While away from their base camps [and wagons] many herders took a simple tent with them—just as protection for them and their dogs from the wind, rain or an occasional snow flurry during the late spring in higher elevations. During the winter months, herders stayed in close proximity to their sheep wagon[s] as those herders with a family often had both a sleep wagon and a cook wagon.

CHAPTER 6

Sheep: The Object of Attention

THERE ARE AN estimated 1 billion sheep in the world, with only 5 ½ million in the United States [most of them in Texas, Wyoming and California]. One need only drive down state or county roads in many other states to witness small herds. While many sheep exist in small flocks [pasture sheep], there was a time in the middle west states where herds of as many 4,000 head roamed their grassy domain tended by individual graziers [sic] or herders.

Sheep are a relatively hearty and healthy animal that has been domesticated in several different parts of the world.[28] They can live on rocky, uneven ground as long as they have ample grass for grazing—which because of their almost nonexistent muzzle—can crop grass very close to the ground [*a major issue with cattlemen as cows could*

---

28   With their heavy coats [before shearing] and an unusually oily skin, sheep can withstand very harsh winter weather for extended periods of time. Most herders contend that sheep can survive snow and cold better than horses or cattle in most situations. [None of the three can stand intense cold and overwhelming levels of snow for long periods of time as snow limits their access to grass on the open range]. Despite a regular fall shearing, the heavy/thick coat of sheep has grown back quite thick.

not graze after sheep had cropped the grass so short].[29]

There is some difference of opinion as to the intelligence level of sheep, as some conclude that a sheep can remember the faces of up to 50 other sheep for two years and can recognize human faces as well. Concerning the relatively defenseless nature of sheep, Mathers contends that "sheep. . . are the only animals that have self-defense bred out of them. They will not fight to [even] protect their young" [Mathers, 1975, 2]. He might well have added that sheep are just NOT physically equipped to defend themselves.

Tom always said "you treat sheep real gentle." You talk with them in quiet tones of voice. And, you teach your dogs to be pretty "easy on em'" as well. In some senses, Tom Stone seemed more considerate of the feelings of sheep [and most other domesticated animals] than he was of people. One thing for sure: he trusted most of "his animals" more than he did people. I have heard him say more than once: "They won't lie to ya."

It didn't take Tom long to learn that you don't really *herd* sheep—you control their wandering. The only things that will make sheep move fast [and this is used in a relative sense] is the smell of water and grass. And once they find that grass, they will stay until they have nubbed it so low they cannot eat anymore—then they are ready to move on. Depending on the stand of grass, they are ready to move about every 2-3 days. The herder's job, when it comes to food and water access, is to control the movement as sheep will rarely move more than 4-6 miles in one day—10 miles was highly unusual.

Sheep need less food than cattle [plains sheep are much smaller than cows]. And, sheep will eat things [types of grasses and even brush] that cows and horses will not. In that sense, sheep are easier

---

29 On the open range, cows eat about 6-6 ½ hours per day and consume some 25 pounds of hay in that time as well as 10 gallons of water. Sheep tend to "flock" instinctively, which makes them easy to handle in large numbers but those flocks will rapidly decimate a grazing area. Herds of 1000-2000 with a grazier [herder] and a dog [or two] and as many as 3000-4000 with a vigilant herder [with horse] and two good dogs was not uncommon. When grass was plentiful, a herd might stay in an larger area 4-6 weeks before moving on to a new grazing area.

to manage and find food for which results in higher levels of profit-ability especially during "tough [drought] times." So, during times when rain was scarce and there were sparse amounts of hay or grass to eat, stockmen, often grudgingly, turned to raising sheep as a more manageable income "crop." Arguably, sheep, although they *do need* a herder to protect them from predators, actually "winter" better than cattle.

Sheep will sometimes move on their own [smell of water or fresh grazing]—and, surprisingly, they can actually run quite a distance. Generally, however, they drift. They gravitate toward water and nat-urally drift as they graze. Losing them is an important concern, as sheep often wander off by themselves or in small bunches [4-6] and are easy prey for a coyote who might appear at most any time.[30] Just by drifting, a herd of sheep will move about a mile in some 30-40 minutes. If they are "spooked" by a predator [coyote, wolf or an occa-sional mountain lion, cougar or bobcat—the latter two will occasion-ally come down from the hill country] or an overzealous sheep dog, a herd of sheep will run—not very fast and not very far, but they will scatter and it takes time to get them back in a "round." In such cases where a herder is trying to "reassemble" the herd, it is the dogs' job

---

30   On the plains, one rapidly learns that the coyote is one of the most cunning and vicious creations of nature. Most frequently [though not always] running in packs, the coyote is much the same height as a standard collie—the male coyote [on the plains] usually weighing less than 75 pounds. Coyotes are relentless in their hunting and will strike an unsuspecting ewe or lamb with little or no warning—most often right around sunup. The physical damage a coyote can do to a full-grown ewe is indescribable. They start at the rear of the throat of the defenseless sheep and tear the rest of the body apart, eating as they go. Generally speaking, a coyote will eat only the heart and liver of their prey but might kill several members of the herd on a given day. Herders know a coyote works 7 days a week—and takes no time off for holidays.

While coyotes were the main predators of sheep, other enemies included wild dogs [who also ran in packs], bears, big cats [mountain lions, cougars or bobcats], wolves foxes and eagles—and in the Badlands, rattlesnakes. At the same time, sheep, as previously mentioned, are relatively helpless against most predators. They don't have sharp teeth, have little power in their kick and running away is not a tactic to which they normally resort. Usually, they stand in a defenseless posture and emit a pathetic bleet.

to approach the herd from the "right" side, move to the front and turn them in the direction the herder wants them to go.

We have suggested previously and with some conviction that Tom Stone loved "his" sheep. While he had never even seen a sheep before he got into the "north country," he developed a deep concern for them that came partly because "they needed somebody to take care of em'" and partly because *he* had been hired to do just that. This young Georgia man had an intense sense of responsibility—especially when it came to caring for something—or someone—who could not take care of themselves. That description fit the plains sheep perfectly.

There were numerous times when carrying out this responsibility to "his" sheep meant that he could not be with his family. His thinking was that Mary was there and she could handle it—he was right. There were also times when carrying out his "duties" to the herd nearly cost him his life. In some way, Tom Stone had developed a deep sensitivity that justified such an ultimate sacrifice. Our Mom--and Tom Stone would argue this often—finally gave up on the issue of his "over-dedication" to his wool charges--telling us "that's just the way your Dad is."

CHAPTER 7

Sheepherders: The One Behind the Herd

THERE ARE NOT many people in this world cut out to be sheep-herders because the "tasks" require a very special type of person. To be even moderately successful, the sheepherder must be dedicated FIRST to the welfare of the herd. The decisions the herder makes must have the herd as their primary concern. A successful sheepherder does not have a life of their own but a life that revolves around the herd. For the herder, a "vacation" or "holiday" was virtually unheard of.

Although he had no idea what would be involved in either the short- or long-term, herding sheep turned out to be an ideal job for a man like Tom Stone. He could "live his own life his own way" and nobody "paid much attention to ya—they left ya to yourself." Except for irregular visits from his boss [usually another hired hand] to bring supplies and his pay, Tom rarely saw anyone else on the trail. There were few roads on the plains of eastern Montana and western South Dakota at that time. And what roads that were there were impassible much of the time. The "lack of potential traffic" suited the sheepherd-er just fine. Quite frankly, herders seemed to have a strong desire—even need—for solitude.

In one sense, at least for the immediate future, Tom had found his "calling." He could "be his own boss," he had no immediate supervision and had to "please nobody"—at least on a short-term basis. He was totally in charge and his own man. For him, nothing could be much better than "when a man tells you what he wants done and *then leaves you alone to do it.*" In addition, it was obvious to ranchers in the area that knew of him, he was the type of herder that could be trusted with their valuable assets. All was well on the plains.

One has to read a good deal about the person who *chose* the life of a herder to understand such a decision. While it was a job that most might not have considered for themselves, a few unique "souls" gravitated toward this life in which they spent much of their time alone on the prairie. Weidel describes the "profession:"

> *A tough solitary, and* low prestige job, herding attract-ed a variety of personalities for different reasons. For many men, the reason was simple: herding provided a job, a roof over one's head, and guaranteed food. Often little or no experience was required to become a sheepherder—only a willingness to give it a try. One learned the job best by doing it. Should the job be-come unbearable, a man could quit, although actu-ally taking leave of the job presented some obstacles as the herder might have to wait for a visit from the camp tender or rancher to get transportation to the nearest town. [Weidel, 2001, 81-82].

Considerable note is made of the "loneliness" attached to the job [life] of the sheepherder. Most sheepherders frankly distinguished be-tween being "lonely and being alone." The latter was often an unde-sirable situation. Being alone for weeks on end, fit Tom Stone's needs quite well when he first moved to Montana. "That's just the way I like it. It don't matter if nobody else wants to live this way."

Sheepherders are intrinsically loners and that may be one of the few things they have in common. And, they come from all parts of the world[31] and many different walks of life—and gravitate to this loneliest [according to some] of jobs for a variety of reasons—some of which they don't even want you to know. Almost to a man, they enjoyed their lives as herders and developed strong affections for the animals around them—most surely their dogs and horses—if they had them. Stories are told of herders that even got quite attached to the sheep as their own—even *naming* some of the older ewes.[32]

Dogs, even those provided by the herd owner, often got so attached to "their herder" that they would not work for anyone else and would mourn the herder if/when they left for another job. Horses, too, though on the job to work [carry the herder on his rounds and pull the wagon when it came time for the base camp to move], were much more than beasts of burden to the herder. In actuality, herders spent more time with their dogs and horses than they did with people—even when the herder had a wife [and/or family] at the base camp, in a cabin court in the nearby small towns or at the home place [ranch/farm] of the owner.

Sheepherders understood that sheep needed "humans to watch over and protect them from sudden storms, and from predators such as coyotes and mountain lions [Weidel, 2001, 20]." *In that sense*, sheep are quite different from cattle and sheepherders are quite different from the western cowboy.

Michael Mathers, a professional photographer, spent some of his early days actually living in sheep camps and interviewing sheep

---

31 Some of the older herders would swear [literally] that, if you look close enough, every sheep is different—at least in the face. Some herders went so far as to name of their favorites and talk with them on a regular basis. And, as frequently noted, most herders were *kind* to their charges. There are countless stories concerning the affection that herders felt for their flock—not necessarily biblical, but a sense of caring for animals that, for the most part, did not possess the ability to care for themselves.

32 Sheepherders have been known to come from such places as France, Italy, Scotland, Portugal, Germany, China, Ireland, England, Finland, Romania, Norway, Russia, Mexico and many other areas of the world. While sheep were raised in many different areas of the world, sheepherders in the United States did *not* necessarily come from a background of herding in another country. [See: Weidel, 2001; Doig, 1978].

herders in Oregon, Washington and Idaho about very personal matters relative to their chosen profession. His comments add a great deal of insight to the nature of the herder and his flock. After his living experiences and interviews, Mathers notes:

> What kind of men are sheepherders? Why do they choose to live alone? I find them to be a unique breed of people. One boss of a sheep operation told me that they had to be crazy to live like that and, if they weren't to start with, they became crazy in time. . . they're peaceful people. [Mathers,1975, 7]

For some, the sheepherder's life was not an option—others chose it precisely because it provided them with a lifestyle they truly enjoyed.[33] Some herders wanted nothing else and would live and die with "their" herds [most herders did not own the sheep they tended] or in their wagons—the only home they knew. While the herder generally saw another human being no more than once a month when they brought them supplies or their pay, these graziers could be isolated from civilization for weeks—even months at a time. In most cases, the only company these early herders had was their horse and their dog—and the woolies. They knew the only visits they would have were by the infrequent herd owners' hired man that came to replenish the herder's basic supplies: beans, coffee, flour, sugar, tobacco, meat [beef/bacon/jerky] and occasionally a keg of syrup or a drum of strawberry jam—and plenty of salt for the sheep.

---

33 For one of the most entertaining and comprehensive accounts of herding sheep in this area [South Dakota particularly] see: Archer B. Gilfillan [1929] Sheep: Life on the South Dakota Range. Minneapolis, MN: University of Minnesota Press. This Ivy League, Phi Beta Kappa graduate followed a lifelong interest in sheep and spent 20 years living the life of a sheepherder on the plains of western South Dakota. Archie Gilfillan's description of his life in Harding County [near Buffalo, SD], is one of the most graphic and entertaining first-hand renditions of life as a sheepherder in print. His contention that a man would have to be "mentally unbalanced" to make a conscious choice to live the sheepherder's life was not challenged—at least in public.

While herding sheep did not [necessarily] require much experience, the first trials associated with being in charge of a herd most often provided a brand-new experience. Gretel Ehrlich describes *her* first experience as a totally inexperienced sheepherder. Thrust into service on a morning when the "regular" herder vanished, she observed:

> To herd sheep is to discover a new human gear some-
> what between second and reverse—a slow steady trot
> of keenness with no speed. There is no flab in these
> days. But the constant movement of sheep from water
> hole to water hole, from camp to camp, becomes a
> form of longing. But for what? [Ehrlich, 1985, 59].

Sheepherders rarely (it is estimated less than 10%) ever get married and those that do marry generally leave their spouses [and family] on the ranch or in "town." The life, especially in the winter months [October through March] was tough enough for a single man and was "no place for a family." Be clear, the only place to live was in a wagon [cook and/or sleep]. These wagons were primitive in nature, hot in the summer months and very cold in the winter months. There was no running, or even well water and very little privacy. Little room was available for personal possessions and scant space for sleeping accommodations. Base camp was a place for one [two at most] persons, the horse[s] and dogs. Tom and Mary Stone, as they would do in many other instances, went "against the grain."

It was commonly accepted that most "career" sheepherders drank [often to excess]. When they got into town, they frequently got drunk. Before they returned to base camp, if they had money left, they brought beer or whiskey back with them. Some graziers would return from town with enough booze to last them for a few weeks. While the *heavy* consumption of alcohol when tending herd was not generally approved by herd owners, some owners supplied a limited amount of libation to their herders—as a nominal reward. It was not uncommon for a veteran herder to become addicted to alcohol. This not only "ate up" their meager incomes but controlled a good part of their lives as well. Alcoholism was not unusual.

There are countless stories about herders drinking and carousing with women. Surely not all herders drank to excess as reported [even admitted] by many in the profession. After months of solitary existence, however, more than a few herders felt the need to "tie one on" for periods of a few days to a week. They most often spent all the money they had saved [drinking, buying drinks for others, loaning money to "friends" and entertaining ladies] while on the range. Most returned to their herds a bit worse for wear but ready to do the job they loved—and to replenish their "stake" for another trip to town.

While there certainly are countless rationale offered for the sheepherder's drinking, it seems most of them admitted they drank because it made them more sociable. Many a herder was known to loan money to "new-found friends" and buy "a round for the house" until their money ran out.

For the herder out on the prairie, the dangers were very real. If you got sick, there wasn't anybody to nurse you or go to town for help. If you fell or were thrown by your horse and broke a leg or arm, you got to the home place [or the closest town] as best you could. Getting hurt on the trail was serious. Sadly, even with serious injuries, the distance to help was the same--no matter your condition or the weather.

And then there was the cold. Temperatures often well below freezing for days at a time were not uncommon—and the "wind chill factor" had not even been conceptualized. While you may have been able to find limited "shelter" [i.e., draws or tree stands] for your herd, you just couldn't find any heat in the great outdoors. The herder had to live with the same weather as their charges although they had their wagon [to stop some of the wind] and his stove inside the wagon[s]. But while you can melt some of the ice on the rivets holding the steel rungs on the top of your wagon, there is only so much you can do to raise the temperature when it is 30-40 degrees below zero outside.

And, in many cases, the herder was outside with his herd during some of the most brutally cold times—keeping the herd from drifting and "fending off" ever-aggressive predators.

The open plains has always been a place for rapidly-developing and often very harsh weather. Violent thunderstorms with drastic lightning and high-level winds are not uncommon during the spring, summer or fall. Many instances of sheep being killed by lightning have been reported by herders. Tornadoes frequently touched down and raised havoc with everything in their path from wagons to animals—even people--as Mother Nature does not play favorites. A tornado will destroy a sheep wagon in seconds. And, if the herder is inside. . . .

Again, one would ask the question, more logical than rhetorical, why would anyone willingly subject themselves to this kind of life with its solitude, danger, low pay and very few obvious "fringe benefits?" To that question, there are likely as many different answers as there were these lone herders. Although it may be hard to believe, some men cherished this solitude—some may even have needed it. Some liked the sense of being in "total control" of their own lives with no "boss." The herder was, indeed, unique among all individuals—each having their own life's story. Many of those stories will/can never be told.

A few lone sheepherders [and the vast majority of herders did live and work alone--except for their animals], disappeared on these open plains and they were never found. Some just left the job because they "could not take it anymore." Some undoubtedly got ill and could not get the help they needed. It's also possible that a herder could have gotten in the sights of an angry Winchester on the "wrong side" of a prairie fence or stream.

The sheepherder needed a couple of good dogs, most often a horse, a cook/sleep wagon [for one person they were same wagon] that they usually left in a nearby "base" camp, and a Winchester carbine [for the wolves, coyotes, snakes and to stand up to the occasional unrelenting cattleman] for, although sheep are relatively docile, they are virtually defenseless and require a vigilant caretaker at all times.

With herds the size that Tom Stone worked, you needed lots of open grassland, water and room to move. And it is important to note that the "open range" was an idea that, in reality was changing. As the demand for land grew, the competition for the special vast [and somewhat flat] grasslands of Wyoming, Montana and South Dakota drew more attention—and became an object of serious contention as well.[34]

And what could be said about the "control" the herder could exert over his surroundings? Wasn't that one of the biggest "calling cards" for the herder. "At least ya didn't have anybody always tellin' ya what to do," Tom would often observe. He knew he couldn't control the relentless prairie winds or the intense summer heat. He knew he had no input into the overwhelming snowfalls and life-taking temperatures of the long winter months. And, although he could look for fresh water and good grass, he was aware that there were times when the "good stuff" was just not there. And even early on, he could see

---

34 There were "range wars" between sheepmen and cattlemen. And during a fifty-year period of history [c. 1870-1920] in some areas of Texas, Arizona and New Mexico and later in Colorado, Wyoming, Montana and Oregon, some "128 violent incidents occurred; over 50,000 sheep were killed; 28 sheepmen and 16 cattlemen died" [Weidel, 2001, 138-145]. The "Smiley Sheep Outfit," [including M.J. Smiley, Al Young, Ed Graham, Charles Smiley, Charles Marlette, and Bill Conway) with nearly 10,000 head of sheep moved out of the Rawlins, Gillette and Moorcroft area into South Dakota during 1903-04, for that very reason. While "looks," were exchanged and a few "western words" were spoken, no incidents of a "sheep war" were reported. While stories of conflict *between* cattle owners and sheep owners were often true, there many cases where *ranchers owned both sheep and cattle at the same time*. It was anecdotally suggested that ranchers owned cattle for prestige and sheep to make a living. And while the sheep did make it nearly impossible for cattle to eat immediately after they had grazed there, either herd [cattle or sheep] moving to a "new" grazing area made it possible for them to coexist in most cases. Such moves were, of course, predicated on the ready availability of good grazing land and water. *It seems unreasonable to conclude, as did some, that cattle would not eat or drink where sheep had been.* The common predators faced both cattlemen and sheepherders: coyotes, wolves and snakes [especially in the Badlands]. While coyotes rarely bothered humans or horses, these prairie rattlers did not discriminate and attacked anything that provoked them—including horses and dogs.

times and conditions changing--cattle ranches brought more control and more fences.

What he could control, however, was his reaction to these maladies. He knew he couldn't make the grass grow or clean water run in the creeks, but he could find where grass did grow [higher elevations in the spring after heavy snows] and places where the water was clear and cold [the Belle Fourche River]. He knew that winter would come and the heavy snows would fall. These were the times to move the herd in closer to the hills and off the flat plains—away from draws where drifts would trap the unsuspecting sheep. No matter what he did, the very bitter cold would plague he and his charges. But he knew that closer to the slopes [of the Black Hills] the temperatures would usually be some ten to fifteen degrees warmer—*and out of the brutal and life-taking winds* for the most part.

Tom knew he couldn't avoid the weather and what it brought. He knew he wasn't "in charge" of it either. But, he learned very early on that he could adjust and adapt to it. He could move his herd [before the days of barbed wire fences] to locations much more favorable.[35] As he learned the lands of eastern Montana and western South Dakota, he rapidly became one with it. The north Georgia transplant not only acclimated to a climate and set of conditions so very different from his home in Whitfield County, but he soon called this new, tough environment, his.

Clearly, those who did not adapt to the weather did not make it on the plains. The weather was what it was. It could be drastic, it could change within the hour, it could take a life without "emotion." Tom Stone knew it was "bigger" than any force on earth.

---

35   Some of the places Tom moved his herds were *not* locations anyone else seemed to want to use. For instance, Tom regularly moved his herd to spots along the White River [literally white in appearance] in the Badlands of South Dakota. This was not a venue for most herders. While cattle did [and still do] live there, grazing is not plentiful and the "scrub" that is available is edible by sheep but not a welcome menu for cows. The water in the White River is not drinkable for humans but sheep didn't seem to mind. The summer sun was scorching, the prairie dog towns [holes] were dangerous—especially to horses—and the rattlesnakes were in abundance—and deadly.

CHAPTER 8

Sheep Dogs: Special Talents— Intense Dedication

IT MIGHT BE argued that a "dog is man's best friend." That was not an argument on the trail—the sheepdog *was* the herder's best friend—and likely his most trusted "associate." There is little question that herder's dogs are an essential part of the "team" as herds of 2500-5000 would be virtually impossible to handle without skilled, working sheep dogs. Most sheep dogs are relatively small. And, there is a general consensus that

> A dog's herding ability stems from genetic behavior shared with wolves and coyotes. Though centuries of domestication and selective breeding have diminished the killing instinct, the desire to circle and gather a target is strong in border collies and some other breeds. [Hunhoff, August 2009, 82].

Sheep dogs instinctively know how to move sheep. And they understand that their work must be conducted in a calm manner—they know not to panic the herd. Good sheep dogs under-stand that it is important to get the *lead sheep* to begin heading in a particular direction or cross a stream first—then, the others will follow. Believe it or not, this is often accomplished by the talented dog's *eye contact*. If this does not work, the accomplished sheep dog is not hesitant to nip the target [lead] ewe to motivate her to move in the desired direction—knowing that the rest of the herd will generally follow.

Sheep dogs are extremely loyal to their herder—once the relationship is established, one would swear that is it something that is "innate" to the dog. Dogs develop this strong relationship with the herder *and rarely leave his side* unless told to "mind" the sheep [especially in times of danger] or move them to new grazing territory. The "understanding" that exists between a herder and his dog[s], is apparent even to the outside observer—even if these observers can't *explain* it.

Ehrlich [1985] effectively amplifies *the difference between* dogs *that were used with cattle and those used as sheep dogs*. She is quite explicit:

> Dogs who work sheep have to be gentler than cow dogs. Sheep are skittish and have a natural fear of dogs, whereas a mother cow will turn and fight a dog who gets near her calf (Ehrlich, 1985, 66].

Tom and Mary early on had *two* sheep dogs. The first was one Tom inherited from Mr. A.E. Blackford before he and Mary met. If Tom Stone *could* love, he loved that first dog. Since the dog was black, Tom named him Nigger. Not unlike most sheep dogs, Nigger stayed with the sheep much of the time—as he was told to do. And, although most older sheep dogs didn't attach themselves to new "masters" very fast, this one took to Tom right away—some time before either of them met Mary. He was loyal, he rarely barked [good sheep dogs don't bark much], he had "good manners" and knew how to take care of the herd—a skill a good sheep dog seems instinctively endowed with and honed to an art under a good herder. Tom talked to his dog often, fed him well and made sure he had a warm place to sleep if and when he slept at the base camp.

It was clear that a trust rapidly developed between them as Tom learned that the dog knew his job well. If there was trouble with the herd, Nigger sensed it and got to the root of the problem as he could run through or *on top* of the herd to meet the issue head on. The dog rapidly learned Tom's voice commands as well his subtle hand commands so they could readily communicate if they were out of hearing range. Tom's frequent compliment was that "he was a damned smart dog. He just knew what to do with them sheep."

It was not until after Tom and Mary were married that a second dog appeared on the scene. Always referred to simply as Dog [that bothered Mary as she thought he needed more of a real name] he had just wandered into camp one day. "The poor thing couldn't have weighed over 25 pounds," Mary lamented. He had a pretty bad case of mange in addition to being severely malnourished. He had some open wounds on his back haunches and on his face indicating that he had likely been in some fights and not fared very well. But as Mary made clear: "He's alive Dad and we're going to do what we can to help him." While Nigger was black with very small white spots, Dog was just about the opposite—mostly white skin with some black fur in spots. Because of the mange, most of his little body was pink/gray skin without much fur at all. They could not have thought at that time that he would stay with them for long.

In a romantic novel, Mary would have fallen in love with him at first sight. She didn't. And Dog didn't take to them right away either. He didn't come within 25 feet of the wagon but didn't drift much further away than that either. Against Tom's practical objections ("we ain't got food for another dog" or "he ain't never gonna make it"), Mary took some bacon and fried potatoes out to where the new arrival was "camped." He watched her carefully in an almost coyote-like manner. He wasn't moving closer, but he wasn't leaving either. Dog kept his distance at about 25 feet. After Mary had gone back to the wagon, failing in her attempts to get him to "at least come and eat something," he moved toward the food, snatched it and ran a few feet away before swallowing—he didn't stop to chew.

"The poor thing is close to starving," Mary observed—half pleading to an unsympathetic and more practical Tom.

"It ain't our job to feed ever' body that needs somethin' to eat. We got to take care of ourselves ya know," Tom countered.

After the new "guest" ate what he had taken in his first trip, he returned to get the rest—some pieces of fried potatoes. He snatched them up and moved away again to swallow them almost without chewing. By that time, Tom was coming out of the wagon.

He had two biscuits from breakfast and a skillet half full of water. Tom set the pan down on the dog's "circle" and laid the biscuits next to the pan and moved back away giving the new arrival room to maneuver toward the food and water. Dog moved cautiously and took a drink—pausing with each gulp to look up at his new and not-yet-trusted acquaintances.

"Good thing Nigger ain't here," Tom thought. "He'd a taken this 'un."

The sun was going down and even if Tom and Mary weren't newlyweds, it was time to go to bed. They left the water where it was and closed up the wagon. And while they really had no idea what their "guest" would do that night, they thought the best thing they could do was "wait 'til morning" to see what he had decided. At this juncture, nothing much would have surprised them.

At sunup, Tom was up getting a pot of coffee ready. He stepped out of the wagon and looked to the spot where the visiting dog had been—he was not there.

"That'll likely be the last we'll see of him. He probly only needed somethin' to eat," Tom concluded.

As was his habit every morning--he looked under the wagon where Nigger often slept only to see that his trusted dog had some company. Not really questioning *how* it had happened, it looked like Nigger had found a new companion. It also appeared that the canine guest was comfortable being taken in. Tom would later remember that "in all the years we had those two dogs, they never once fought or even growled at each other." While it was clear that Nigger was the alpha of the duo, once Mary had nursed Dog back to good health, he did his share of work with the herd. Nigger taught his new trainee well and Dog learned fast. He rapidly became part of the "family."

In most cases with "working dogs," one generally takes charge and "teaches" the other one what to do in dealing with a large variety of circumstance—mainly dealing with the sheep, understanding the commands of the herder and, probably most important, dealing with the ever-present issue(s) of predators. The new "kid on the block" quickly learned how to deal with adversities presented by snakes, coyotes, and other predators. Dog was a fast learner and the two "workers" soon contracted to share the responsibilities of working with both Tom and the herd. There was never a doubt, however, which was Tom's number one assistant. Nigger made that very clear.

Most sheep dogs worked hard and Tom considered his dogs an essential "part of the crew." In some instances, after a summer in the more difficult high country [better and more plentiful grass] many working sheep dogs were taken back to the homeplace for some re-cuperation. And while this may have been the case for the herder's riding horses as well, it was *not true for the dedicated herder*—he stayed with "the bunch."

There were practical reasons for herders with smaller herds to have only one sheep dog at a time—one was much cheaper to feed than two. But, with most larger herds [2000 and up] herders found it worthwhile to have 2 dogs. It was not unheard of that something happened to a dog [you "lost" them] and to be totally without a dog would have been a serious issue in herd management. In actuality, the dogs were good companions [for each other and the herder] and the work they did far outweighed the extra food [mostly scraps] that was needed for them.

Because of the considerable distances that dogs often got away from the herder, voice signals couldn't always be heard. And, al-though herding dogs are initially trained with vocal commands, such directions are soon substituted to nonverbal cues—hand, arm or even finger movements. In some cases, the movement of a raised finger in a specific manner [direction] told a smart, well-trained dog [and most of them were] just what they were expected to do. One other problem with dogs—especially younger ones: rabbits [jacks or cottontails], ground birds, or prairie dogs. If a sheep dog, who is not highly disciplined, and there would likely be *very few* of them, saw a jackrabbit or other "ground animal," they may likely give chase—it's instinct. Most sheep dogs won't grab a rabbit or hurt it—they just love the chase. Sheep dogs will often mess with things like a skunk or porcupine too. They invariably regret that confrontation.

Again, with larger herds, many felt a horse was necessary. When Tom Stone arrived in Montana, he actually had no idea how to saddle and bridle a horse, how and what to feed it much less how to ride one. Actually, when he got to Montana, he knew nothing about how to care for sheep either—in his life, he had *never even seen* many sheep.

Not one to admit he didn't know something, Tom didn't tell anybody about his lack of horse knowledge or riding skills for at home he'd only known his Dad's mules—and there's considerable difference between a saddle horse and "old Jack" [R.L. Stone's lead mule on the north Georgia farm].

Being able to ride, and ride well, was a given in Montana and this part of the west. He soon discovered that the acres to cover in keeping track of even a slow-moving [large] herd could be more than a man on foot could do. The relative ease of movement that a horse made possible more than balanced the extra feed [generally oats] in the wagon and the often-difficult task of picket roping a mount each night[36] so they would not wander too far from camp. A second problem with a horse stemmed from the winter snow and cold, for horses need some shelter from brutal winds and can freeze to death if

---

36 You would picket stake a horse in the summer so they could not wander off too far but located where they had plenty to eat and considerable room to maneuver [away from a pack of predators—coyotes, wolves or a mountain cat]. You never staked a horse in the winter because they would be unable to protect themselves by moving to shelter during a bad storm—and again, they became easier prey for predators.

left too long in the elements or hobbled during a harsh winter storm. And, herders knew that horses don't take care of sheep—they just got the herder to the places where that work could be done much faster.

When he and Mary were married, Tom worked for the A.E. Blackford "spreads." Mr. Blackford owned "a lotta stock and had a helluva lot a land." While exactly how much Blackford owned likely few people knew, his holdings of sheep, cattle, horses, hogs and land was immense. The word was that he had "over a hunnerd thousand acres in Montana alone." Tom Stone also knew that very few women were ever around the home place or on the trails except "missus Blackford and their five girls." Wisely, the newlyweds decided not to even bring the subject of their marriage up to anybody at the ranch and headed right out to the base camp with the herd. Tom also knew he had to relieve his temporary replacement who had already been there for 4 days.

What Tom Stone did know was that A.E. Blackford took good care of his men. While some herders in the area actually waited for their pay until shearing time and the wool was sold, others didn't pay until after the sheep were driven to the railhead and shipped. This was not the case with Mr. Blackford. A.E. Blackford paid in cash every month when he sent one of his "hands" out to each one of his several herds in different parts of the eastern prairies. The "packer" delivered a month's provisions at the same time he brought wages. "Wages wasn't really very important" to Tom since he rarely had a chance to spend any money [rarely went into town and didn't drink much]. But, he believed "a man should be paid for his work on a reglur schedule."

A.E. Blackford had a reputation in this country of eastern Montana and western South Dakota. It was a solid reputation. His "word was good." If you worked for the Blackford spread, your word had better be just as good—or you didn't work there long.

During his first year with A.E. Blackford, Tom drew $35 a month in the spring, summer and fall. During the winter months of November, December, January and February he was paid an additional $5 each month. The extra salary was for working under more "trying" winter conditions. Notably, about 3 months after Mary and Tom were married, Mr. Blackford began sending them an extra $5 every month. Neither of them ever asked for the extra money—neither of them questioned getting it either. The first month they guessed it was a wedding present—because the word about the "exciting" wedding was all over Carter County. But the extra money kept coming in every month after that as well—no matter what the base pay was.

Make no mistake, $5 extra each month was a great deal of money to Tom and Mary at that time. And it wasn't an amount inconsequential to A.E. Blackford as well—at least symbolically. Like other successful owners, he paid his help well. Blackford paid for the loyalty and longevity of all his men—who protected his very large investments. From his early days as a hand himself, A.E. Blackford knew you had to put a great deal of trust in all of your men—especially his herders because they were on their own most of the time. Most of the *cowhands* lived in the bunkhouse at the main ranch unless they were riding fence in a remote part of the ranch for a few days. They then stayed in a line shack.

Blackford also knew that once you got a good herder—one that would stay with the herd "no matter what--" and stayed sober most of the time, you did what you needed to do to keep him. The "good herder" took care of the owner's property as though it were his own. While virtually all herders lost some sheep [some losses were inevitable], you didn't stay on the payroll long if you lost too many—and the word circulated fast about who was a "good herder" and who you didn't want taking care of your stock.

A cowboy from the main ranch named Trotter visited the Stone's base camp every month [spring, summer and fall] and winter when the weather permitted. He rode out and trailed a pack horse with supplies and Tom's monthly pay [in cash]. Trotter first arrived at the camp one morning just before dinnertime [noon]. Tom was at the base camp for a noon meal and he and Mary both met Trotter as he rode in. Tom had his 30-30 leaning up against the cook wagon about two steps away—This was a typical precautionary measure.

"Aftnoon," Tom opened the conversation not knowing what to expect for a response.

"Afternoon," the lone rider responded as he got off his horse. "Name's Trotter and I work for Mr. Blackford at the main ranch. I rode out here to bring your supplies and pay."

"That's a pretty long ride," Mary offered. She could tell a good deal about a good rider when she saw them "set a saddle" and mount or dismount. This was a cowboy who had spent many hours sitting forward in the saddle.

"Can you sit and have dinner with us Mr. Trotter?"

"It's just Trotter ma'am and I'd be obliged for some dinner and some coffee," he answered politely.

"We got both and you're welcome to join us," Tom answered—almost happy to have some company from the main ranch—but only for a short time.

"How are things at the ranch?" Mary asked, making what she thought was a good conversation starter.

"Good," Trotter responded, seemingly closing off any "question/answer" session.

"Ever get to Ekalaka?" Mary continued, trying to open up the exchange a bit.

Just maybe, she thought, he might know something about her sister—or even her brother-in-law Gib. She had been gone for quite a while and had left town on less than favorable terms. She still loved her sister and wanted to know if she was OK.

"No Ma'am," Trotter replied—again politely but still very much matter-of-fact.

Mary Stone had already learned from her husband to respect another person's [man's] right to "say nothin' if they didn't have nothin' they wanted to say." She didn't look over at Tom to see what he was thinking—she already had a good idea what that would be. And she could almost hear him later telling her [not always politely] that "you don't get into somebody else's business if they don't want you to." Tom expected her to know that—he certainly followed his own advice in life. She was appreciative that he didn't say it at the time, but she knew what he was thinking at the time and in the years ahead she would hear it often enough to make up for the times he held off from saying as much.

Mary made some biscuits, warmed a pan of beans and cooked some thick bacon. That, along with plenty of strong coffee made a good meal—much better than most people would expect [or get] when they are out on the trail. Nobody talked much during dinner although Mary *wanted* to ask him all kinds of questions about things back in Ekalaka. So, she didn't ask. Just as well, he wouldn't have known anyway since he had only been to Ekalaka once in his life even though the Blackford ranch was less than 20 miles northwest of there. Tom and Mary soon got the impression that Trotter spent most of his time working and very little time in "social settings."

And so, Trotter was the only name they ever knew him by—and they didn't know his first name, last name or a nickname. They *did know* he was a "decent sort" and they learned to depend on him to do what he said he would do. Not surprisingly, as was likely in that part of the country that nobody knew much about many of the "hands" at the ranches that were often 20-30 miles apart.

Trotter came to the base camp on a "regular" basis—much of the movement in that country was dependent on the weather in any time of the year—mainly in the winter months. During the bad months of the winter, he still brought supplies: food for Tom and Mary, some oats for the horses, salt for the sheep and Tom's pay.

Mary wasn't there for most of the bad winter months [November through March] as she generally moved into a small cabin court in the town nearest the base camp—especially once they started having kids. During the worst days of winter, if there was a break in the weather, you could expect Trotter to ride into camp during that break. Plains ranchers learn to "read" the weather fairly well as a matter of survival—for themselves, their hands and their herds. They were rarely wrong and made plans based upon the weather patterns [*which were somewhat predictable*].

It is hard to imagine the winter weather in this country. Nature was truly in control of life in many ways. The cold, especially when it was accompanied by strong winds, would freeze a man to death if he was in open country in a matter of hours—or less. Those who knew the true nature of this country did NOT challenge it—nor did they take any unnecessary risks with the weather unless their family, a fellow worker or some of their stock was at real risk.

During "good weather" [and there were some good days even in winter], those who needed to move, did so. Trotter arrived about dinnertime [middle of the day], unloaded supplies, had something to eat and headed back for the ranch—he did not stay for supper. During the winter, he normally arrived later in the day, had supper, spent the night at the base camp, sleeping inside one of the wagons and left in the morning [after breakfast] the next day—if the weather held. Tom remembered Trotter as a "pretty good feller."

This would have meant that he did his job and didn't talk much. That would have been Tom's definition of a "good feller."

Even though Trotter was Tom and Mary's primary contact [actually, only contact] with the "outside world," they did not talk much. He asked Tom about the herd [Tom suspected that Trotter had once tried herding sheep but abandoned it for a more regular life on the ranch] but did not volunteer much information about the "main" ranch as he probably knew Tom wasn't too interested. You soon learned in this country that people just didn't talk much—whether they knew something or not—they just didn't talk much. The three of them did not talk about anything in Ekalaka even though Mary was "itching to ask him about her sister Grace"—and her brother-in-law but she never did.[37]

The last time they saw Trotter, he gave them some bad news. It was late fall and he rode up to the base camp just before noon. Tom had been on the back side of the herd so he saw Trotter coming and got to camp just about the same time as the cowboy and his pack horse. The look on Trotter's face was the same as it always was as he tied his horses to the second wagon.

"Mornin." Typical Trotter.

"Mornin." Typical Tom Stone.

"Got your supplies and your pay. Got some bad news.
Mr. Blackford took sick and died."

While Tom had met Mr. Blackford only once, this was a shock. A.E. Blackford was a legend. He was the sort of man who didn't die. He was a man like other men—he grew older but "he did not die." Mary had never seen the man but felt a lump in her throat—like more bad news was coming.

Trotter seemed to know what questions were on their minds. He uncharacteristically volunteered more information.

"I don't know much about what's gonna happen, but
they said Missus Blackford is movin' back east with

---

37 Mary would not be reconnected with her sister for nearly 30 years when she discovered Grace living in Portland, Oregon with a son, Connie. They visited each other and corresponded until Grace's death in 1977. Mary found her brother Bill some 40 years later in Arkansas and they visited once before his death in 1986. Mary and her brother Louie, who had moved to White Lake [SD] and later Rapid City [SD] with his family, stayed in close contact with the Stones but only visited on occasion as it was some 175 miles [to Pierre, SD] and the Stones did not have a car.

one of her daughters. They're sayin' the older girl and her man are gonna run the ranch."

"What'll you be doin?" Tom asked the obvious.

I'm stayin' on," Trotter continued. He might have added that he liked his job and had no other place to go that would have been any better. Tom and Mary got the impression that Trotter had been with the Blackford's a long time and you could hear what sounded like loyalty to the family in his voice. He didn't ask Tom or Mary what they planned to do even though that seemed a logical question. It was one of those things you just didn't bring up at the time. If somebody wanted you to know something, "let them tell ya."

Tom and Trotter unloaded the supplies off the pack horse and noticed that there were obviously some *extra* supplies on the horse. Trotter had loaded some extra oats for the horses [in the winter months, horses were usually fed oats twice a day] and it looked like enough food to last for well over a month. Tom said nothing about the extra provisions but the two men sensed that it might be some time before more supplies came out to the base camp.

Mary fried some potatoes and a piece of beef steak [from the new supplies] as a sort of "celebration" dinner—knowing that they didn't really have anything to celebrate. In some ways, this may have been more of a farewell meeting. As she made some fresh coffee and a pan of biscuits, she did consider that this might be the last time they would experience their monthly visit with Trotter. After dinner, Trotter and Tom both followed custom and washed their own dishes. Trotter gathered up some firewood for Mary and put it in the wood bin on the cook wagon. Nobody said anything. There really wasn't much to be said—or that needed to be said.

Things were likely going to change. Tom Stone didn't understand change very well—and liked it even less. Still, both he and Mary knew change was inevitable. Later that night, long after Trotter had headed back to the main ranch, Tom and Mary talked about what the news might mean. Would they be let go? Would the new owners get out of the sheep business? Would these two just starting out their new life together have to make other plans? The "security" they had felt in their herding job didn't seem very secure right now. The Stones may not have been scared—but they were fast becoming very concerned about their *immediate* future.

This life was a good one for them—newlyweds who did not want any connections for now. They were quite happy with their life that provided them with "isolation." But they had just gotten married and were not going to "let the shine wear off" their new life together. Both of them felt a sense of a "new" start doing something together that they really enjoyed—and there was nobody around to whom they had to answer at every turn they took. They didn't owe anybody. They didn't have any bills to pay at the first of the month. They had plenty to eat and a warm [most of the year] place to sleep. Their thoughts were about each other, the sheep and their surroundings. It was a pretty simple life—and simple was good.

When you have contact with very few people on a weekly or even monthly basis, you tend to analyze those you do meet more fully. And, while Tom and Mary did not see Trotter very much, he was one of the few people they did see on a "regular" basis and actually felt they "knew" him. Some things seemed obvious: he was quiet, polite and stuck to the task he had been assigned to do. You could be sure that Tom Stone respected those traits. Still, Mary thought some about what kind of life he must have had. She assumed he was not married since very few hired hands ventured into matrimony--at least not for very long. She also concluded that he was quite private. While most "country people" stay "to themselves," not all do. And, when given a chance to talk about things at the "homeplace," he declined to do so—with no particular show of reason.

Even in his quietness, the Stones learned some things about Trotter. He was a hard worker who knew his job—and gave a full day's work for a for a day's pay. He was a "cow person" and not a sheep person. He was not one to mince words—he said what he had to say in as few words as possible. And the thing that Tom admired most, Trotter was very loyal and respectful to the Blackford family.

While herders did not tend to adopt a particular sheep as a pet [there were exceptions], they often hand-nursed a newborn lamb whose mother may have died during the birthing process, been killed by a predator [or disease] or a ewe who *rejected her new offspring for some reason.* Tom Stone would often make a seemingly out-of-character remark about how "them little ones really needed someone to look after 'em for a few weeks." And he [or Mary when the herd was close to the base camp] were the only ones around to do that.

The strongest connections herders had, other than a spouse in rare cases where the herder was married and the spouse was willing/able to accompany them on the prairie, were with the dogs and horses they depended upon so heavily. True sheep dogs instinctively understand what needs to be done to take care of a herd. While the sheep dog will rest when the opportunity arises, they have a strong sense of the needs of the herd and seem to circle the herd constantly--looking and listening for trouble. Most of the time, a pack of coyotes can be heard "howlin' and yippin'" in the distance. The sheep dog[s], along with the herder, were on patrol during much of the night—especially when there was any sense of danger. That danger usually meant bad weather or a pack of hungry coyotes.[38] And a "pack" usually meant trouble.

At times the herder directed his dogs, generally with a flick of a wrist or even a finger, and the sheep dog moved to encircle and turn the herd in the desired direction—often by nipping the slower sheep in the "backside" to get them moving. It was not uncommon to see a

---

38 While the similarities among coyotes is readily discernible, there are some differences in size and weight—adult males are usually between 60 but rarely over 80 pounds. Generally, coyotes seemed to either be sleeping or on the hunt. In appearance, most coyotes look as though they are near starvation. They consistently appear gaunt and with little strength. As common prey, sheep have little sense of fear of the coyote who is vicious and cunning. Luckily for the somewhat unsuspecting sheep, a smart sheepdog and knowledgeable herder *did not underestimate a coyote—especially those in a pack of three or more.*

large herd, tightly compacted in a grazing area, with one or two dogs *dashing across the backs of the flocking sheep* to get to an area where they could then turn the herd in the desired direction.

Not all herders lived on the open plains with their herd[s]. Some graziers actually kept the herd near the ranch at night and moved them to differing close spots each day for grazing—returning to the relative protection of the "homeplace" at night. This provided a considerable amount of security for the sheep [who tended to wander at times on their own] and allowed the herder the luxury of sleeping in the bunkhouse and eating a couple of meals at the ranch each day. This plan never interested Tom and Mary Stone. "We wanted to be out on our own," Tom asserted—not surprising for a loner and a newlywed.

One can better understand Tom Stone if they understand the sheepherder's life "in general." Tom had learned early on that the life of a herder was 24 hours a day, 7 days a week and 52 weeks per year. But, while herding sheep dictated one's lifestyle and demanded a total commitment to achieve success, it had advantages for some people. "Some people" *liked to work every day*. Some people wanted to be left alone to do their work without much supervision and no criticism. These "loners" thrived on the responsibilities that went with the job of herding. Tom Stone was among that group of "some people." In his way, the herder's life "suited him fine."

It's also important to get a feeling for his relationship with the land—especially "this land." It would be too easy, and perhaps a bit trite, to suggest that Tom Stone loved this land. While that may be a bit extreme, it would be in line to suggest that this north Georgia transplant had a *respect* for this new, wide open land. It was not at all the same feeling he had for his home in Whitfield County. This new respect was not out of some kind of fear—he was not afraid of much and this land—including the weather. In life, not much made him fearful. The land was almost like a friend—but he had already had some winter experiences that "friends don't do to friends." If this country was a "friend," this one was brutally honest at times. Still, it helped him to get what he needed and wanted most of the time. And he knew he didn't [nor ever likely would] *understand* this land totally. Yeah, it would seem appropriate to stay with the notion of *respect*.

Although it might sound a bit strange, Tom Stone felt "this land" actually had some concern for him as well. The land was tough. It was unpredictable. It treated everyone the same way. But, Tom mused, it must have cared "some" about him since it had not handed out anything that he couldn't handle. Maybe their respect, his for the land and this country for him--was mutual. Then maybe he'd been living out in this desolate place too long. Anyway, he "loved" it where he and Mary were and he was going to stay--at least for the foreseeable future.

This strong feeling for—or about—the land—perhaps even affection—was a sense that was germane only to his "new home" in Montana and South Dakota. And while some of these "mixed" feelings may have had more to do with the people "down there," Tom knew he had a *different* connection with his *new home*. With some confidence, you could conclude that he *understood* this place he had chosen for his new life. And, for survival's sake, a thorough understanding of your surroundings [most surely including the weather] was critical.

After living in this country for a while, you tended to forget how big it really was—how open it was. That was not a problem since only a small part of it affected you at any one time. What you "damned sure didn't want to forget about this country was that it would turn on you overnight." Tom wasn't suggesting that the country was vindictive or held grudges although he often talked of it in as though the country had human qualities. And, he concluded that it could be "just mean as hell." That meanness showed in the 30+ degree below zero nights when the wind blew across the flat prairie at 25 miles an hour—often harder.

This same "meanness" showed in the heat of July and August when you knew the temperature was over a hundred in the shade—and there was no shade to be found. The country showed its obstinance when it wouldn't rain for close to a month and you got to a point where you were afraid to move your herd because they would drop over from heat exhaustion. Tom so often said, "You better learn to get along with this country cuz' it ain't gonna change for you." When you were trailing a herd, you constantly looked for any sign of trees—especially cottonwoods—because chances were that they were growing near a creek bed [or what had been a creek]. Cottonwood trees are "seeded" by floodwaters that usually come during the spring of the year. While the creeks often dry up in the hot summer, the cottonwood trees often remain and may grow to be large [20-30 feet high on the plains—40-70 feet tall along the Missouri River]. So, there was at least a chance there was water there. And when it got really dry, a "chance" was better than nothing.

> "So why stay here?" Mary asked that question of Tom
> many times during their first 20 years of marriage.

Many times his answer was not to answer her at all. In his way, that was an answer. It might have meant I don't have any good reason. It might have been because he didn't feel he should have to answer to anyone for staying where he was—even his wife. Perhaps it was because this was *home*. Many times during those early years of marriage there wasn't much. No house. No car. They owned nothing except the "clothes on their backs and the boots on their feet."

> "Because this is home Mother. We're doin' just fine
> right here."

And as most of their family discussions went, "that was all there was to it." He didn't have to say that because she knew. They had both come to the conclusion early on that things were "gonna be pretty much how *he* said they were gonna be." At this time in their lives, she accepted this as reality.

We keep suggesting that Tom Stone was "his own man." And we recognize that would be an understatement. However, he could be "his own man" *only* in an environment like this one. As his environment changed in the next few years, his ability to control his own destiny diminished markedly—to the point that it nearly destroyed him. And, when the environment did [inevitably] change and he did not, would not, or could not adapt to it, he "packed up and left"—everything and everybody. He physically got away from the things in his life he could not control or did not like [sometimes family]. He might move to another place to live or even, at times, to another state—as he did more than once without telling anyone else—even Mary.

It would seem to fit the classical Freudian "fight or flight" syndrome. Maybe it did. Psychology aside, this was Tom Stone—and he continued this behavior until he got too old to "pull up stakes" and get away from all things undesirable to him—family, work, neighbors or the place he lived. Most of the time It was moving away from something undesirable rather than moving toward something that suited him better.

CHAPTER 9

The Sheep Wagon: The Herder's Home—Their Only Home[39]

FOR TOM AND Mary Stone, not unlike virtually all other sheepherd-ers, the sheep wagon was their home. For over 20 years, with the exception of the short time[s] they spent at the homeplace in Georgia and small cabins for limited times in winter, it was all they knew. Still, they "made do" because *that was all they had and all they really knew.* In many ways, it was enough for them. They were very happy most of the time. Their lives and needs did not differ much from most herders—quite a simple existence.

Sheep wagons came in two major "styles." While most herders both lived and cooked in the same wagon, herders with families often got a *sleep* wagon as well. The sleep wagon was basically the same size but configured differently inside. Generally, sheep wagons were 12 or 14 feet long and 6-7 feet wide. Most herder's wagons contained a bed, stove, 2 windows [one usually above the bed and the other

---

39 An exceptional work, devoted entirely to the *sheep wagon* has been thoroughly researched and very well-written by Nancy Weidel [2001]. Weidel has devoted chapters to such things as different styles of sheep wagons, the herding life, women in sheep wagons and even modern-day herders and their domiciles. For a better understanding of the sheep wagon and the people who called it "home," Weidel's work is most highly recommended. This excellent work also contains some outstanding photography and an excellent bibliography for reference work.

on the opposite *side* of the wagon], wooden shelves built along the inside to store metal plates and cups, canned fruit, vegetables, coffee, etc. Sheep wagons had a hinged [fold-up] table on the wall and a kerosene [or coal oil] lamp. Most importantly, they had a stove--for heat and cooking.

The inside of the wagon was small and had to be organized very carefully to provide the needed space. Sheepherders had few personal possessions. Many did not read and those that did had few books in their possession [when they did get a newspaper from town with supplies, they kept it for months—reading and rereading]. Their clothing was simple—and very practical. There were virtually no frills in a sheep wagon [although Mary did begin "decorating" after the first few months with simple curtains on the windows].

Virtually all sheep wagons were built with considerable storage space [compartments and shelves on both the outside and the inside]. Such compartments were used judiciously. Tom and Mary learned early to plan very thoroughly. They did not waste anything. It was obviously better to have provisions left over when they got their new supplies than to run out with no way to get any help. [40] This was a "lesson" that herders learned early on.

One essential space [inside] was a metal-lined flour bin that was usually built near the stove. Flour, along with beans, coffee and sugar, was one of the *essentials* to the existence of the herder. Most sheep wagons [sleep or cook], had storage spaces built above or between the wheels as well. Little space was wasted in this primitive domicile. Building sheep wagons was an art--and still is to this day.

In some ways, sheep wagons generally resembled the larger

---

40 It was essential to be fully supplied with food for both the herder and their horses [oats]. Such supplies needed to be in closed shelving [outside so scavengers did not help themselves and inside so they did not fall when moving the wagon from one base camp to another]. More than ample supplies were prized by the herder as they were often isolated for more than a month on a secluded trail. What they had for supplies in the wagon *was all they had*. They could not go to a store to buy more and they might not, in difficult times, be able to rely on supplies getting to them from the main ranch. For the most part, and herders knew it, they were on their own.

Conestoga wagon but unlike the Conestoga, *extended over* the large, steel-rimmed wooden wheels. Sheep wagons were generally covered with a canvas top [usually double- or triple-layered] *stretched tightly* over the steel rungs/hoops that served as the roof to the wagon. While many sheep wagons were "custom-built" by their users, there were a number of companies that also specialized in building sheep wagons [Bain Wagon Company, Peter Shetler, James Julius "Cooster" Svendsen, The Studebaker Company, etc.] Some sheep wagons were covered with corrugated aluminum, which was better in dealing with most weather although heavy rain and hail made disturbing noises for the occupant. The typical sheep wagon was tall enough for a six-footer to stand up straight [in the middle]and was fairly comfortable for two people—not a family of three or more. The floor was generally constructed of double-layered wood [to keep the bitter winter cold out]. Inside the wagon, protection from the elements was actually *reasonable.*[41] And, during the summer, if you kept the Dutch door [on the end of the wagon] open, [top only to keep out varmints—mostly pack rats] and one of the windows, you could get some cross draft and it was quite pleasant inside. Make no mistake, it was hot in summer but out of the direct sun and during the evening the prairie cooled off considerably most days.

Fall was easily the best time of the sheepherder's life. After that part of the herd that was to be sold had been delivered, the "heavy work" was done, the herder found considerably more time to relax—to read if they did, to be with family if they had one, and to ponder and enjoy the life that most of them truly loved.

Don't make the mistake of thinking this was anything like "camping out." This was home. And it was generally the *only home most herders had.* This was notably true for both Tom and Mary Stone. It was their only home for nearly a quarter of a century.

---

41 One must remember that herders, if not always their families, were people who were able to *adapt to this type of living*—many enjoyed it. In addition, these were days where homes were heated with fireplaces—and there was no air conditioning. In the most extreme weather, hot or cold, Living on the plains was often harsh. Living in a sheep wagon was just somewhat worse.

After they started a family, Mary and the kids would most often go to a small cabin court in a town close to the base camp rather than winter in the wagon[s]. This is not to suggest that the months of October to March [even some of April] were not bad. Quite the contrary. Early or late snowstorms were not surprises. They were just more tolerable since they were relatively short-lived. The prairies often rained *hard* and most wagons leaked around the doors, windows and every other joint. "You just couldn't stop the hard wind and rain from comin' into the wagon when it was really blowin."

And, the wide-open prairie where the grass grew best was also flat and open so there was little to stop the sometimes vicious winds that blew in virtually every season—40 to 50 miles an hour.

The earliest sheep wagons were built in blacksmith shops and on local farms and ranches. Commercial builders generally charged under $250 for a sheep wagon complete with the running gear and canvas cover[s]. More complex sheep wagons cost around $600 [See: Home Comfort Model] with sheep wagons manufactured in the 1970's priced between $9800 and $15,000 [Wilson Camps of Midway, UT].

More modern-day sheep wagons have changed somewhat. Although they have changed little in size, they are somewhat better constructed to withstand the cold, the wind, the snow and the rain— and they have *rubber tires!* Most sheepherders have a battery- powered radio and some even have a windup clock [for whatever reason I don't know] while others have a battery-powered TV. If a herder reads, it is a real treat to get a newspaper from time-to-time. And herders will assure you they read cover-to-cover and even scan the classified ads.

In the winter "it was cold as hell" out on the prairie where herders spent nearly all of their time—in the summer, the same place was "hot as hell." It still is. Tom would talk as though he never even thought much about this. It was reality. In the winter, the herder moved the sheep to a winter bedding ground [when and if such a location was available]. This was an area with ample grass [not necessarily as good as the open range] but could provide some much needed [actually lifesaving] protection from the winter winds and snow. Rest assured, the plains of eastern Montana and western South Dakota both had brutal winds and plenty of snow. There was less movement in the winter as neither the herder nor the sheep wanted to travel very far. Sheep wagons were not as comfortable as a normal "stick-built" house—but then, *most herders never had or knew any other home than their wagon.*

During the bad days and nights of winter, Mary remembered that

> "it was so cold inside the wagon that ice froze on the steel rivets attaching the metal rungs holding up the canvas roof. When Dad got the stove going, the ice started to melt and dripped until everything below got wet."

It was still "a helluva lot better than sleeping on the ground with nothin' to cover you but your overcoat or a slicker," Tom would caution.

These words were spoken by a man who had done just that on many a winter night when he couldn't get back to the base camp and needed to stay close to "his" herd. Mary related times when he was out that

> "he froze the tip of his nose, cheeks, ears and his toes. My God, he even froze his private parts—just to watch after those sheep. But that was your Dad."

In Tom Stone's mind, it wasn't about living conditions. Instead, it had to be

> "all about them sheep. You had to take care of 'em becuz' them poor devils couldn't take care of themselves. It was your job and you did it."

Tom Stone didn't think the same way about his horses or his dogs as he did about the sheep. When it came to horses, he thought they were the *most loyal* animal he had ever seen—next to his dogs. [Remember, he did not have any horses in north Georgia].

> "If you asked him to, a good horse will run himself for
> you until he drops over dead."

He spoke as though he had witnessed it. While he admired his horses, he likely loved his dogs.

> Dogs," he often bragged, "are pretty damned smart.
> They know what to do most ever' time without bein'
> told."

This strong feeling for dogs would stay with him for the rest of his life. He always had a dog and always treated them in a very "human" way. Mary regularly noted that "Dad liked his dogs better than a lot of the people he knew."

Here again, a large part of this praise was based upon the loyalty he felt was inherent to both horses and dogs. Such loyalty, shown by either humans or animals, was most surely one of the major components of what he had learned in his early years and "who he was." It remained critically important in [his] life—a fundamental value.

In contrast to the respect he had for his dogs and his horses, Tom never talked about the *intelligence level of sheep*. He did talk about their *habits and their tendencies* as this was critical to know in caring for them. When it came to sheep, it was not about whether "they could or couldn't." It was about *"his job to see that they was took care of."* To Tom Stone, this was an inescapable sense of responsibility.

This sense of responsibility was a trait Tom and Mary Stone would try to instill in all their kids—*along with* the idea of self-reliance as an *ideal to strive for* and practice in real life—whether their kids agreed with them or not. The insistence upon such a standard would cause considerable dysfunction[s] among the family members in the years to come. You can be sure Tom Stone could not imagine any person worth much that "couldn't stand on their own two feet."

CHAPTER 10

Trailin' Sheep: Times Could Get Tough

HAVING TRAILED SHEEP for nearly 3 years before he met Mary Danley, Tom Stone was well aware of how tough times could be on the sheep trails of eastern Montana. As her Uncle Gib's "hired hand" and his only "bronc buster," Mary Danley was tough enough for "a sixteen year-old woman," but she did not know the life of a herder. She would soon get baptism under fire. On March 22, she was a serious, but young, single teenager. On March 23, she was a married woman with what seemed to be insurmountable immediate and heart-breaking legal problems with the local sheriff. On March 24, she was the adopted "mother" of 3000 head of sheep and living with them on the grasslands of eastern Montana.

> "It ain't no place for you if you ain't tough," Tom
> would often remind his new bride.

Mary Stone found out pretty fast. And, Tom did not hesitate to remind her if he felt the need to do so. If his new bride wasn't ready on day one, she soon got that way. In two months, it would be shearing time—another new experience.

Life on the prairies *does not wait until you get ready*. There wasn't much that was fun about it. Still, this was the life Mary Ellen Danley had chosen—*even if she didn't know what she was getting herself into.* If you could outlast the winters on the trail, if you could survive the solitude, if you could make it with lean rations and not much pay to show for it, "you could make it."[42]

One thing Tom and Mary knew for sure: the decision they made to get married meant there was no "going back." Both of them knew that would have meant admitting failure--and survivors, like Tom and Mary Stone, didn't include failure in their repertoire.

Tom and Mary had their first child in the middle of May early in their 3rd year of marriage. But, while Tom and Mary "stopped" to have Bob [Thomas Robert, May 14, 1927], all those that lived in this country knew that the spring of the year was "time for lammin." Of course, that part of Mother Nature's plan wasn't going to be interrupted for any other part of her grand designs.

While not all ewes lambed ["cull ewe" was the name given to those who did not], most did. And, it was not uncommon for a strong ewe to have more than one offspring [more likely in the eastern United States than it was in the west—as a result of better food/grass]. As a rule of thumb, if you had 2000 head of ewes [which would be broken down into smaller "bunches" at lambing time] you expect upwards of 2000 lambs. If you had help during lambing "season" [time], the herder could expect a "crop" of 125% since ewes had twins that often. These twins would more than make up for the lambs that could not be saved at birth or some ewes that just did not lamb. Herders, their spouses [family if they had any] and often some extra hired hands, if they could be found, worked very hard and fast during the lambing season. Lambs, were, of course, a large part of the

---

42 During this time cowhands usually got about $25 per month plus room and board [bunkhouse] and feed for their horse—cowboys usually owned their own horses and their own tack. *Sheepherders generally got more than cowhands—* nearly half again as much.—especially during the winter months. The wagon[s], their horse with all essential provisions supplied for them. That wasn't really an issue with cowhands as they didn't *care much for the sheep business and did what they needed to do to avoid sheep and sheepherders.* In their financial remunerations, there were not 401Ks, IRAs or other retirement accounts for either of them.

owner's profit picture.

Lambing occurred in the spring when there was plenty of grass that helped ready the milk of the expectant ewe. Lambing was compressed into about 3 weeks [or less] and it didn't matter much if "you was ready or not, the new lambs was goin' to come." If the winter moisture was limited and grass was not ample for feeding, Mother Nature tended to limit the lamb crop and delay the birthing time a bit as well.

Ewes have their first lambs at two years of age, and many of them need some help during the delivery—at that age as well as when they are older and still delivering. On occasion, a ewe will, for a variety of reasons, abandon [ignore] her offspring immediately after birth.[43] It is then that the herder or someone else helping during lambing *must* step up if the "orphaned" lamb is to be saved. Tom and Mary both worked long and hard hours during lambing season helping the ewes as well as the newborn orange-colored lambs [first days].

> You needed to save every one of 'em you could," Tom would remember. "That's how we made our money in the fall when we took'em to the railroad. Every one you lost cost ya ' money."

---

43 If a ewe had more than one lamb, it was not uncommon for her to feed *only one*. She would sometimes care for twins but certainly not a third [which was a rare birth occurrence]. When a third lamb is born to a ewe, they are usually destroyed. Nor is it unheard of for a ewe to "adopt" another lamb *before hers is born*—in such a case, *she will not feed her own when born*. There were times when a ewe would get sick during delivery and was unable to feed her newborn. Then too, some ewes died during the birth of their lamb[s] and the herder most often assumed responsibility for feeding the new arrival [if they had the "manpower" to do so]. Orphan lambs [called bums] that were not nursed by their mothers were generally fed goat's milk by the herder. Another option for the bums was to find an older ewe who did *not* have a lamb and "convince" her to adopt the orphan. Scientifically, vaginal stimulation [VS] of a non-lamb-bearing ewe may induce "maternal behaviors" on the part of the ewe to accept [and feed] a lamb that is not really hers by birth [See: Lynch, Hinch and Adams, 1992, 139]. If a ewe's lamb died at birth, it was not uncommon to skin the dead lamb and drape the hide over a bum [one that had no mother]. 80%-90% success rates were reported for adoption when a bum was covered with the hide of the ewes dead offspring and the two were isolated for a couple of days to "get acquainted" by smell.

The first hour after a lamb's birth is especially critical. If the lamb gets to its feet and feeds, it will be fine. If it fails to get up—and therefore does not eat—it will die. Lambs who do not get up and feed must be helped by a person to survive. Regardless of the normal maternal instincts of a ewe, she cannot help her new offspring get up. For the first few days, the lamb is somewhat off-balance with crooked, spindly legs. The ewe will stand over her lamb, lick him and make strange noises but cannot, by herself, get her new baby to "stand" and eat [most lambs actually eat from their knees].

It's both rewarding and amazing when you see a new lamb some 8-10 days after their birth. They have lost their orange color, run full speed, jump over small objects, play games with other lambs and eat ravenously any time they get a chance. When you see a lamb feed, it is difficult to understand why their mother *would not move away from them*. They charge their birth mother, fall to their front knees and ram their head into the underside of their mother until they "hook onto" their precious source of nourishment.

When lambs are born, it is critical to see that each lamb is connected with its "rightful" mother—paired up. Tom Stone always said that you can "just about tell which one goes with which one." Mary was not so sure. In addition to finding a surrogate mother for an abandoned lamb, you might need to take the newborn into the wagon and put them next to the stove for a short time-depending upon their condition. As previously mentioned, finding a mother for every newborn lamb was critical. Herders used any number of differing means to keep the newborns alive. Not only was every lamb important to the financial well-being of the herd owner but to the herder's job as well.

Another responsibility that fell to the herder at the time of lambing was marking lambs. Each lamb was "docked" [their tail was clipped off]. Clipping the tail was a very practical issue: the sheep stayed cleaner in their rectal area and they had less difficulty breeding when the time came for ewes to be "joined" with a ram herd.

Finally, one of the lamb's ears was split so the lamb's age can be determined at a later time. In addition, sheep were "branded" regularly [because of annual shearing] with paint [blue, yellow, red or green]. Colors were then registered with the state of domicile. While it was rare that lambs got "lost," painting seemed to provide some sense of insurance of ownership.

Herders [and lambers] help keep the newly connected pairs [lambs and their mothers] in separate groups and separate bed grounds—such groups growing to no more than 500 [which requires at least one man to handle each separated bunch]. This was especially true when lambing occurred on the "wide" open range.[44] Little did most of these *male* newborns know that they would have less than one year on this earth and then be shipped off to "slaughter" houses.[45] Their *female* counterparts, on the other hand, would live 3-5 years on the prairie so long as they could adequately produce and care for little ones.

Tom and Mary continued to have kids of their own—Sissy [Phyllis}, Jody [JoAnn], Dorothy Jean [who lived only a short time] and Rosalie [Lindy Lou] and John. Mary would often comment about John who was born in the late spring of 1943—a second May baby—as he was born in the midst of lambing:

> "I had worked so hard during lambing that when John
> was born, he looked like a tired, little old man."

---

44 If the winter was mild and the range was flush with "good grass," certain ewes might lamb in the *early* spring and often in the "high country." In such cases, the ewe and her offspring are separated from the remainder of the herd and left to "bond." The difficulty of lambing in the "high" country was that there was little help if Mother Nature decided to produce numerous offspring at one time and the herder needed considerable help in the process. Second, separating the new couple meant that at least part(s) of the herd could be out of sight—somewhat dangerous.

45 Lamb meat [under 14 months] is highly sought-after by restaurants in all parts of the world. Generally, lambs of this age produce the somewhat petite lamp chops and the tastiest leg-of-lamb. While lamb was a *regular* part of the fare of herders and families who owned large herds of sheep, lamb is most often used nowadays for special occasions, holidays and religious celebrations for various faiths.

The work was hard—very hard and tiring for a young woman let alone a young mother—she never complained. This was the life she had chosen. Tom Stone admired her toughness but rarely said so. It was not his nature to tell someone they had done a good job—*that was what you were expected to do.* "Mother," as he came to call her for the rest of his life, "learned pretty quick what to do and she did it." Looking back, neither one of them probably thought they had any other options for their lives at the time.

Like many other offspring, new-born lambs are relatively help-less—and they depend entirely on their mothers for live-giving milk. They eat often, and except under rare circumstances, will eat *only* with their birth mother [and, again with few exceptions, a ewe will feed *only* her own lamb]. It is worth noting that "if ewes are separated [immediately after birth] from their lambs for the first 24 hours, as many as half will not accept their own lamb" later [Lynch, Hinch, Adams, 1992, 137].

Ewes and lambs recognize each other [for the first couple of weeks after birth] by smell. They often spend considerable time try-ing to find each other between feedings as lambs tend to wander off and play or explore between feedings. Most lambs will nurse about 2-4 weeks in the field while those raised in domestic surroundings have been known to feed for up to six months. At that age, the lamb is more than half the size of his mother [Lynch, et. al., 1992, 137].

Not all herders move toward or have access to "high country grass." Such grazing provides "great nutrition" but some unwelcome issues for the herder. For instance, it is often somewhat more diffi-cult to keep the herds bunched—and bunching is quite important in the herder's efforts to protect the herd from predators. Of course, the higher one gets in the "hills," the more likely the herd will encounter predators in addition to coyotes [wolves, bears, mountain lions, wol-verines, etc.].

Generally, moving to high country for summer grazing meant trav-eling on horseback *without* the wagons [for either sleeping or cook-ing] as the terrain was often difficult and there were frequently no passable trails for a wagon. Therefore, all necessary supplies had to be packed in for the duration. Understandably, this terrain is rougher on the herder, the horses and even the dogs. The sheep actually did quite well. They are enjoying their "lush" menu and eating to their hearts content. For the herder, the sheep are putting on weight [and wool] which will add to the price paid for them when they are taken to the railhead [often *directly* from the high country] at the end of the summer.

Admittedly, sheep are a bit harder to control when they get away from relatively *flat* grasslands. While the "high country" does have some areas of good grazing, it also has some rocky peaks and areas where sheep will cluster and can't be seen—by the herder or the dogs. A second concern with high country is that weather often changes "at the drop of a hat." Electrical storms occur frequently and more than one herder has been struck and killed by lightning. Not surprisingly, hundreds of sheep have been reported "lost" during such weather flare-ups.

In addition, because the "high country grass" is spread out in different areas, the grazing sheep tend to disperse more [than they would on the more level prairie]. The disperse nature of the grass is often located amidst such terrain that includes numerous rocks and jutting peaks that potentially limit vision [of the smaller clusters of sheep]. It is easy to see how protecting the larger herd [or the smaller bunches] from frequent predators was a major issue. Tom often remarked that it was always important to "keep the loop tight" and not let the sheep get "too wide" or spread out. While it is primarily the job of the dogs [and this is why you really needed more than one], it was a constant trial.

While it varied in different parts of sheep country from California to South Dakota, and the nature of the weather where you were herding, when lambs are about 3-6 months old, it was time for getting your herds together and move them to more permanent [stable] corrals for docking and tail removal that may not have been done shortly after lambing. [In a word, docking is castrating the young lambs and, concurrently, removing the tails from virtually all the sheep in the herd].

So, while docking and tail removal were standard, such practices were different in various locations of the country.[46]

Docking is a procedure that may be a bit unsettling to one who has never seen it done before. [The method used to castrate lambs is the same "operation" used on calves as Tom would later discover].

Sheep were rounded up from their grazing ranges and brought to a central set of corrals. At the corrals, a small number of sheep were herded into a narrow passage on one side of the corral as the young and bucks and ewes were separated. Generally, two herders work a castration. One would grab the lamb, hold it to their chest while the second clutched the small sack with their taped fingers, squeeze it so the testicles were pushed to the surface, then made a slit across the bag with a very sharp knife. Almost immediately, the cutter thrust their head into the crotch of the lamb, not letting go of the sack, and sucked the testicles and the attaching cord from the young lamb, cutting the cord just before spitting the testicles into a bucket that was close by.[47] These new wethers were then marked with a special waterproof paint and turned loose.

---

46 Herd owners had their own timetable for docking their young lambs. Blackford's ranch nearly always *completed* docking and tail removal within 2-3 weeks after the lambs were born. This was a time when the small lambs were much easier to work with than waiting a few months [4-5] to complete these essential tasks. Lew Thurber, one of Tom's later bosses and a major sheep owner, always insisted that the newborn lambs were too young to go through such a shock and lambs treated this way would become disoriented toward their mothers [he said they would smell different] or just give up and die—lambs at this age, Thurber said, were not very strong and generally didn't make it without their birth mother.

47 Not all outfits used this "manual" method for docking. Some herders, when the lambs were about three weeks old, used a large pair of *fencing* pliers to squeeze and pull the testicles off. To Tom Stone, this always seemed much more painful to a young lamb so he preferred the "slitting method" although he did not actually do any of the castrating himself. Strange as it might seem, the primary herder often emotionally connected with his herd—and Tom Stone's behaviors over the years clearly showed he cared about "his" sheep." While there is some argument, the most illustrious label of "rocky mountain oysters" likely originated in this setting.

The buckets of "rocky mountain oysters" would be cleaned by a couple of herders as they separated the remaining tendons from the testicles before they were floured and pan-fried for a special dinner. If you were a "real" sheep person [or cow person in cattle country], you were *expected* to join in this very traditional meal when it was offered. You didn't have to eat many but should try to "enjoy" at least a good handful [or mouthful as it were] of "mountain oysters."

The entire "surgical process" that transformed a potential buck into a wether took less than a minute. The lamb's ear was then cut [marked] for future identification as they readied them for market in the fall and reconnect them with their birth mother for some much-needed comfort food. [Oftentimes *both* ears were notched to provide additional "identifications"].

Tails were removed on all the ewes. Herders used a red hot knife [or heated iron bar] to slice off the tail. The removed tails were thrown in a pile to be disposed of [buried] later. Tails were removed on the ewes to make breeding easier and to help keep their anal area relatively clean. Keeping a sheep clean is very important as "clean wool" is much more valuable than wool that is tarnished or stained during a year on the open range.

The spring of the year was also a time for shearing the ewes.[48] [Lambs born in the spring were not sheared]. Ewes were not sheared until *after* they lambed as the danger of dropping a ewe during the shearing process might injure [or kill] the pregnant ewe or the unborn lamb. While most herd owners hired a shearing crew to come into the herd [usually at the base camp] to do the job, the herder normally joined in. The *camp mover* generally prepared all the meals for the shearing crew—who worked hard and ate plenty. If the herder's spouse was with him [most herders were not married and those who were most often were not accompanied by their mate on the trail] she was expected to prepare meals. *Whoever* was responsible for meals,

---

48 This is *body shearing* and should not be confused with *eye shearing* which actually took place in the fall and removed heavy wool from around the eyes of the sheep allowing them to see more clearly and feed more easily.

there was always something to eat and plenty of hot coffee from sun-up to sundown—anytime during lambing or shearing.

After the shearing was completed and the wool bagged to ship, most herders separated their lambs [for shipping to market, often Sioux City, IA) and moved their ewes to summer grazing land to prepare them for the [tough] winter months.

Summer grazing land, for those who moved, was often in "high country." As previously noted, sheep can negotiate rocky and mountainous areas—and the path to some high country grazing often required a finding a stable trek for both herders and their charges. [For a great visual depiction of such strategy in action, the PBS video **Sweetgrass** is highly recommended. Language may be an issue for younger viewers].

Wool was profitable! And as you watch skilled shearer work, you can also see that the shearing of sheep is, in a rough sense, an art that few really do well.

The clippers *were* generally manual [in Tom Stone's day] and the shearers worked rapidly.[49] Needless to say, many a ewe got nicked and the noise level indicated their plight—during both shearing and lambing time, the bleating of sheep was nearly constant. Still, depending on the size of herd and the crew, shearing usually lasted less than a week and was done for the year. The time it took to shear the entire herd was dependent, of course, on the size of the herd, the number of people in the shearing crew and the weather.

During shearing time, it was most advisable to move the herd close to a place [building] where the wool could be stuffed into large bags and stored [to keep it dry]. Often this was near a railhead if there

---

49 A few shearers had a gasoline engine that ran power shearers. [Today, virtually all shearers us electric shears and trim at least a dozen sheep an hour]. Shearers during the 1920's and 1930's were paid good wages which was about 30 cents a head. They could earn as much as $30 per day. The worked *fast* [10-12 sheep per hour] and for long hours each day. The only things that stopped them were exhaustion [back pain] eating, the dark of night and rain. Most shearing crews had a person who bagged the wool [herders usually helped] and stored it inside to keep it dry until it was taken to be shipped. Nowadays, shearers get "in the neighborhood" of $280 per 100 sheep and each shearer can complete around 200 head per day. This cost has become prohibitive for many sheep owners.

was a place to store the wool for a short time—again to keep it clean and dry so it would fetch a higher price. To supplement this storage, sheepherders sometimes convinced school officials to call school off so the bagged wool could be stored inside the school building for a short time. Older school children were often provided the opportunity to make money by helping with bagging [tramping or tromping] the bags of freshly-sheared wool.[50]

Shearers were unique people. Although the work was very hard on the back, they worked diligently and earned good wages when they were able to work—only for the month or two of shearing. When the shearing crew was in "camp," they were provided a "bedding spot" and plenty of food to eat and coffee to drink. What they could make shearing, however, was not enough to keep them "going" for the remainder of the year and many good shearers found steadier work on ranches [or with herds] and did not leave their steady work for one month of "really good wages."

Sheep-shearing still goes on in modern times. Many current shearers actually wear a harness that *connects them* to the ceiling of the building in which they are working. They suspend themselves over the ewe while shearing to "save their own back." Others in the current market merely sit on the ground while shearing. Their output of sheep sheared in a full day has remained about the same but as the number of sheep in the U.S. declines along with the price for wool, shearing is not as rewarding a profession as it once was.

Shearing sheep still takes considerable talent and demands a high level of concentration to work fast, yet not nick the sheep "too much" during the process. It is also important to not shear the sheep too close so the sheep's skin will not blister while it is growing its winter coat.

The shearer had only one way to make money. The owner of the sheep, had additional profit opportunities for their risks. In that

50 Initially this may seem like a weak excuse to close school. However, In communities where large numbers of families depended on the sale of wool for making their living, schools were often quite cooperative. The same was true in other parts of the country where the existence of families, and even communities, depended on local agricultural production for their existence.

sense, sheep ranchers had two profit "windows." First, in the spring they could make considerable income from their sale of wool. The fall brought additional income when they sold their older ewes and lambs to slaughter houses.[51] And, even though the price of wool fluctuated some, it was quite profitable during much of this time as wool would bring over a dollar a pound on the open market.[52]

A sign that much-loved and revered traditions often continue even though they have rendered themselves wanting for negligible net profit was Don Hafner's wool warehouse in Newell, South Dakota. In 2012, the Newell operation handled some 3 million pounds of wool. I can personally attest that the sales were attended by many long-time South Dakota sheep people--including myself.

Early in the fall,[53] it was time to take the "eligible" sheep to market. Depending on where the herds were at the time, this generally

---

51   *Lamb* meat [i.e., lamb chops, leg of lamb] comes technically from sheep that are less than 14 months old. *Mutton* comes from sheep that are over 14 months of age. Wool, the renewable commodity of sheep, is still gathered during the fall of the year in sheep country. The price of wool, even "clean wool," however, has dropped markedly so that raising sheep to make profit from the wool and/or meat is marginal.

52   Records show that Charles Bair's 300,000 head of sheep produce 1.5 million pounds of [clean] wool that filled some 44 railroad cars and paid Mr. Bair in the amount of $1,635,000.00. Depending on their size, a sheep will produce from two to 30 pounds of clean wool per year. At the time of this writing, U.S. domestic wool was selling between 27 cents a pound to nearly $1.15 per pound at the end of 2011. Synthetics and foreign imports of wool have drastically reduced the high prices paid during war time [uniforms and blankets supplied to soldiers] and times when American wool was used for a good number of products. Even in the 21st century, certain breeds of sheep may still bring close to $4.00 per pound of wool. Valued for his potential breeding ability, an 8-month old Scottish ram name Devon-shire Perfection was sold for £231,000 [$380,000] in 2009.

53   Sheep are still being raised all over the world. And, as conditions are different for sheep ranchers from Scotland to California and from New Mexico to South Dakota, the *timetables* for such things as lambing, shearing, and marketing will follow different schedules. Such differences are dictated primarily by nature: the availability of good grazing [grass], water and general weather conditions [rain, temperature, etc.] While the markets for wool and lamb/mutton do vary in a limited sense, their impact on the production of sheep has not impacted the industry in a *positive* sense for many years—there is just not as much demand for wool or mutton/lamb as there was in the "booming sheep days." There are, as a result, fewer sheep ranches, fewer sheep being raised and fewer professional herders.

took 5-8 days. Herders would separate the wethers [the castrated male lambs] and all the ewes that were getting older. You could determine the age of a ewe by how many teeth she had. The first-year ewes had two teeth, two-year olds have four, etc. By the time the ewe is about five years old, their teeth have worn down significantly and have often broken off. Rarely would you keep a ewe that had reached the age of 7, although she could possibly be used for another 3-4 years for breeding! However, she no longer feeds on the open prairie and has trouble sustaining herself to get through lambing on her own. Keeping the *aging* ewe in a moving herd on the open prairie rapidly approached non-profitability.

As a natural consequence, the older ewes were rounded up and moved to the railhead. While distances to the railhead varied in different parts of both Montana and South Dakota [as early years provided few rail lines in the western half of the latter], one tried to move their herd progressively toward the railhead as fall approached. Rarely would a herder be more than 75 miles away from the line when it was nearing time to ship their "eligible" sheep to the markets. The herder knew that they and their dogs could move the herd [depending on the herd size and help you had] about five to seven miles a day. This assumed fairly level country, available water, decent weather and few distractions [predators, cattlemen, etc.]. In any such cases, it was the job of the herder to adapt to virtually all conditions—man or nature-made.

For most herders, the fall of the year was their favorite time for work. The lambs had all gone to market and the ewes, after a couple of days, had adjusted to losing their offspring. The shearing had been done in the spring and the shearing crews were long gone. Herders were on their own again and that's just how they liked it—just the herder and his sheep. And even though Tom and Mary Stone knew that the coming year would be somewhat the same as the last, they were also aware that they had some time for family and themselves.

"Those were good days in camp," Mary would remember. "Dad was able to spend time with the kids and we were a normal family."

As normal as a family of 7 could be living in two sheep wagons in the middle of the prairies of western South Dakota.

Tom was content. He knew "winter was comin' but he had been here long enough to know pretty much how to get ready for it—as ready as you could get. He also knew he'd had a "pretty good year." "We shipped a lotta wool and close to four hunnerd head of sheep on the railroad." He knew that those numbers meant something good to his boss.

By early December, it was time to get the ewes and the "buck herd" together for breeding. While all parts of your herd are essential to the owners profit-making, it is *critical* to have high-quality bucks. Estimates vary when determining the buck-to-ewe ratio [how many bucks it will take to "service" how many ewes]. Owners for the first 30 years of the 20th century, used about one buck for every 150 ewes. Later herders reduced the number of ewes that one buck could/should service and placed one buck in the herd for each 35-40 ewes. Other than the times that the bucks and the ewes were breeding, the "buck herd" was kept separate and usually handled by a veteran herder. In this scenario, the herder could exercise considerable control over the times that the lambs were to be born and plan accordingly. Such planning obviously increased a successful lambing season and high production.

While some smaller sheep owners drew from a larger "community" herd of bucks as they entered their breeding season, most of the big ranchers [Blackford, Hoover and Thurber] had *their own* herd of bucks. In so doing, they could more easily control the quality of the bucks, replace them when necessary and carefully manage a significant investment [productive bucks were quite expensive—though necessary and worth the monetary consideration so long as you took good care of them]. Having your own "buck herd" also allowed you to "breed" your herd precisely when you wanted to rather than hire an outside contractor and take them on someone else's schedule of availability.

There should be little question that the sheep business was truly *big business*. Owners had large investments in their sheep and knew that "managing" their herds [with competent herders] was critical to their success—and profit.

Sheepherders aren't considered nomadic *just because* they move from place to place—although there seems to be considerable substance to such a theory. Sheepherders move because of the very basic necessity of finding new grazing areas and drinking water for their herds about every 4-6 weeks [under normal conditions]. And there were times when it was important to avoid conflicts that may have developed in the last place they located with their charges. Other considerations, such as packs of coyotes, often spurred a move that normally may not have been planned.

Tom had to be with the herd as much as possible as it was lambing time—and they expected over a thousand new additions the first week. Several of the hands from the main ranch were there to help for a few days but Tom was the herder and he knew it was his responsibility to be there in case something went wrong—and somethings almost always did. Besides that, cowboys didn't like lambing—or sheep for that matter.

If you herded sheep in eastern Montana, you would likely have ventured into parts of western South Dakota. Quite frankly, at this time before there was much emphasis on a state's sovereignty, people moved back and forth without restraint. This was very apparent with sheepherders. They didn't know much about borders. They really didn't care much about borders. As always, they knew good grass and clean water. And, for the most part, they had never experienced much restraint on their movement—with even large herds. The "drive" to move to new territory "pulled" at Tom Stone. He looked east more and more.

So, it was not surprising that Tom and Mary started spending much more time in Western South Dakota and almost none in Montana. It wasn't that Montana had "wore out," it was just that South Dakota looked like a new and exciting adventure. And part of the herder's life was geared toward adventure—finding the next clear creek or lush grazing land. That truly was their nature.

CHAPTER 11

Moving Further Into South Dakota

SOUTH DAKOTA IS often referred to as "The Land of Infinite Variety" for a number of good reasons. It is just that. In the 77,047 square miles, the Mount Rushmore State boasts at least three very distinct regions. Approximately one-third of the state [in the east] boasts a truly productive agricultural [crop] base. This region also houses most of the population centers in the state of 814,180 [2010 census, a 7.9% increase over the 2000 census]. The middle one-third of the state, while utilized primarily for raising livestock and food grains [wheat, corn, soybeans, etc.] is relatively arid with a base of shale, especially along the Missouri River.[54]

The western one-third of the state, while still demonstrating

---

54 For many years, the Missouri River flowed [often rampaged] out of control— especially in the spring. After years of devastating floods, the Federal Government moved to correct this problem with the Pick-Sloan Missouri Basin Program. It is important to note what a major impact the entire Pick-Sloan project has had on this vast area along the Missouri River. With the creation of the Flood Control Act of 1944, the U.S. Army Corps of Engineers planned and built a series of 6 major dams [Canyon Ferry Dam in Montana, Garrison Dam in North Dakota, Oahe, Big Bend and Fort Randall Dams in South Dakota and the Gavins Point Dam in South Dakota and Nebraska] on the Missouri River. Initially designed for much-needed flood control, these dams and the lakes they created, provide millions of gallons of water for irrigation/sale, vast lake areas for recreation [camping, boating, fishing, water skiing] and the creation of a system of hydroelectric power generation [that is sold nationwide]. See: Bureau of Reclamation [July 29, 2004] Pick-Sloan Missouri Basin Program.

"some" bent for agricultural [cattle and large hay crops], depends to a large degree on tourism [both domestic and foreign]. With its unique historic landmarks from Bear Butte to Mt. Rushmore, historic Lead and Deadwood, the Crazy Horse Monument, Custer State Park, Hot Springs [Evans Plunge], the Badlands and Wall Drug, western South Dakota has unlimited offerings for tourists of all ages and interests. In addition, the roundups, the Sturgis Rally, rodeos, and great camping and fishing areas [Deerfield, Pactola, Sheridan, and Sylvan] provide some of the most beautiful, natural and unusual sites in the world. Add to that, the unique small towns of Hill City, Custer, Keystone and others. Infinite variety indeed!

Early "settlements" in South Dakota were still being established by trappers and explorers—even after the expansive explorations of Meriwether Lewis and Captain William Clark and the Corps of Discovery [1804-1806]. Large portions of land near the Big Sioux River[55] and in the southeastern portion of South Dakota [the Yankton Triangle] began development in 1859. The majority of the early settlements in this area were trading posts and small military installations.

As late as 1870, population still lagged as the Dakota Territory [*south* of what would become the North and South Dakota border] recorded only 11,776 residents. The next three decades, however, showed phenomenal growth as the state of South Dakota [admitted to the Union in 1889] had a population of over 400,000—by 1910 nearly 600,000. There were growth figures upwards of 700% during one period during these early days of expansion.

As Tom and Mary Stone moved southeast into South Dakota from Montana, they found themselves faced with some frustrating new job concerns/decisions. The long nights and days on the open prairie for all these years was beginning to exact a toll. Trying to raise a growing

---

55 The Big Sioux River is a 419 mile-long tributary of the Missouri River. It starts some 40 miles north of Watertown [SD] in Roberts County and runs nearly straight south near Brookings, through Sioux Falls and joins the Missouri in Sioux City, IA. By one measure, the Big Sioux was listed as the "13th dirtiest river in the nation" but boasts some of the state's largest cities built along its banks. [See: AP, May 7, 2012].

family in sheep wagons and cabin courts was not working well. "The kids need to go to a real school," Mary would often assert, fondly remembering some of the *most pleasant times* of her own experiences in Ft. Madison [IA] and Ekalaka [MT]. Though Tom did not share his young wife's enthusiasm for school, he knew she was right. And, to his credit, Tom Stone always wanted his kids to get *some* formal education. He may not have known what going to school was all about, but he "figgered" his kids deserved better than what he had been afforded.

Ironically, it was this newly-embraced "push" to get into a town [where there were *regular*—not *country*--schools for the kids] that would serve as a "death sentence" to the lifestyle he loved. It's difficult to decide if either Tom or Mary thought about the "impact" of "town-life" on *him* or not. Still, Mary's continued insistence would eventually win the day—in the not-so-distant future. As they both would later remark, she did not "harp" on the eventual move, but she was planting the seeds.

South Dakota borders on the southeastern corner of Montana, though at this time, few paid attention to formal borders between states—especially the nomadic sheep herder. While South Dakota and Montana have some differences, the similarities of this area between the two, were the only things that mattered to Tom and Mary Stone at the time. South Dakota, though similar to Montana [in the *northwestern* area], is less than half the size of "the Treasure State" in actual square miles. Tom was not as interested in *land area* as he was in *sheep land area*—and to the east of Alzada [MT], he saw plenty of what he liked.

"There was pasture for grazin' as far as you could see," Tom would observe. And, if the pasture was green, it meant there was likely plenty of water. Tom had been to Rapid City with Lew Thurber [his new boss] so he had seen good "trails" from Alzada [MT] through Belle Fourche and Newell near what he described as the "prettiest little river he had ever seen" [the Belle Fourche River]. 40 years later as we retraced his "trails," he repeated his feelings for this river and this part of the state [SD] that was dear to his heart's memory. There were several creeks that fed into what is now the Belle Fourche Reservoir [North and South Indian Creeks and Owl Creek]. They all contained "plenty a good drinkin' water for them sheep." Looking at the land and living through one summer and one winter, you could tell the weather was about the same as that in Montana—"Colder n' hell in the winter and hotter n' hell in the summer."

This is not to suggest that weather was not an issue—it was in both the very hot summers and the very cold winters. And, in most cases, animals, with "guidance" from herders, usually fare reasonably well during the weather extremes.[56] Of course both humans and animals were lost during times of extreme weather. In a recent tragic incident, for example, west river South Dakota ranchers lost approximately 100,000 head of cattle in a surprise [early] snowstorm in October of 2013.[57]

You could also tell that this was good sheep country by the availability of reasonably clean water [White River was an exception] and plenty of flat grassland. You could also tell if sheepherders had been there before [often sometime ago] by the presence of the occasional cairn built along the trail or randomly in a pasture. A cairn, sometimes called a "stone Johnnie," is a number of flat rocks—often a large number approaching 40-50—piled [stacked] in what seemed to be some sort of meaningful structure. On the open prairie, this collection was most likely carried from different areas to be placed in this "most unusual structure." Dedicated to the sheepherders of days gone by.

---

56 The highest temperatures ever recorded in South Dakota were at Usta in 2006 and Gann Valley in 1936: both 120 degrees. See: South Dakota Magazine, July/ August, 2017, pp. 15,19. The coldest temperature recorded in South Dakota was 58 degrees below zero—not taking into account current calculations of the wind chill factor.

57 An early fall storm, with heavy snows and over 70 mile-per hour winds, [October, 2013] left as many as 100,000 head of cattle dead in the west river area of South Dakota. The cattle, many of whom suffocated in massive snow drifts, were in "summer pastures" and had not yet grown their winter coats. In a short time, these herds would likely have been moved to more "protected" areas. Financially, these losses of livestock were estimated to be nearly $1.25 million dollars. [Manuel Bojorquez, CBS News, October 14, 2013].

For most, the "stone Johnnie" is still somewhat of a mystery—at least from a *meaning* perspective.

The first sheep had been brought into South Dakota in the southeastern part of the state but not in sizable numbers. Sheep appeared on a Ft. Pierre inventory in 1844—right on the Missouri River. The first significant herds of sheep in west river country were brought to the areas around Battle Creek and Spring Creek, just south of Rapid City by Jakie Mills sometime after 1877.[58] The leading sheepman of the time, however, was rancher/politician John "Jack" Hale who left an indelible mark on both the sheep industry and "the business of politics."[59]

Major sheepherders tended to concentrate their herds in the counties in the northwestern and north central parts of western South Dakota [Harding, Butte, Meade, Perkins, Corson and Dewey]. It was here that M.J. [Myron John] Smiley [previously discussed] and his "bunch" had moved their large herds from Wyoming in an attempt to avoid the cattle-sheep wars.[60]

Few were surprised that Smiley and his fellow herders were met at the South Dakota border between Belle Fourche and Spearfish by armed cattleman who were determined to "block" Smiley's entry into "their land." The cattlemen were apparently not aware that Smiley, in anticipation of their efforts, had hired a group of "Mexican gunslingers" to act as "guides" on this foray into South Dakota. At the initial point of confrontation, one of Smiley's "gunslingers" was said to have roped a cowboy and dragged him around the herd of sheep in a

---

58 Herbert T. Hoover, ed. [2005]. **New South Dakota History** [Center for Western Studies], 282.

59 Pioneer cattleman and horseman, John Dickinson "Jack" Hale was born in Grayson County, VA [October 22, 1847] and died in Sturgis, SD [May 9, 1929]. Hale served in the SD State Senate and ran sheep, hogs and cattle in both SD and Wyoming. Hale was elected to the Cowboy Hall of Fame in Oklahoma City in 1967. He founded the Pleasant Valley Stock Farm near Tilford in Meade County [near Sturgis].

60 Jami Huntsinger, "Pioneering Black Hills Sheepman: Myron John Smiley," in South Dakota Leaders, ed. Herbert T. Hoover and L.J. Zimmerman [Vermillion, SD: University of South Dakota Press, 1989], 261.

display of bravado. The cattlemen soon backed off as Smiley and his fellow herders conducted their large contingent of sheep into the new territory. It was clear that Western South Dakota was rapidly emerging as a major territory for sheep. It was perfect timing for the influx of woolies:

> "The hard winters of 1881 and 1887 eliminated or greatly reduced the large open-range cattle companies. When the large companies left, more land and water opened up for grazing sheep. Three factors made western South Dakota good sheep territory— the climate, the abundance of open range, and the variety of feed on that range. Black Hills miners provided a ready market for mutton as well as beef.[61]

Smiley's own herd soon grew to nearly 50,000 head at his home place near Belle Fourche. And, by 1930, South Dakota boasted some 1,139,000 head of sheep—valued at $10 a head, this amounted to a value of $251,000.00 in the markets of the time.[62]

While there are comparatively few sheepherders working in eastern Montana and western South Dakota today, they truly left their mark on both the history and the land of this wide-open prairie country they *claimed* and called home. A drive through the countryside will reveal an occasional "disengaged" sheep wagon sitting in the yard of a farm or on display at a hotel/motel or a restaurant. And, though it is rare, one can find someone who knew a herder—or maybe even was a herder themselves.

In reality, the sheep industry didn't leave much on the land in the form of houses, corrals, or fences. That was not what they were all about. But be assured, sheep, their herders, their wagons and their

---

61 Cowboys and Ranch Life [nd.]. [Pierre, SD: South Dakota State Historical Society Education Kit], 4.

62 Ralph V. Hunkins and John Clark Lindsey [1932]. **South Dakota: Its Past, Present and Future** [New York, NY: The Macmillan Company.

dogs made an historical mark. Countless books and articles have been written about them and the places they called home including the small "rock statues" that dot the country where their charges grazed.

Often called the "sheepherder's monument," or "Stone Johnnies," [see p. 121] there were a large number of "carefully constructed rock "towers" built [without mortar] to be found over much of the range country where these tradesmen trailed their herds. Often referred to as "cairns," these piled up rocks/stones were just that—stacks of rocks. Early settlers in Dewey County [1902] found such stone monuments built on the top of high buttes—most likely [they assumed] by Indians to mark springs that may have been located at the base of a particular butte or canyon. Later, these intricate stacks of stone were likely constructed by sheepherders in a similar—appearing manner in areas "west of the Missouri River" and in Wyoming and eastern Montana as well.[63]

Historians and other writers have offered a number of plausible reasons for the construction of these unusual stone structures that frequent herding areas. Some suggest that the markers were carefully constructed to suggest specific geographic positions or indicate water locations. Others say sheepherders spent time carefully piling up the rocks to pass the boredom of the long days and nights. Some passersby suggest that these hundreds of stacks of rocks might even be a burial site or monument of worship. Still, others contend that the cairns sent a message to other traveling through the wide-open prairies that showed little or no signs of other human beings. It has also been hypothesized that the cairn was a navigational instrument that guided other herders to specific watering areas—even indicating the

---

63 Shirley Baughman O'Leary has written a most informative pamphlet entitled: **Stone Johnnies: Vanishing Landmarks of the Lonely Buttes** [November, 2005, Belle Fourche, SD: Sand Creek Printing] that discusses these historical markers in considerable depth. The author provides an extensive number of pictures as well as considerable background information. She is meticulous in denoting locations of these stone monuments in counties where sheepherding thrived in eastern Montana and Wyoming through the west river country of South Dakota.

distance from the spot where they were built. Still others felt these "herder's fingerprints" were used to scare off predators on the open prairie. Whatever else they may have been, the "Stone Johnnie" was unique and indisputable evidence that sheepherders had spent more than a brief time in a specific area. In the final analysis, it is a bit difficult to ascertain any agreed-upon meaning for the "Stone Johnnie."

The biggest livestock owners [both sheep and cattle] in eastern Montana at this time were the Hoover brothers, A.E. Blackford and Lew Thurber. It was estimated that Thurber had upwards of 20,000 head of sheep at the time. While Tom had worked for all of them at one time, he felt more at ease with Lew Thurber as Thurber put him "in charge" of his herd and "left me alone." That was just what Tom Stone wanted.

So, the Stones had a new boss and a large sheep owner-Lew Thurber. While Thurber owned *both* cattle and sheep, he had asked Tom to take control of his largest herd of sheep—remembering all the time that this was the "money crop." Thurber gave you the impression that he and this country were one—almost like he had been in Montana since the day God created it. He was comfortable in this country "just the way it was." The changes that would take place in the next 20 years would cause him considerable mental anguish.

Tom remembers well how good Lew was to him and the rest of the Stone family. Tom Stone returned that "goodness" with his trademark loyalty and hard work. Interested in helping Tom get a start in the cattle business, Lew gave him a good bull one spring to be used [rented] to start his own herd. If that meant using the bull for stud fee—that was OK. If that meant getting some cows that the bull could breed, that was alright as well. Lew was willing to help Tom get started and build a foundation for himself and his family.

Knowing the openness of the territory in which they lived, Tom kept his new bull close to the base camp wagons. Still, his new prized possession turned up missing one day. The would-be "rustler" had used a pickup truck and loaded the bull in the back of it. The tracks the pickup left were easy to follow so Tom and Bob [who was now nearly 12] saddled up and followed the tracks. They eventually located the pickup with the bull still in the back. Tom unloaded his bull and proceeded to empty his 30-30 into the cab and the engine of the pickup. He then took his Winchester 4570 [3 load] and did the same. "Dad never said a word," Bob recalled later.

Bob remembered "that since it was near our base camp we saw that old pickup sitting in the same spot for weeks til' we moved on." In Tom Stone's mind, "no worthless son-of-a-bitch was gonna steal his property and get away with it." One can only imagine what would have happened had the "rustler" been with the pickup and his bull when Tom found them.

There was legal recourse that could have been followed. A "report" could have been filed, but it seemed few availed themselves of such action in this part of the country. They took care of things themselves—and nobody would have faulted Tom for doing what he had done in this case.

Back to his boss and friend. "Lew was a good man. He would just as soon take a shot of whiskey as drink a cup of coffee—and he had plenty of money to pay for all of either that he wanted. He was always good to us. And even though we didn't need much, he saw to it that we had all that we needed. That's just how he was."

In a business sense, Lew Thurber was a good livestock man even though "Mother and I always guessed that if he wouldn't of had a *good sheepherder*, he most likely would have sold them all" [his sheep]. There was no question that Lew Thurber was a cattleman and wanted to own an even larger spread than he had. He knew he *needed* the sheep because they provided him both good and stable income from both the wool and the mutton—giving him a sizable annual income to build his cattle herds—that was the major reason most of the large cattlemen had sheep in the first place. Ironically, most cattlemen didn't much care for sheep, but knew they needed them to make the rest of their "empires" grow. For many years, it was a reasonable trade-off in this part of the country. History showed, cattle were the future.

The relationship between Tom Stone and Lew Thurber was more like a friendship than one of employer-employee. Lew and Tom regularly went into Rapid City and would spend a couple of days [and nights] in the Red Room [the bar] at the Harney Hotel. One would have to think some serious drinking took place.

Lew Thurber was also a different type of stock owner than A.E. Blackford or either of the Hoover brothers. For instance, he would drive an old Ford pickup to the base camp himself much of the time to bring provisions and Tom's pay—rather than send one of his hired hands or ride a horse. He spent considerable time talking about the sheep [since he didn't know much about them] and asking Tom what he thought could be done to cut losses and move to ground that would provide better grass and water.

Tom often remarked that he "wondered why Lew ever got into the sheep business since he didn't seem to know a damned thing about em'." Even though Tom and Lew were more like friends, Tom Stone still took his job "just as serious as if the sheep was his'n." And, as was his way, Tom Stone never forgot who was "the boss."

Come spring, it was time to move. Looking toward the sunset, Tom could see high mountains [Rockies]. Looking north, he saw Rim Rock and decided against moving in that direction although there were a good number of smaller herds in Harding County [SD]. Southeast of his current basecamp lay the Black Hills. Not the least impetus for moving was the fact that Tom and Mary Stone were about to have their first baby.

Thomas Robert Stone was born on May 14, 1927 in Alzada, Montana in a small log hut near the northwest end of town. At Tom's almost panicky requests, they found an experienced midwife to help Mary during the delivery and the first couple of days after Bob was born. She stayed with Mary and Bob while Tom rode back and forth to the herd—at the base camp just southwest of the small Montana town.

On his trips to Rapid City with Lew, Tom had seen at least the northern part of the Black Hills. He was convinced his sheep would not be able to navigate that area well although he did see it as "a good spot for winterin'" at the *base* of the Hills.

After giving the new lambs about four weeks to get used to their mothers and standing on their own four feet, Tom decided it was time to move. By this time, Lew had known Tom for over 3 years and trusted him implicitly with the herd. He knew that if Tom decided to move the herd, then that was what needed to be done. It was new territory—it was unknown territory as well—and they didn't know if anybody had ever run sheep down in that country. That didn't stop them. It was time to move. Tom told Mary about the plans to move further into South Dakota. Where Tom went, Mary went. It was that simple.

During most of their lives together, they did not talk much about decisions like "where to move or when to move." Both of them seemed to understand that the needs of the herd dictated where they would live and how long they would live there.

Mary Stone had learned plenty about sheep in the time she had been with Tom. She was a big help during lambing and took good care of both the cook wagon and the sleep wagon—she even gave some "woman's touch" to the wagons with curtains made from emptied flour sacks. As Tom often said, "the wagons was clean and there was always plenty of food to eat and coffee to drink."

Mary had learned some things about cooking while a young girl in Fort Madison, Iowa living with her aunts. She had learned a great deal more from her sister Grace in Ekalaka. And, she was rapidly learning one of the "laws of survival."

> "You made do with what you had. You couldn't run
> to the store to get a loaf of bread or a can of beans,"
> Mary often remembered years later.

Importantly, Tom knew that if there was an emergency, "she could ride good, knew her directions and wasn't afraid to get her hands dirty." Although he was unlikely to say it, Tom Stone very much admired her willingness to pitch in when it was necessary and "without havin' to be told what to do. Besides, her biggest job was to take care of that boy." The decision to move did not really require that much "packin' up" to put them on the trail.

It was obvious that Tom was really "taken" with his new son even though he didn't really know how to show it. He tried to take this new "addition" as just a matter-of-fact but *never* suggested Bob was not something different or special. It wasn't that he had never seen babies before—he had just never seen one that was his own and carried his name and that of his Dad. They didn't make a big deal out of that either, but it was important.

So, Tom and Mary, with their two "homes on wheels" and a new son, began to head southeast—into South Dakota. This was not a typical "base camp move" as the main ranch normally sent a couple of hands to load up and "skin" at least one of the wagons. Since this move was to be so far away from the main ranch, Tom and Mary knew they were on their own. Since they only had four horses, they hooked two to each wagon. Traveling "two up" would be slow moving but they were not in any hurry. This was all part of "trailin.'"

The move into South Dakota required no permits or licenses and there were no signs of the state line or mile markers. Nor, as a matter of reality, were there any guarantees of rain, or grass or safe passage. If these prospects bothered them, neither Tom nor Mary talked about it. If they were scared, they didn't show it at all. Their life was not built on certainty. Quite frankly their life could not tolerate much in the way of *hesitation* either. Their very existence continued to be built on their *instinct for survival*—for them, their new baby and the herd.

They had no idea how far they would be able to go into South Dakota until the grass ran out or the water dried up. "We'll go as far as we can, Mother," Tom told his wife. "If we run into any trouble, we'll turn around and go back. We gotta give this a try," Tom resolutely declared.

They had plenty of supplies [provisions] in the wagons for themselves and the baby and a good supply of oats for the horses. Tom was better prepared for the trip than one might have thought. He had asked around enough to believe that there was a route that was fairly level and would take them into the Badlands. He had been told that the Badlands—despite the name—had ample water and feed for his herd. That information was not completely accurate in its totality. Regardless, he felt it was worth taking a chance. And, again, "they could always turn around and come back if things got to lookin' too bad." At this time, Tom was pretty sure this move was just going to be for this one summer as he would return closer to a railhead for shipping in the fall.

On clear days you can see for what looks like "a hunnerd miles in this country" Tom would often remark. The northwest corner of South Dakota blends in with the southwest corner of Montana. And, since there were no [very few at this time] fences and virtually no landmarks, you really didn't know "what state you was in" at any given time. What's more, it didn't much matter.

Actually, you never even thought much about moving from one state to another. You moved because the range was open and you needed plenty of grass and water for your sheep. So long as the grass was there and they could find grass and water for the sheep, Tom and Mary edged south-southwest. They stayed south of Owl Creek and near the Belle Fourche River—which was "the best drinkin' water for the sheep in the area," Tom had concluded some time before. [The Belle Fourche River had flooded quite badly in 1923, but since that time was clean, safe and reliable].

Good water and plenty of grass are major comforts to a sheepherder. They did not move fast. There was no reason to move fast. They had at least the next four months to find good spots for their base camp as well as grazing and water for their herd. Along with watching over their new son, their concerns seemed minor.

From his base camp just east of Alzada, Tom Stone took Lew Thurber's large herd [nearly 2500 head] and started trailing south and east—along Indian Creek and just into South Dakota until he settled just south of Belle Fourche. This would be base camp for the remainder of the summer. It was good land, plenty of good, clean water and close enough to get back to the main ranch land in Montana when it was time to get the lambs and older ewes ready for market.

It was time to stop. Mary was pregnant with their second child and was having a bit of trouble. Belle Fourche, a reasonably-sized town, seemed like a good place to "settle" for the winter—even if Tom had to move the sheep back to Montana in the fall. That's exactly what he did.

He moved Mary and Bob into town to a room they rented from an older couple whose children were raised and were out on their own. Irene and Milt Jessup took to Mary and Bob right away and assumed the role of the parents she never had. That's the way some people were in those days in times of need. Irene looked after Bob like a grandson—they were in good hands and over the next month Mary relearned about "glass plates and cups and real silverware." She relearned about sheets on a real mattress and how some people even ironed their pillowcases. Mary stayed with the Jessups for just over two months.

Sissy [Phyllis Joyce] was born on December 29, 1929. While Bob had been "long and lanky," Sissy was petite and had a full head of curly hair. The snow was typical for January—heavy and moist and over 30 inches during the last part of December and the first month of the new year.

Tom would share his time with the herd at the base camp that was close to his growing family in Belle Fourche. Lew had strongly suggested he should do just that. "We'll look after the herd when you're in town," he reminded Tom.

Late January came and Tom and Mary Stone knew it would soon be time to resume their journey toward the Badlands. Tom, Mary and the two kids made their way from Belle Fourche back to the main herd. Lew and his men had already taken some of the oldest ewes and the lambs to the railhead but kept the base camp where Tom had left it—a decent place to winter.

Just northwest of Belle Fourche, South Dakota [at one time spelled Bellefourche] they learned some new things about the state they would call home for the next 40 years. The area where they crossed into South Dakota was the starting point of what was known as the "gumbo belt." When it rained the dirt turned to a very different type of "mud" they came to call gumbo. Gumbo turned into a near-cement mixture—and stuck to everything. Neither horses nor sheep could navigate the terrain so you sure weren't likely to pull a wagon through it. And, when it was dry, "it was hard as a rock with black dust every-where," Tom vividly recalled. But at least it was passable right now.

With the heavy winter snows, the spring grass came full and plentiful to the areas around Belle Fourche. The Stones would spend the spring right here not far from the main ranch so Lew and some of his men could help with lambing—a job Tom and Mary knew they could not do on their own. They also became aware that they were now part of the South Dakota sheep industry.[64]

Sheep were still relatively new to South Dakota. Historically, there were some small herds in the eastern part of the state during the early 1800's, but large herds of sheep were not reported in the western part of the state until 1844. This was "when J.D. Hale had trailed three thousand woolies into the Black Hills in 1878, however, he became the first to place sheep in the area set aside as the Great Sioux Reservation by the Fort Laramie Treaty of 1868 and opened to non-Indians by an act of Congress in 1876." M.J. Smiley and several of his fellow herders would follow in 1904.[65]

South Dakota was new territory for both Tom and Mary Stone as sheepherders. Tom had only been as far as Rapid City on his trips with Lew Thurber a couple of times so he knew a little bit about this initial

---

64 While still in its stages of infancy, South Dakota would soon be moving toward becoming one of the major sheep-producing areas of the Midwest. Production actually peaked in 1943 when South Dakotans herded some 2.4 million sheep on their prairies. Profitability in both meat and wool remained somewhat steady until 1967 when incentive programs for sheepherders were discontinued by the Federal Government and the markets for both wool and mutton were marginal at best.

65 Jami Huntsinger [1989]. "Pioneering Black Hills Sheepman: Myron John Smiley," in **South Dakota Leaders: From Pierre Choteau to Oscar Howe**, ed. by Herbert T. Hoover and L.J. Zimmerman [Vermillion, SD: USD Press], 260.

"trail." But, he had not been this far south [of Rapid City] or this far east [near what is now Scenic]. Still, they had been encouraged and excited as they crossed the Montana border heading south toward Belle Fourche and were welcomed by the same big skies and seemingly endless grasslands they had grown to know and love in Montana. Sadly, except for two short visits, they would not call Montana "home" again in their lives.

But now it was spring again. In the fall, Tom had brought in a buck herd for breeding—and now the benefits of that breeding would be realized: lambs. As veteran herder Eric Thane tells provides his narrative:

> . . . first off in the fall they've got to breed the ewes. The bucks are kept in a band by themselves and when the boss figures its breeding time, he'll turn them in with the ewes. It don't take many bucks. They breed at night, and one buck can take care of a hundred-fifty ewes during a night. Then they send the ewes in a band down into the valleys and me, Old Joe, I watch'em all winter long until lambing time. [Eric Thane, **OutWest Magazine**, December, 1953, 20].

Lew and some of his men came to help with lambing and all "the extras" [docking, etc.] that went with it. Once this was done, it would be time that Tom and Mary—all alone—would be moving into South Dakota with their herd of over 2000 head of seasoned ewes and a large group of young lambs.

Mary was back to her cooking for the "lambing crew." They had an understanding that Lew would bring one of the cooks from the main ranch to help her since she had the two little ones to look after. For a man who had never been married, Lew seemed to know quite a bit about "a woman's work." Mary got a release from helping with the ewes who were having trouble during "birthing" and spent that extra time with the kids, baking plenty of bread and biscuits and keeping a hot pot of coffee on the fire at all times. It was a welcome relief to have that extra time with the kids, and both she and Tom made it clear to Lew how much they appreciated the "extra measures" of help he provided for them.[66]

About four weeks after lambing season was over, it was time to load up the wagons and get on the move—this time Tom was determined to make it all the way to the Badlands. He knew about how long it would take. And, he knew that any trouble they faced, it would be just he and his wife. That did not deter them. They loaded the wagons, rounded up the sheep with the help of the dogs and set out for unexplored territory—at least for them.

As long as you stayed out of the higher elevations of the Black Hills, western South Dakota offered plenty of fairly level land and good grazing for large herds [of both sheep and cattle]. Just as important, most of the rivers were full of water for the sheep to drink. Finally, and it was a critical concern, there was not much fence strung in the western part of the state so you could move large herds with relative ease. It seemed ideal for the Stones and their large "bunch of sheep."

Lew went back to the main ranch but sent some of his men along for the first 30 miles or so to help set up the first base camp just south and west of Sturgis [Ft. Meade]. His men got the wagons to the base camp and got everything set up—making sure Mary had plenty of water in the casks and all he wood she would need for cooking the next couple of months [they likely wouldn't need any wood for heating in the sleep wagon as the summer months were pretty warm]. They waited until Tom got to the base camp with the herd [though Mary said that wasn't necessary]. After spending a day at the base camp,

---

66   While Tom never said as much, Lew Thurber was as close to a *good* "father figure" as he had ever known. There was *mutual trust and concern* for each other—and it was genuine. And even though there was nearly 30 years difference in their ages, they just seemed to know what the other one was thinking much of the time—even when they had been apart for months. They talked things over and respected each other's position—even when they disagreed. Tom and Mary Stone would never forget Lew Thurber and what he had meant to them and their young family.

the ranch hands headed back to Alzada.

Tom regularly rotated his large herd on the grasslands between New Underwood, Wasta and Elm Springs, keeping Elk Creek to the south of them and the Belle Fourche river to the north. The winter just got tougher. Tom would admit the following spring that he "couldn't find much cover around the area except some draws near the Cheyenne River" which he located quite a ways to the east. He assured Mary that he would move the base camp and the herd "a helluva a lot farther east come spring."

They had gotten a "head start," [because spring had come early] and Tom had it in the back of his mind to push his herd a little bit further south and east this time than he had the year before. Not only was he always looking for grazing and water that nobody else was using, it was just part of his nature to want to "see what was over the next hill." Even though this land was open grazing, it was pretty important to stay "out of the way of the some of the big cattle herds that was in this area." As they moved, they took the herd on side trips for water and then brought them back to the "main trail" that would take them parallel to the Black Hills, past Rapid City and toward the "grasslands path" he had been told about that would lead him to the Bad Lands. In his mind's eye he could see it. He was right.

Tom and Mary were consistently heading *away* from "security." And although they would leave the base camp where it was for about a month, Tom would move the herd further south, just north of Elk Creek. The next move for the herd would be south and east of Rapid City—their next lengthy base camp would be established somewhere near the rather unpredictable Rapid Creek—from there it was straight southeast to the Badlands. Although Tom did not know exactly where he would wind up in the Badlands, he was looking for the White River—the name was more than ominous—it was somewhat literal.

Lew Thurber had always treated Tom and Mary and the kids as though they were *his* family. Although neither Tom nor Mary knew much about how he treated his other employees, they were pretty sure he had never been married and didn't seem to have any siblings—at least he never talked about any kind of family. You could tell Lew Thurber was a natural-born son of Montana.

As Tom's boss and friend, he had always made it clear that he wanted all of them to move to the main ranch. There they could have a house "of their own." A house—with floors and doors and windows with glass. Surely that would have been a much more comfortable life for Mary—and the kids. But it would also mean surroundings that was much "too close" for Tom Stone. And, although Mary would not have minded working in the large kitchen, feeding over two dozen hands every meal, Tom knew it would mean taking care of *cattle*. At this stage in his life, Tom Stone was a sheep man.

The summer of 1930 was good for the Stone family. That fall and winter were typical--average and not too bad. While there was a massive [nationwide] economic depression raging in the rest of the country, the Stones didn't feel the impact of such "mean" conditions where they were. Their needs were pretty much the same as they had always been. No matter what the stock exchange did during the week, they still needed [and had] a place for their sheep to graze and water for them to drink. For the family, the needs were also simple: a warm and dry place to sleep and enough food for them and the kids to eat. The "value" of the few dollars they had [and were to earn] meant very little to them. They got paid in cash and saved it—hidden safely in the sleep wagon—one day they might need their savings to buy something. 1931 came and went. Everyone was fine.

JoAnn [Jody] Tom and Mary's third child, was born on one of the coldest days of the year: January 22, 1932. Tom had taken Mary into Newell, South Dakota—just north of their last base camp east of Rapid City. Like Bob, Jody was "long and lanky" like her big brother. Tom said "she'll be sittin' a horse before she's 5 years old." She was.

So now there were 5 members of the Stone family—living in two wagons [a modified cook wagon and a sleep wagon] for most of the year [at least 8 months]. Tom always said the kids loved "the outdoors." Mary seemed to answer by saying "they never had anything else to compare it with—except when they lived in town for short periods of time in relative 'social isolation.'" But it would not be long before Bob was ready for school. And there were some schools around—in private homes and even tents. Mary's desire to send her kids to a "real school" was persistent. Tom heard her but his work was a--even the--priority.

Personally, the summer of 1936 would be what was the most difficult year the Stones would experience in their marriage. They had three children and were about to have a fourth.

Mary Stone was strong. Yet, after having three babies, she knew this pregnancy and the upcoming birth were going to be different from the others. She didn't say anything to Tom. She did talk with her friend Lee about it. Mary was worried—things just didn't seem right. It was something a woman knows.

After spending the shearing and lambing time at the basecamp, Tom had moved Mary and the kids. back into Wasta into a cabin court. There was a small kitchen and a separate bedroom. By the end of July, Mary was "settled" there. She was close to her friend Lee and Bob and Sissy could go to school with Larry Collier, Lee and Percy's son, in Wasta. Bob Stone was over 9 years old and Sissy, though small in stature. was ready for first grade.

That summer on the prairie, there was little rain which made it easier to manage the sheep as they could move without the restrictions of swollen creeks. On the negative side, the shortage of water means a shortage of grass. These are the two things sheep need the most. So, even in late summer, Tom was thinking about moving the sheep to decent [stable] winter grazing. At the time, his plan was to move nearer to Wasta. While it was not an ideal place to winter the herd, it would be close to Mary. Such a move would mean that Tom could come to Wasta every couple of days to see how she was doing. Mary's friend Lee was there and was a great help. She checked on Mary every day.

The Colliers lived fairly close so the kids could play together. Lee and Mary spent time working on sewing [embroidery] projects together and watching over Jody, who was still the [knee] baby. Still, Mary knew she was not "carrying" this fourth child very well. She never mentioned anything to Tom as she knew he couldn't do anything and "he had his work to do."

The baby girl was born on August 27, 1936 with help from both Lee Collier and a midwife and, although the little girl seemed very small, she was only a week short of being "full term." As was their "new tradition," the entire family decided on the baby's name. The new arrival was name Dorothy Jean and she was officially a member of the growing Stone family—now numbering 6.

The three older children [not much older] were like most brothers and sisters. They were interested but thought that this "new thing" got too much attention. Still, they wanted to play with her and hold her. Mary, however, for the first time with any of her children, was very cautious. She still felt this baby was different from her other children—and needed a special kind of attention and care. Dorothy Jean did not eat very well nor very much. She gained very little weight. Mary would remember that "she didn't fuss very much. She didn't cry at night although she never seemed to sleep more than two hours at a stretch. She was so pretty. She looked at me like she was asking for help but I didn't know how to help her. I kept thinking—praying-- she was going to be OK."

If there was ever a case where "a mother just knows," this was it. Mary never let Dorothy Jean out of her sight. At less than six months the baby started coughing. Mary walked her and rocked her. She provided steam from a boiling pan on the stove to make sure all her breathing passages stayed open. The coughing continued. The baby's mother held her tears in front of the other kids— she cried quietly at night when the baby would sleep for an hour or so.

Mary Stone often said she "loved all her kids the best but for different reasons." It would not be difficult to figure out why she loved her new baby "the best" at this time. With Dorothy Jean, the reasons became apparent. Though all the kids were little [young] *this new baby needed her momma the most—all the time.* Lee pitched in more than anyone could imagine—as she had Larry, who was only 9 at the time. Percy and Tom took care of the other kids as much as they could but weren't a substitute for a "mom."

Tom took care of the herd though his heart was with his new daughter and his wife. They got through shearing, thanks to the men that Lew had hired and Tom decided not to move anywhere for the winter—right where they were was going to *have to be fine.*

Spring came and it looked like time to move—but they made no plans to do so. Lew didn't come down so Tom knew whatever he decided was OK. Spring brought a freshness—good grass and clean water in the creeks all over the prairies. Everything looked bright and fresh—except little Dorothy Jean.

Even during the days when the weather was warm and the baby *should have been out in the sunshine,* Mary kept her inside the small cabin as the outside exposure seemed to increase her bad coughing spells. Even after 9 months, the baby hadn't gained much weight. Her coloring suggested anemia and she showed no signs of even rolling over on the bed. Her mother so often remarked to no one in particular that "she is the sweetest little thing."

Tom knew something was wrong. He had decided, in what was "his way," to not talk about it. Tom Stone didn't talk much anyway, but you generally knew "where he stood" on things. This was one of those times, and there weren't many, when you had *little idea* what he was thinking. If anything, this almost stoic, tough, independent, north Georgia man didn't understand "what was goin' on." And then, maybe he didn't want to admit what was happening.

When Dorothy Jean got even sicker the following winter [they diagnosed her with pneumonia], Tom was reminded of his family's loss of "Little Jim." And even though he didn't want to talk about it, Mary knew he was concerned about their baby. He wasn't angry. He wasn't short-tempered with the other kids. He wasn't at the cabin except to eat and sleep. Tom Stone just stopped talking.

Dorothy Jean Stone died during the day on January 17, 1938. She didn't cry or make any kind of fuss. Her labored breathing stopped. She stopped living. Mary had held her much of the time hoping against hope that "love would keep her alive." Her mother was holding the little girl when she breathed her last. It was not dramatic. It was not climatic. It was heartbreaking.

The Stones buried their baby in a small cemetery just outside Elm Springs, SD. It was a pretty resting place—well cared for by the members of a local church—quiet and even "country serene." Her grave is right in the middle of the cemetery.

One could justifiably argue that if you never lost a child [no matter what the cause] you can't understand what a parent feels when their child—still a baby—dies. Tom and Mary still did not talk about it. Mary felt she had failed her little girl—she felt that a mother should be able to do something to keep a child alive once they have given them birth.

Years later Mary would talk about it in 'bits and pieces" when one of we younger kids got sick or when we asked her about Dorothy Jean. Relating the story of the loss of her baby showed a type of pain few can relate to and even fewer have personally experienced.

While one's *capacity* for pain is not always something that is measurable, Mary Stone was most certainly exposed to what one could imagine was the maximum "dose." Still, she survived. She knew her husband and the other children *depended on her* and she was not going to let anybody down. In the opinion of her children, she never did "let any of us down."

For some very practical reasons, Tom and Lew had talked about keeping a base camp in South Dakota year 'round. Moving sheep took considerable time and there were always some losses. "If you have a good spot, stay there," Tom advised. He was becoming very much aware of his surroundings. He was also very much aware that things on the prairie were changing. There were increasing numbers of cows—and that brought barbed wire fences. Every year the lands "reserved" for sheepherders and their flocks got smaller.

Mary agreed with Tom's insistence on keeping a base camp in South Dakota:

> "Dad and Lew had agreed that it was not a good idea to move our large herd back and forth from Alzada every fall. It took a great deal of time, the 'route' back was becoming increasingly private [harder to cross] and it took its toll on the herd in both weight loss and lost numbers. They decided we could just as well winter right here in South Dakota. So we stayed for the winter."

With the 3 kids Mary wasn't riding herd nearly as much as her husband during these times, she could see some of the same signs as Tom did. "Their [precious] open land" was disappearing. Perhaps it was avoidance, but Mary would remember later, "Dad and I didn't talk about it. This was the only life we knew. *This was the only life we had.* We surely did not want to think about it disappearing."

Tom regularly rotated his large herd on the grasslands between New Underwood, Wasta and Elm Springs, keeping Elk Creek to the south of them and the Belle Fourche river to the north. The winter just got tougher. Tom would admit the following spring that he "couldn't find much cover around the area except some draws near the Cheyenne River" which he located quite a ways to the east. He assured Mary that he would move the base camp and the herd "a helluva a lot farther east come spring."

He lost quite a few head of sheep that winter—more than he would normally have lost. And, they lost a mare. She may have gone off by herself, been "enticed" by some wild stallion, been attacked by wolves, or even stolen. She was Mary's horse and it broke her heart—horseflesh was personal with Mary Stone.

Tom's "plan" was a good one. The Cheyenne River had plenty of water [not as clean as the Belle Fourche but drinkable for the herd] and there were quite a number of other small [and full] creeks along their trail. The sheep moved well and really demanded very little "herding." It was wide open country with almost no other sheep, cattle or ranches. Best of all, there was no barbed wire. For Tom Stone and his sheep, this was ideal country. Supplies were a bit of a problem as nobody came from the home place to bring them provisions for over two months—but they had planned and, as always, Mary knew "how to make do with what she had."

This far away, Lew only came a couple of times a year to see how they were doing. He would bring them a good load of supplies—all he could get in his new model A Ford [his years had moved him to a more comfortable riding vehicle]. Knowing that they would likely *not* be getting back to the home place, Lew made arrangements in Wasta to have supplies delivered to them every month and paid for them in advance. This was the sort of agreement you could make in this country and in these days and rest assured the "contract" would be fulfilled to the letter. People were honest and reliable. Their word was their bond.

Lew got Tom's wages current [he relied on Tom and Mary to let him know what he owed them] and brought some things for the kids as well—though some of the toys didn't work very well on the high prairie grass, "his heart was good as gold." Lew went down into both New Underwood and Wasta and hired a crew to help with spring lambing and stayed for most of it himself so he could pay the lambing crew. Lambing went off with only a few "snags" as the workers showed up and the weather held good. Most of the men [and two women] Lew hired had worked at lambing before and knew what they were doing without being told. The herd grew as never before.

Lew and Tom made a trip into town to spend some "planning time" and contacted a third party who knew a couple of good shearing crews that would be in the area in the fall. As long as the people he hired held up their end, things would work out all right. Remembering, that In this part of the country, you could count on people to do what they said they would do. Since Tom knew how to deal with the shearing crews, Lew left those matters in his trusted friend's hands.

They agreed on some specific dates and locations for shearing, nearer to Wasta, and Lew told Tom he would be back to help in the fall [with the shearing] and to pay the crew when they finished their work. Tom Stone had learned that Lew Thurber was a man of his word as well. Lew Thurber knew the same thing about Tom Stone. They never once doubted each other.

Unless he was with Tom, Lew always traveled by himself. For the first time since he had been working for Lew, Tom was a bit concerned. Lew was getting up in age [nobody really knew how old he was, but both Tom and Mary guessed some over 60] and had some trouble with his sight and hearing. He regularly carried a lot of cash with him--but he also had a loaded 30-30 right beside him. "And he damned sure wasn't afraid to use it." Besides, he knew this territory like the back of his hand. He was born and raised here. He was as much a part of this land as it was a part of him.

Lew made arrangements with the Chicago North Western Railroad [the CNW RR had established a railhead in Vale by 1927] to carry his sheep to market the following fall and shared all the details with Tom while giving him the name of the contact person on the line. Tom knew the timetable for getting to the railhead and had enough experience in selling sheep to know what price they should bring from the buyers there. While Tom Stone was a master at his craft of herding, his close association with Lew had taught him a great deal about the financial end of selling his product to buyers. It's easy to see why Lew trusted him to deal with this end of the process.

It was a fairly good winter. Tom did not expect to get through any of the winter months without a good deal of snow but rationalized the heavy snowfall by knowing that "it would bring a good crop of grass for spring." Mary and the three kids moved into Wasta where Mary was close to her friends Percy and Lee Collier. The Colliers had a son [Larry] the same age as Bob so the boys could play together. It was a good, new relationship and one that Mary cherished and maintained for many years after the Stones left the sheep business and moved to Pierre. Such relationships were not something she had been able to build before with someone her own age.

Tom would come to town on a regular basis and spent some time socializing [playing cards] with the Colliers. He later said he "didn't care much for it" but kept coming back into town about once a week. Mary and Tom had rented a small house in Wasta so they could "entertain" the Colliers for dinner and cards at different times as well. This was the first time in their married life Mary and Tom Stone did some of the things a normal married couple did. It was one of the best winters Mary remembers on the many "trails they traveled."

When Lew got back to the base camp the following spring, the shearing crew he had hired were not where they were supposed to be at the time they'd agreed on. This was a big surprise. He made a couple of trips to some smaller herds in the area and found a crew that would soon be done there. He hired them to work his herd when they finished. The shearing was over in about 10 days and the wool was bagged and ready to be shipped. The new lambs and the older ewes who were less productive, would stay "in herd" and be readied for the drive to the railhead and the market in the fall. Although it would be some 6 months before time to ship to the markets, Lew and Tom agreed that Lew and a couple of his hands would "carry" the sheep that were being sold to an area near the shipping yard so Tom could stay with the main herd—with Mary and the kids.

When the wool was sold, Lew came right back to the base camp. It was a good market and *clean* wool was still bringing a good price—especially for military use [uniforms, coats, blankets, etc.] While Lew knew that Tom wasn't responsible for the good market prices that the wool brought, he knew that Tom was responsible for keeping his "investment" intact.

The same was true for the meat [both lamb and mutton supplied good financial returns]. Tom's movement of the sheep to good grass and water *was largely responsible* for that return and Lew Thurber knew it. Lew had been around the sheep business a long time and he knew the herder should be given credit for the number of healthy lambs and surviving ewes that he was able to take to market. His "good herds" were not a matter of luck. They were a product of a knowing herder who managed their movements and kept them from most of the dangers that would confront them in this "unfriendly country" [predators, weather and even cattlemen]. Any large herd owner knew how important their herders were to his successes. And, while Tom Stone was Lew Thurber's friend, he was also a valuable and knowledgeable sheepherder.

In that vein, Tom Stone was ready to act on the decision he had made the year before—he was going to the Badlands. This was much more than an ill-conceived adventure for Tom always felt it was important to find "new" land for both water and grass. While he may have not wanted to admit it, he could see the changes taking place—especially the barbed wire. "Closed" land [primarily because of fencing] would signal the end of sheepherding as he knew it.

So, he methodically gathered his herd and he and Mary got their young family ready to move. While some wives and mothers might have objected, Mary Stone did her part. She made sure about all the provisions they could carry. Three of Lew's men were there to help [they had brought provisions] and they helped load heavy things such as her Maytag [gas driven washing machine] and her Singer sewing machine. Most of the other supplies were the standard fare: plenty of coffee, sugar, beans, flour, salt, bacon and some oats. They didn't load much wood or water—both weighed a great deal and both she and Tom "figgered" they could find enough on the trail. *If they were going to make it, that belief had better become reality.* Luckily, it did.

Tom [foreground] and Mary Stone [holding baby Bob]
just after shearing. Wool "stomper/tromper"
is filling bag of wool in back. 1927

They headed southeast. The weather was beautiful. Tom and Mary both "skinned" one of the wagons. The girls rode with Mary and Bob rode with his dad. They stopped often to "get their bearings" and take breaks for the kids—they were understandably restless and needed to just run. The dogs kept the sheep moving as well as could be expected [with lots of good grass, the herd wanted to stop and eat quite often—remember, sheep eat constantly]. Forcing sheep to move is somewhat akin to pushing a piece of string. Tom guided the dogs and the dogs took care of the herd.

Keeping the herd along the Cheyenne River as long as he could, Tom had discovered a passable route moving across Spring Creek and turning more directly east just south of Rapid City.

They headed southeast toward the Badlands and started across Leonel Jensen's[67] farm [from whom Lew had gotten permission for Tom to cross], near Scenic. This turned out to be a fairly level area all the way to the White River [which eventually joins the Missouri]. The land got a bit more rugged [not mountains but hills and valleys] but still provided a "path" for the large herd to move through. Luckily, the overfilled wagons had only slight navigation issues. Both Tom and Mary knew how to handle their home on wheels.

Soon, Tom and Mary noticed a markedly different landscape. To be sure, the Badlands has been described in many different ways from desolate to breath-taking. Mary saw it as "beautiful." Tom remarked that it "was one of the roughest lookin' places" he'd ever seen. Regardless of their surroundings, here they were—and here they were planning to stay for at least the next 3-4 months. They had seen enough to know they could make it that long if they could find

---

67 Leonel Jensen was one of a group of 5 influential men in this part of South Dakota who shared a vision that the Badlands of South Dakota was something very special and should be preserved as a most unique shrine in the midst of their home state. The others that helped to create the Badlands National Monument were Ben Millard, owner of Cedar Pass Lodge, A.G. Granger of Kadoka, Ted Hustead [owner of Wall Drug—now world famous], and G.W. Mills, a prominent Wall physician. The Badlands National Monument was formalized as a national park of nearly 244,000 acres by President Franklin D. Roosevelt on January 25, 1939. It is home to the largest native grass prairie in the United States.

some supplies for themselves—they found Interior, South Dakota.

The White River is aptly named—but it is drinkable for sheep. And while it was in the southern part of the Badlands, Tom knew he had to get to a constant source of water for his sheep. It would work--it had to.

The grass cover in the National Grasslands was plentiful from the winter snow runoff and lasted even longer into the summer than the grass further west. Further into the Badlands, there was also plenty of grass and yellow-flowering sweet clover [which was hearty enough to stand the normal summer drought] and the sheep would eat that as well. And there were no fences. While Tom was likely the only sheep herder in the Badlands that summer, sheepherders were becoming somewhat more evident in Montana's neighbor to the east.[68]

While the major problems for humans in the Badlands were the intense heat and the utter desolation [the latter condition appealed to some], the issues confronting the sheep were "hundreds of damned rattlesnakes and a helluva lotta coyotes." This was balanced out by available water [only the White River] and enough vegetation [sheep would even eat the plentiful sagebrush—a plant that lives for some 200 years without human tending] for feeding sheep and the fact that nobody bothered you. That latter condition was a true positive for Tom Stone.

Tom and his dogs had trailed the herd further into the Badlands, past Sheep Mountain Table, a mesa just southeast of Scenic and head-ed closer to the White River. They did not set up a base camp and just "stayed the night in several somewhat "protected" areas [where the sheep wouldn't wander]. They had learned a long time ago that their

---

68 Currently, the sheep industry remains a fairly significant force in South Dakota al-though nothing like it once was—many of the herds are small and considered pasture sheep. More than 2 million pounds of wool are sheared and sold in South Dakota every summer as sheep still number about 375,000 in the state. At the same time, there are estimated to be some 1.6 million beef cows and a reasonable number of dairy cows in the state along with over 100,000 breeding bulls. Herds of woolies are still evident as one drives along roads/highways in both east and west river country in the state.

"living style" would, to a large degree, be determined by the needs of the herd. While not the biggest thing in their lives, the "safety" of the herd was a prime consideration. And, they did not forget, they were in new and somewhat uncharted territory for them.

The terrain on both sides of the White River was made up of serrated sand buttes—with plenty of gaps so sheep could easily move down to water in large groups at a time. This they seemed to do naturally. The White River would serve as drinking water for the sheep but not for people, the dogs or the horses. It was milky white from the stone it collected along its banks as it trailed *north* out of Nebraska and through the Badlands before heading east and eventually into the Missouri near Chamberlain, SD.

By the end of the first couple of weeks, Tom had decided that he could "summer" here [and likely would again] but had talked with one rancher who gave him enough information to convince him that he *could not winter* in the Badlands. This was truly "open country" and a herder *could* stay in one place as long as he wanted to. It was, however, mainly for summer grazing as the winters were, as Tom remembers "tough as hell and there wasn't much shelter to be found." The novelist Frederick Manfred penned the Badlands as "painful beauty. . . poignant desolation" in his novel **The Golden Bowl.** While Tom probably never saw Manfred's "painful beauty," he certainly recognized the Badlands as one of the most desolate places he'd ever seen.

The Lakota Sioux called the Badlands of South Dakota [North Dakota also has a Badlands area], *Mako Sica* meaning "land that is bad" and the Eighteenth-century fur traders who traveled the area spoke of *les mauvaises terres a traverse* or "the bad lands to cross" [Griffith and Floyd, 2009, 196]. The Badlands, wrote Champ Clark, "assault the senses. They affront sensibility. They are the biggest and the baddest" [Clark, 1974, 21]. Had Tom Stone read Clark's accounting, he probably would *not have cared* anyway. He was one who "needed to see it for hisself." He would be able to tell quite soon if his sheep could live there or not.

If the sheep could make it in the Badlands, its isolated and open nature would be a logical place to bring them in the late spring and keep them there until late summer. He knew there were at least two rivers that provide his sheep drinkable water—the Cheyenne [on the way down] and the White. He later found a third water source aptly called the Bad River but it was quite a ways north of him. He would use the Bad River on one trip out of the Badlands at the end of a summer as he headed north toward Cottonwood and Quinn, trying to get back closer to the familiar territory south of Wasta. He found the Bad River to be dry later in the summer with little water until it gets close to flowing into the Missouri River at Ft. Pierre. This "trial route" straight north out of the Badlands was a long trip with some very tough terrain.

When it rained in the Badlands, it was a typical South Dakota "cloudburst" that rushed through newly-formed creeks and into the surging White River—dramatically changing any of the landscape that it touched. And, while it receded by the next day, it was dangerous to unwary sheep. Tom soon learned the importance of moving them to higher ground at the first sign of a storm.

It's a common observation, even though a bit exaggerated, that "the wind blows all the time in the west"--drying out what was not already dry. And, it was "hotter than hell." The wind does blow quite a bit—in the summer and winter—and it surely is *very warm*.[69]

After late spring, the summer months brought the blazing sun that baked the dry ground so that it "buckled up" with cracks. That first fall Tom stayed too late. He and Mary got caught in an early fall storm with howling winds and near freezing temperatures. This was his first and last experience staying up into the days and nights of early fall. He'd been told: the Badlands was OK for summer but not anything

---

69 The average annual temperature in the Badlands of South Dakota is 48° F. The range of temperatures in this "natural phenomenon," however is 158° F between the record high of 116° F in 1910 and a low of 42° F in 1916 [Clark, 1974, 29]. It's not unusual to bed down sweating and wake up 4 hours later need some heavy covers to keep you warm. **South Dakota Magazine** [July/August 2017] recently reported that the highest temperature reported in South Dakota was 120° F at Usta on July 15, 2006 and Gann Valley on July 5, 1936.

140

past August. It surely was no place to try to raise a family. There were few human inhabitants and virtually no towns for miles. It was obviously one of those places where few had chosen to live.

It was a "noble" experiment. Tom found out what he needed to know: the Badlands *was* an option. But, "like a blister on a clean face, the Badlands stood in stark contrast to the normally flat and nondescript high plains of western South Dakota" [Straub, 2010, 85-86]. In addition to its most unusual geophysical appearance, the Stones found that the Badlands too, had its share of coyotes.[70] Doig vehemently agrees.[71] Along with the coyotes, were the ever-present prairie dog towns. That meant plenty of holes [the dog's homes]—and the cause of countless broken legs on a rider's mount..

And there were virtually always rattlesnakes to contend with in the Badlands—mostly prairie rattlers which are somewhat different from diamond-back rattlers as they are a bit smaller but may be even more aggressive and dangerous. This area was particularly suited to the prairie rattler as they blended in especially well with the terrain and its natural colors. And, while they thrive in the "semi-desert terrain," you could most often find dens of them near areas of water— the same places Tom took his sheep.

Rattlesnakes, Tom knew, would strike anything—a horse, a dog, a sheep, a human. Their venom is potent. While it didn't always kill a person or an animal, the bite sure made you sick enough to "wish to hell you *was* dead." He was convinced they had killed his second dog [Dog]. One night he didn't come back to camp with Nigger—very

---

70   The coyote deserves special attention because of its most vicious and seemingly relentless drive to stalk and kill. Champ Clark [1974] notes that the coyote is "the most eclectic of all prairie predators" and will "eat anything living—or recently dead." [Clark 1974, 100]. While not the only enemy of the herder and his sheep, the coyote surely looms as one of the most cunning, relentless and cruel.

71   "Coyotes, sheep killers that they were, were hated as nothing else in that country, especially on the lean foothill ranches where the loss of livestock hurt like a wound. They were eatin' the lambs just about as fast as we could turn 'em out. And you could hear those coyotes in a park up on the side of the mountain yippin' up there early in the morning and evening." Ivan Doig [1978] *This House of Sky: Landscapes of a Western Mind* [San Diego, CA: Harcourt Brace and Jovanovich, Publishers, 42].

uncharacteristic. Tom looked and called but he never found him. He was sickened to think the coyotes would.

The trip back to south of Wasta took much longer than Tom had planned. He had to reverse his path a number of times as he would get into canyons that had a way in but no way out. And, the wagons couldn't handle the rugged terrain even as well as the sheep did. Tom and Mary were frustrated. Luckily, they had time to get back to Wasta before fall really set in and the weather actually got better as they "climbed" out of the Badlands. Another lesson learned: don't take this *return* route again.

When they finally got south of Wasta [a safe haven for them and the herd], Tom and Mary took "accounts" of their overall Badlands adventure[s]. Tom described in his own way:

> "It's hotter' hell and they ain't much that wants to live there except a lotta coyotes and them damned rattlesnakes.[72] You got some birds [meadowlarks] but they get pretty scarce til' it rains—which ain't very offen. There's a lot more grass down here than people think and the water is alright for sheep. You ain't gonna have many come down here because no-body says anything good about this place. We'll try it for one more summer since it's free grazin' and there ain't many people around. So, you're at least left alone."

Mary agreed. She could take "tough" but didn't see any reason to be in the Badlands when there was plenty of other good grazing land available that was not as far away and not as nasty. But, she assured her husband, "If you want to go back Dad, we'll go back. We just

---

72 Actually, a number of species live in the Badlands including badgers, ferrets, bull snakes, mice, ground squirrels, pocket gophers, magpies, prairie dogs, owls, hognose snakes [puff adders], toads, mule deer, cliff swallows, sharp-tailed grouse, grackles, hawks, pronghorn antelope, countless plants and blooming flowers as well as other living creatures—including a few 600-pound bison.

don't need to stay so long."

In its very own way, the Badlands of South Dakota is quite beautiful. There is, quite likely, no other place like it on earth [some might argue for the Badlands of North Dakota]. Tom and Mary Stone found some of the things they "wanted" with the very open access and grazing and the available water—and even the isolation. Mary even found some things for canning in the abundance of chokecherries and buffaloberries as well as some wild plums. Gathering such wild growth provided fun for the kids as long as an adult was very close to watch for predators—especially snakes.

They also found some things they didn't "want." There were the always-present rattlesnakes, the vicious coyotes, an occasional mountain lion or even an agile bobcat. The relatively unpredictable weather was a daily issue. You learned to live with the heat—and the cold nights of the approaching winter. But, the sudden storms and flash-flooding that took place near the larger creeks and the White River were, in no uncertain terms, life-threatening.

Seemingly harmless were the frequent prairie dog "towns." These communities were often a square block of holes to provide the varmints [sized between a squirrel and a jackrabbit] with both entrances and exits. You tried to avoid even going into them. However, the herd usually "led" and they were oblivious to the coffee-can sized holes and curious little creatures poking their heads out to see what was going on. Many a larger animal [sheep and/or horses] broke their leg stepping into such holes.

It was good to be back in Wasta. The kids would have some new playmates, Bob could go back to school and Mary could go over to Lee Collier's and get her chickens back [she had left them with Lee because she didn't know if they could make the trip down to the Badlands—much less survive a summer there]. It would be good to have some fresh eggs. Then too, with the coming of fall and winter, they would be *staying put* for at least 5 months—even though Tom would move the base camp a time or two.

Tom set up base camp just south and west of town between Wasta and New Underwood. It was nice to be back "near" civilized country again—even for Tom. He wanted to go back up near Newell to get another dog, but thought it was too far to ride just for that and he was sure he could find somebody who raised dogs much closer to Wasta or New Underwood. It wasn't hard to find a dog—even to find a sheep dog. The task was to find a *good sheep dog*.

Sheep dogs can work by themselves. With herds the size that Tom Stone had, however, he needed *two* good sheep dogs. And while Tom didn't like to think about it, Nigger was getting older, You could see the gray around his muzzle--though he rarely lost a step--because he knew his job so well. Still, with his herd size, Tom knew he needed two dogs. That meant dogs that could/would work *together*—which they often instinctively do.

The new dog would have to get along with the aging Nigger. While the old "master of the flock" was not as quick on his feet as he was 5 years before, you could tell his mind still worked well and his basic instincts for herding had not dulled one bit. One thing more: Tom knew that Nigger would have to be *in charge*—no matter what other dog joined their "crew."

When it was time for shearing, Lew sent two men from the main ranch to the base camp south of Wasta. Their job was to help Tom hire, manage and pay a shearing crew. Once the shearing was done and the wool was bagged and shipped [from Vale at this time], the men from the main ranch would stay with Tom and the herd while the buck herd serviced the ewes. They brought a small truck full of provisions, some new equipment for refurbishing both the sleep and cook wagons [they had taken a beating in the Badlands] and Tom's salary for the last 6 months. The wagons were both "rebuilt" inside [and retarped outside] and the Stones were as ready for winter as they could be with their wagons. As had gotten to be their practice, Mary and the kids would stay in a two-room cabin in town while Tom and the dogs [he got a new dog in town] stayed with the sheep at the base camp.

For the first time in her married life, Mary Stone took her three kids into town [Wasta] with Lee's help and *they went shopping*. They always needed shoes [boots for Bob] and now some coats and caps for winter. Since they had gotten paid, she had the money.

Tom had "expanded" his territory to the Badlands. That appealed to him because nobody else was there. He was on his own [which had both up- and downsides] but they made it alright. The trip into the Badlands was fine [through Scenic and the Grasslands] but his choice of a path "out" had been a mistake. He lost some sheep and the terrain was hard on everything—from the wagons to losing so much time. But they made it back--sadly without their Dog.

Most of the problems that faced sheepherders were fairly simple ones. First, they needed open grassland that was unencumbered by other herds of sheep, cattle or fencing. While not a necessity, most of the experienced herders preferred their "herding domain" to be free of human inhabitants as well. They were loners.

Obviously, when ranchers moved to fence open grasslands and fresh watering areas [with barbed wire], *large* herds of sheep were restricted from the free movement they needed to survive. Second, large herds needed to move quite frequently in an unrestricted manner. Not unlike grazing lands and water, such access for movement need to be open to them on a year-round basis. Third, large sheep herds needed railheads. To be sure, "expansion" didn't mean the same thing to all those who lived on the plains of western South Dakota.

"The patterns of settlement, growth, business and community in any region are heavily reliant on the transportation systems available to that region" [Hufstetler and Bedeau, 2007, 4]. For those who relied on both cattle and sheep for their living [many of the big ranches], that form of transportation was exclusively the railroad—especially in the sparsely-populated west river country *before* highways and transport trailer-trucks.

Before the railroad was established in *western* South Dakota, [railroads had been plentiful in the eastern part of the state for years], horse-drawn freight wagons [sometimes mule-drawn] were the major means of getting supplies to the remote parts of the state and towns like Newell, Belle Fourche, Vale, Deadwood and a number of other adjoining communities. And, while there were Indians on the plains between Pierre [river "port" in the east] and Deadwood [the western stopping point], they were generally friendly and even helpful.[73]

Such freight lines, however, carried basic food supplies and household provisions and were not used to carry the large volumes of wool and mutton to markets in the east [Sioux City, IA and as far away as Chicago]. Such a task would be reserved for the much larger and more powerful "iron horse."

Tracing the development of these railroads in South Dakota reveals a great deal about the nature of the state. Remember, the railroad was *essential* to the development of both the cattle and the sheep industry in eastern Montana and western South Dakota. Without railroads, these industries would *not* have achieved the huge production and financial empires they did. It is safe to say that adequate railheads and regular rail service were crucial to the development of the area—surely for sheep and cattle.

The first railroad "service" in South Dakota began in 1872. The Winona and St. Peter Railroad constructed their line from New Ulm [MN] to Watertown [SD]. The line provided only 34.48 miles of track in the state of South Dakota. But it was a start.

While early railroads had little difficulty becoming established in eastern South Dakota, it was a totally different situation in the vast plains west of the Missouri River. Early on, regulations prohibited the railroads from building across the native American reservations that took up a large part of the western part of the state. As a

---

73 James Harvey Garr came to South Dakota from the Shenandoah Valley in Virginia in the late 1870's with his brother Benjamin. After they spent some time successfully mining gold in the Black Hills [Lead area], James stopped mining and started a freight line from Pierre to Deadwood. During his trips across the prairies of western South Dakota, he often encountered Indians [Lakota Sioux] and found them not only friendly but willing to help him—especially in bad weather. After a trip back east, James returned with a wife and settled in the Vale community where they raised a family and lived until they moved to Kentucky in 1914.

result, the rails stopped at the Missouri River [Pierre, Mobridge and Chamberlain].

In their efforts to reach the Black Hills and service the newly developing "gold traffic," the railroads actually went west across the state of Nebraska and headed north near Chadron [NB] up through Edgemont and Hot Springs [SD] in the southern Hills to Rapid City, Lead and Deadwood. While not a *prohibitive distance* away from the primary grazing lands of some of the large herds, the *terrain* that had to be covered in the Black Hills was not manageable. Sheep and cattle ranchers were understandably impatient.

In 1904, the Rosebud "lottery" opened some Indian lands on the Rosebud Reservation[74] "for white settlement" [Straub, 2010, 135] and the decade that followed witnessed construction of several railroad lines across the vast west river country. The Milwaukee [Rapid City Line] and the Chicago and Northwestern blazed these early rail lines from connections east of the Missouri River all the way to Rapid City—with strategic railheads along the way in such places as Belle Fourche and Vale. Other "shipping stations" would be established where it was felt economically beneficial.

While this was an essential addition for stock producers, the wanton "invasion" of lands ceded to Native Americans is still being debated—with just cause. This was, of course, only one of many violations of the sovereignty of Native American lands. Nonetheless, the railheads were in place and a steady stream of sheep, wool and mutton made its way to markets in both the east and the west. The

---

74 There are 8 American Indian Reservations "in" South Dakota. Standing Rock, Cheyenne River, Pine Ridge, Rosebud and Lower Brule west of the Missouri River and Crow Creek, Yankton, Flandreau and Sisseton Wahpeton [Lake Traverse] east of the Missouri River. At least nine major tribes are supported by these reservations: the Cheyenne River Sioux Tribe, the Crow Creek Sioux Tribe, the Flandreau Santee Tribe, the Lower Brule Sioux Tribe, the Oglala Sioux Tribe, the Rosebud Sioux Tribe, the Sisseton Wahpeton Oyate, the Standing Rock Sioux Tribe, and the Yankton Sioux Tribe. One glance at a tribal map would clearly indicate that both the Cheyenne River Indian Reservation and the Standing Rock Indian Reservation [located partially in North Dakota] were the major "obstacles" to opening railroad lines across South Dakota's west river sheep and cattle country.

same was true for the cattle owners of the area.

If "home" was Montana, Tom and Mary were moving farther away from "home" each year. But it was much better than trying to move the sheep back there every fall. And herders soon realized that where they staked their sheep wagon was really going to be home—at least for a few weeks or months.

Tom Stone still remembered his early days on the trail when "one wagon was all he needed." He stored all his belongings in it, slept in it and even brought the dogs inside when it turned really cold outside. Even after he and Mary were married, one wagon was enough, although the space would have been a bit confining for someone who had to stay there all day. Before they had children, however, Mary was with Tom riding herd most of the day. Once they started their family, however, the "cook" wagon was not going to work. Even when they got a second wagon for sleeping, it soon became inadequate—they both felt it. Three wagons? Not a realistic option.

Make no mistake—Tom and Mary Stone both loved their life on the prairie. They had little desire to move into a town and establish a permanent residence. And both of them actually loved what had become "their sheep." And if you loved sheep in these days of large herds and open grasslands, you resigned yourself to living right where you worked.

From south of Wasta, they went back to the Badlands two more summers. Tom better understood the trails to follow both going in and coming back out and did not deviate from the plan. There were few surprises. The grasslands east of Scenic were still as green and full as could be. During the second summer, water was a little bit scarce but they "made do" by staying longer in a spot where they found a good stream or creek after a rain, then pushing a little bit further the next two or three days.

Other things in the Badlands were the same. The White River was still just as white as could be. You still heard the coyotes at night, and it seemed "there was more damned rattlesnakes every year." And still, nobody else was in the area with a herd. Needless to say, the trips in and out were tough. They were tough on the sheep, tough on the horses and tough on the wagons. Most of all, Mary's question about "why do we need to go way down there when we've got such good land further north" came up again—and again. Tom finally agreed.

Deep down, Tom Stone knew that the "good land further north" was not going to be there for them forever. He knew that the cattle would come and with them the fences. He knew that the way of life they loved would not last forever. They didn't talk about it.

But here they were—in the middle of western South Dakota with family they loved and doing work they truly enjoyed. They had "everything" they needed *for right now*. As Tom so often said: "We had plenty to eat and a roof over our heads." They did. They also had good horses and a boss that took care of any need that may arise. They were paid well—by herder's standards—and had very few expenses. So, they saved virtually all their salary. Besides, if you don't go into town much, you don't have any place to spend what money you do have.

Then came a letter that was addressed to Tom Stone, Belle Fourche, South Dakota. Somehow it had found its way from Belle Fourche to the open prairie south of Wasta—over a hundred miles away. The rider gave the letter to Tom—Tom handed it to his wife.

They thanked the "postman" and he immediately headed back for Wasta and eventually Belle Fourche.

Mary was excited. It was a real letter. It was postmarked Dalton, Georgia. The date was September, 1937. It had taken over four months for the letter to find them.

Tom was more than apprehensive. While he had no idea what the letter was about, he knew it was from family. He was curious as to the contents and at the same time "didn't really give a damn' about what was goin' on down there . . . .You can read it Mother, but you can be damned sure it ain't gonna say anything good."

Mary didn't respond. She knew very little about any of Tom's family in Georgia. One of their seemingly "unspoken rules" was that she didn't ask and he didn't tell her much of anything about them. Not unlike her husband, Mary Stone had no contact with her family—in Iowa or even Ekalaka [she had not talked with her sister Grace since She and Tom got married—over 12 years before]. The family they had, was the family they had right here—right now.

She wasn't sure how strongly Tom felt about his "whole" family. She knew how he felt about his brothers and sisters. That issue was very clear. But Mary did not have a good idea what Tom felt about his parents—R.L. and Lizzie Stone—now in their late 60's. While he talk-ed very little about them, he virtually always spoke with respect. He referred to his father as "Dad" and his mother as "my Mother." There was never any use of the expressions such as "the old man" or "the old lady." As a matter of fact, he rarely talked about his family at all—especially his mother and father. It was a signal that he didn't want any questions about them from anybody. His family was a non-topic.

Finally, with the letter in her hand, Mary Stone was curious. The only family she had lived in two sheep wagons. This letter was from family she had never met and knew very little about.

Tom said no more. Mary opened the letter, being careful not to damage the return address. Tom would not likely have admitted it, but he wanted to know what was in the letter as well. Mary didn't read it over first—she just began reading it aloud:

> Tom Stone. R.L. and Miss Lizzie are in pretty bad shape. They want you to come home and take care of them. They are at the home place by themselves. No-body else will help them. If you help them, you can have everything they got. Doc Stone

Mary held the letter and looked at her husband straight away. "Who's Doc," she asked.

"My cousin," Tom answered. "He's the only one down there worth a damned," he added. "We went to school together."

"We need to do something Dad."

"You don't know what they're like Mother."

"It's your mother and father. They need some help and it doesn't sound like anybody down there will help them."

"I'm tellin' you Mother, you just don't know what they're like—they're all a bunch of damned snakes."

"Dad, this is not all of them. This is your mother and father. They're old—and it sounds like they can't do for themselves. We've got to do something."

"Well, I don't give a damn and I ain't doin' nothin' for that bunch. You can go down there if you want to—but you'll be sorry you did—you'll see what I'm sayin'."

"We can talk about this later," Mary concluded. She didn't know if Tom would talk about it later or not. She understood him well enough to know that *this* was *not* the time to make any decisions. His mind was "made up"—for the time being. So was hers. This was family—even though she didn't know them. She was going to figure out some ways to help. And, all the ways she thought about involved going to Georgia. She had also decided that *when* they went, it was going to be the *whole family* going.

There were some big decisions to be made.

The next morning Tom admitted: "Maybe we oughta' see what kinda' shape they're in. We could try to talk to somebody down there . . . I still don't think we're gonna' find out anything good."

He wasn't saying anything about going to Georgia, But, at least Tom was willing to talk about it. Then, he reminded Mary,

> "Mother, you gotta see what we got *right here*. We got a good job. We're savin' some money. The kids can go to school in the winter. This is a helluva lot bettern' nothin'. You wanna give all this up? I sure as hell don't."

It was a good question. He had some good points. Right now, they did have a job and they had a big responsibility to Lew Thurber—he had been very good to them. What would Lew say? What would happen to this large herd of sheep? What would happen to the horses and the wagons—all their tack and provisions and personal belongings [the kids' toys, Mary's Maytag and Singer sewing machine, the dogs]?

For Tom and Mary Stone, this was stability. Even more importantly, this was true independence. They could come and go as they pleased. They really had no "boss" as Lew gave them virtually complete control over what to do with his herds. The trust meant a lot but the independence even more. Give all this up?

Besides all those issues, they had no idea how far it was to Whitfield, County in north Georgia. They knew nothing about the route—let alone highways.[75] They didn't even have a car! Have a car--Tom Stone didn't even know how to drive! Mary did. Right now, none of this made any difference—Mary had decided. They were going to Georgia.

The fact that they had little knowledge about "traveling" on "highways" or that they had no idea how far they were going to be traveling or how long it was going to take, seemed not to matter. Right now, they had no real directions [except south] and they had never even heard of a road map. But they were accustomed to not knowing "what lay ahead" from their years on the plains and in the Badlands. They "knew" they would be able to handle whatever came up. Their decision seemed clear to Mary Stone. Tom was still not sold on the idea.

Within the week, they made contact with Lew. He let them know he would help in any way he could. Even though he would "lose" the best hand[s] he had, this was his way--typical Lew Thurber. He would keep their job until they got back—they were counting on a staying in Georgia only a few weeks at this time. He was willing to advance them some salary but they told him they had the money to make the

---

75 Using present-day roads, the distance between Wasta, SD and Resaca, Georgia is nearly 1400 miles—via INTERSTATE 29—and there was no INTERSATE at all. With today's roads, it would take about 20 hours of hard driving to go this distance.

trip—*down and back*. Tom and Mary had saved a good amount of their salary for the last 5 years—they had over $2,260 in cash.

Lew loaded up their stuff in one of his "straight" trucks from the main ranch and took them to Philip. There, Tom and Mary bought a 1935 Ford, 2--door coupe that would carry 5 passengers. They bought it from Dorothy Brothers Chevrolet in Philip, SD. The kids were small and they were used to "roughing it." And they would take Nigger—the new dog could stay with the herd.

Since they had cash money, they had no trouble making a "deal" on a *good* used car—times were different. The '35 Ford would cost them a total of $740.00 with new tires [and a spare], license plates and a full tank of gas.

Though Lew had offered to store their "stuff" at the home place, they decided to take everything they owned to White Lake [SD] where Louie, Mary's brother, owned and operated a Flying Red Horse [Socony Mobil] filling station [present-day gas station]. Her brother, after leaving Montana, lived in White Lake with his wife Eva and his two sons, Bill and Louis.

Lew told two of his men to drive the truck full of Tom and Mary's belongings to "wherever they're goin'." From Philip, the trip to White Lake was about 185 miles. It would take them about 6 hours. The trip was uneventful and the car ran well. Mary, of course, drove all the way.

When they got down to White Lake, they had no trouble finding Louie's filling station. And, since he ran the station by himself, he was there when they got to town about 3 in the afternoon. He had plenty of storage space for the things on the truck and the ranch hands unloaded it. Both Tom and Louie offered to have them stay for the night but the men wanted to get back on the road. So, after eating, gassing up the truck and getting plenty of coffee, decided to head west—as far as they could go before it got dark.

Louie's wife Eva had fixed a big dinner and they all talked about the trip to Georgia. Bob and the girls went to bed early. Tom and Mary had decided to leave early the next morning. Since Mary had not seen her brother for such a long time and really had no good idea when they'd be back this way, she asked Tom to consider spending another night: "It would be good for all of us to rest up for this trip," she argued logically. Since Tom liked Louie [they had gotten to know each other quite well in Montana] he agreed. This would also give them a chance to "map out" their long trip to Whitfield County, Georgia.

CHAPTER **12**

Heading South: Back to Roots

THE NEXT MORNING they carefully started packing the things they knew they would need [buying things on the road was not an option for them]. They packed their clothes sparingly. They packed their cooking gear, several blankets and a tarp [as Mary and Tom would sleep on the ground with the kids on a makeshift bed in the backseat of the car].

They packed two gallon jugs of water [for drinking and for coffee] as they knew water would be readily accessible "on the road." Since Louie had a small grocery store with his station, they got their staples [coffee, beans, flour, salt, sugar, bacon, lard, and baking powder] and only enough "perishables for" three days—they planned on stopping to replenish anything that would go "bad." With Mary Stone's planning, that would likely not happen.

The rest of the day, they relaxed and talked with Eva and Louie. The kids played outside and seemed to have no idea what was in store for the next week or so. It would be a "new adventure." But, up to now, the Stone's life had been plenty full of "new adventures."

As his filling station was on a "main highway," Louie got some customers traveling across country [not many during these days of tough economic times and gas shortages]. Because of that, he had some knowledge about the highway "system" in the United States. It was surely not an efficient "Interstate," but was quite reasonable if you stayed on "main roads" and traveled mostly during the daylight hours.

In some ways, this trip was not unlike many they had taken across the plains of Western South Dakota except that the "ride" was much more comfortable [especially in the rain] and they could cover a great many more miles in a day—one day nearly 200. Louie had given them a 5-gallon can full of gas in case they found themselves in isolated spots. They stopped regularly along the road, gathered up wood, and Mary cooked over an open fire [nothing new for her]. They pulled a bit further off the road at night and slept soundly—the kids in the car and Tom and Mary and Nigger under the stars. This was NOT something new to them either. With only two days of hard rain the whole trip, the weather held generally good.

They stopped at roadside stands [set up by farmers] and bought some of the supplies they needed—mostly fresh fruit and vegetables. They didn't need much. They had brought some bacon and canned meat from Louie's store and Mary baked enough biscuits to last all day—Tom had remarked that this was about "the same thing my Mother did every morning." Because they had no sheep to worry about, the trip went very smoothly.

That is not to say that Tom did not think about "his herd" every morning and every night—he did. But he knew there was nothing he could do from where he was. Still, he thought this whole trip was a "damned fool idea.". . . and he said so nearly every day.

They cut straight down through Nebraska and into Kansas. Their only concern was finding gasoline along the way. They did not need any motels or restaurants—and their bathroom breaks were quite natural just as they had been on the open range. Some days Mary purposely drove further than others—depending more on the mood of the kids than anything else.

Near Wichita, Kansas, they started to veer east toward Kansas City and St. Louis. At St. Louis they would head southeast toward Chattanooga, Tennessee—and Tom would be in "familiar territory." At least he would recognize the names of some of the towns and counties south of Chattanooga—just on the north Georgia border and about [for them and hour and a half] 35 miles to Dalton, Georgia and another 20 miles to Resaca.

It was amazing how well the trip was going—no surprises and no crises. The kids did well and loved playing with the dog [more than he did with them] and the car ran very well [remember, in those days when you bought a "good" used car—it was].

Just south of Chattanooga, Tom calmly said:

> "Mother, before we get down home, there's somthin' I need to tell ya." He was very matter of fact and displayed no humor in his tone.

> Mary was just as matter-of-fact: "What is it?"

> Tom did not hesitate. "Well, a long time before I came to Montana, I was married—I was married twict.'

> "What on earth do you mean? How could you have been married before? You never told me . . . "

> "I never told you becuz' I didn't think there was any need to. I sure as hell didn't think we'd be comin' back down here. I guess I shoulda' said somethin' about it. It shouldn't matter none."

> "Shouldn't matter!" Mary almost shouted.

> "Why shouldn't it matter that the man I've been married to for over 10 years now tells me he's been married before—and more than once."

> "Neither of em' lasted even a year—and there was no kids," Tom explained carefully.

"If wasn't for these little kids, I'd put you out of this car and go back home. Dad, this is the most hurtful thing you've ever done to me. I don't know what to think anymore."

"I don't even know where either of um' is anyhow—and don't care."

That didn't help. "We're not done talking about this!" Mary assured him. "Who else knows about your other two wives?"

"Nobody else knows. I never took em' home."

"Well that's something. This is still not over," Mary said in a warning tone. "We are going to talk about this some more. My God, Dad. How could you? How could you do this not tell me until you thought I would find out? You don't know how ashamed and embarrassed I am.

And what about these children? What are they supposed to think? Their father has been married two times before and never said anything about it? What about them?"

"I don't think it'll mean anything to em' later just like I don't think it means anything to em' now. . . It'll be alright. Just wait."

"I just can't believe it, Dad. You never told me."

"I'm sorry. …….. I am sorry."

That was the end of the conversation about the former wives and "whatever happened to them." Mary never brought it up to

Tom again although she did talk about it with her kids in later years. When she talked about, a look came over face that we had not seen before—it was resolute.

It had taken them nearly 6 full days to get to Resaca, Georgia. Driving long hours all the way from White Lake, South Dakota, through the entire states of Nebraska, Kansas and Missouri and the southeast corner of Kentucky and Tennessee [Chattanooga] and into north Georgia. Once in north Georgia, they would go through Dalton and then straight south into Resaca[76] and Sugar Valley—for Tom Stone, it really was the "home" he had known for so many years. There was no way Tom could have known all that was in store for he and Mary. "Coming home" would prove to be *much less* than a dream come true.

Somehow Tom remembered how to get to the home place. It had been nearly 15 years and the main house was well back in the woods. The road was built for R.L. Stone's wagon and it is doubtful more than a dozen cars had ever taken the "risk." Maybe none successfully. When Tom and Mary drove in, the "road" looked like nobody had used it for some time—even a year or two.

They drove up to the house. It was much like Tom had described it: two story with windows on both floors. Two full stone chimneys were very apparent—one on the north side and one directly in the middle of the house [both were used for heat but the fireplace in the middle was also used for cooking].

There was a large porch on the front with a couple of rocking chairs out there. The fence around what was a "struggling garden" looked in bad disrepair—as though it had not been tended to for a while. It was summer but Tom still expected to see smoke from the "cook" chimney. There was none. There were no pigs in the yard and

---

76 R.L. Stone lived in Whitfield County. Resaca, which is partly located in both Gordon County and Whitfield County was the closest town of any size. The Stone home place was actually, in Whitfield County. The population of Whitfield County at this time was approximately 21,000. Total population of Resaca in 1937 was about 250. Current population of Whitfield County is over 105,000 with Resaca's current population at 781.

no mules either—and lots of weeds. Tom had never known this to be the case at the home place. A stranger might have justifiably concluded that nobody lived here and perhaps had not for some time.

If anyone in the house heard the car drive up, they didn't show any response—nobody came to the door. Tom almost expected his Dad to welcome "a car" with his double-barreled shotgun—it would have been rare for a car to come up the "road" to the main house—at least they should have heard them arriving.

Tom looked at Mary and before she said anything, he was out of the car and at the door. If he was reluctant about seeing "who" was inside, he didn't show it. "I'll see if they're inside," he said as he stepped up on the porch and knocked slightly on the big pine door. This was ONE of those moments. Tom did not know if there was anyone inside or not. It had been about 15 years since he'd been here but the letter—the letter was now nearly 7 months old. In his mind he was thinking "a lot could have happened in that amount a time."

R.L. opened the door. This was another ONE of those moments. Mary knew they wouldn't hug. She didn't think they would shake hands. She didn't know if they would even speak. She heard Bob say from the back seat: "Who is that?" Mary answered in a somewhat proud but low voice: "That's Robert Lee Stone; he's your Grandfather." While she thought that would satisfy him, she had not thought that the kids had no idea "what" a grandfather was. There was going to be plenty of time to explain.

"Lizzie," Mary heard R.L. say: "It's Tom." There was no response from Tom's mother. But, in less than a minute she appeared in the doorway. She was small, and slim, and bent over. Her hair was nearly all gray and pulled back. She had some glasses perched on her nose that centered her slim but not wrinkled face. Mary thought she looked "precious." "And that lady kids," Mary Stone announced proudly, "is your Grandmother, Mary Elizabeth Harper Stone." Kids the ages of Bob (just 11), Sissy [8] and Jody [5] were most likely not impressed. They probably didn't know what to think about his "new chapter in their lives."

Mary was in awe. She never thought she would get a chance to meet any of her husband's family. This seemed so important since she had lost both her parents before she was 9 years old. While not exactly a "dream," for them, this was a critical event in their lives.

Tom said hello to his Mother and Father. He did not make any affectionate gestures. Neither R.L. nor Lizzie offered to do that either. A quick thought rushed through her mind: Maybe she didn't "know what they was like."

She hurried the kids out of the back seat and took them up on the porch to the opened front door. Mary, as was her nature, gave both R.L. and Lizzie a hug—albeit brief. Mary did not even think about how this may have felt to these two seemingly-isolated people—who had never seen nor heard of her before.

She then held each of the little girls up to their Grandpa and Grandma—and "introduced" them:

> "This is Sissy. She's 7 and a half." Mary switched kids and lifted JoAnn. "This is Jody. She's going to be 6 this January." Mary then put her arm around Bob and said "This is Bob. He was 11 in May." Not surprisingly, The kids didn't know what to do. "What, they wondered was family? What was a grandfather? Who was the other person—our grandmother?"

With the exception of a day-and-a-half with their Uncle Louie a few days before, they had never met "family." And, they had no idea what "grandfathers" or "grandmothers" were.

R.L. invited them all into the house and told them to sit down. There were several chairs and stools around the large, single room downstairs. Tom volunteered Mary to make some coffee. She gladly agreed to do so to help break the tension. She found R.L.'s pot. It was full to the brim with what appeared to be solid coffee. She set it back down and found a large pot that was almost empty.

Tom announced: "You all go ahead and talk. I'll get some wood for this fire and some water. Bob, you come with me." Bob jumped up—happy to get out of an uncomfortable situation. Tom drew water from the well and Bob went about gathering some wood. He had done that plenty of times before. Bob stacked it on the porch near the door choosing not to go back inside until his Dad did.

Meanwhile, Mary was looking for coffee. Lizzie offered that there was some in the cabinet on the wall—and then got up to come help Mary find it. Lizzie reached for the coffee sack as Mary's hand came on top of her badly bent-up arthritic fingers. "I'll get it Mother," Mary said. Lizzie softly answered "thank you." They were going to be "friends."

It didn't take Tom long to get the fire going. The old chimney still drew well—that was a relief. No idea what had been living up in there. Tom didn't build a big fire as it was already hot in the house—and they were just making coffee. When the coffee was ready, Mary poured all the adults [and Bob] a cup. The girls had water. "I need to get my pot readied up," R.L. announced as he seemed to feel the need to do something other than just sit. "Maybe I'll just tend to that in the mornin'." He was Tom Stone's Dad all right.

The room was still as they drank their coffee. It was likely that nobody knew what to say. The girls started to go up the stairs to the loft. Mary stopped them. She had been told that the loft was where people slept although it seemed obvious that neither R.L. nor Lizzie could have climbed the stairs.

"It's alright Mary. The kids can go up there. Ya'all will most likely be sleeping up there. We stay down here," Lizzie told them all. "We'll all be turnin' in pretty quick. You might wanna' go and red' up those beds for all of ya," R.L. added. At least it was clear that everybody was going to stay *in the house* and *where* everyone would sleep.

Nobody had yet said anything about supper. From first glance it didn't look like there was much in the house to eat. Mary asked Tom if he would get "things" out of the car—meaning what food they had left. He brought in some flour, baking powder, two cans of meat and a small bag of navy beans. This would be plenty. This had to be plenty—it was all they had--grocery shopping would be "left to first thing in the morning." R.L. had volunteered that .

Mary put the beans in some water to let them soak only a few minutes and then got them boiling on the edge of the fireplace. She started mixing a double batch of biscuits since she knew that would at least be filling. Tom opened the cans of meat and Mary "sliced" it and put it on a plate. Lizzie told Bob [Tommy Bob they started to call him] to go out to the garden and see if there were any ripe tomatoes. At 11, he was used to responsibility—he found 5 tomatoes and picked some other "things" he saw [okra and squash]. It looked like food and he was very hungry.

You could tell Lizzie felt good about contributing. Tom continued to bring things in from the car and take them up to the loft. Bob took Sissy out to show her the garden which he now "knew everything about." Jody stayed close to her Mom. R.L. sat in his chair. There was a new "dynamic" in R.L. Stone's house. One that nobody had seen before.

When supper was ready, they all sat down at the table. R.L. sat in what was apparently "his spot" and Lizzie sat at the other end. There was plenty of room as the table had seats for at least 8 people. Mary poured more coffee and dished up food on the kid's plates—even some fried okra--which didn't go well. R.L. took two biscuits right away and put some sorghum on them. "I like the looks of these 'high-top' biscuits Mary," he offered. "Well, we've got plenty of them," she replied encouragingly.

Everybody seemed to get enough to eat. Mary heated water to do the dishes and she did a bit of cleaning around the kitchen area as she put things away. She could tell that nothing had been done for quite a while around this house. But, Mary Stone was excited. She was here where she could really help her "new family." The kids didn't really know what to think and were worn-out from the long trip. Tom was still pretty anxious—and cautious.

It had been 15 years since he had been here. Much had changed. Nothing had changed. It seemed like a lifetime. In many ways, it was a lifetime.

They did the best they could with the loft to get ready for bed. There were two big beds up there, some quilts for covers and 4 pillows—no sheets or pillowcases. The kids went to sleep right away. Tom and Mary lay in bed but did not talk for a few minutes. They both saw a couple of stars through holes in the roof. "I'll fix that roof tommora," Tom assured her. Mary was pretty good with just about everything. They even had "a roof over their heads."

They slept soundly. They woke up a couple of times in a strange place but went right back to sleep. Tom continued to feel uneasy about what would happen tomorrow and the next day and the day after that—"You just don't know these people. . . "

The next morning they heard R.L. downstairs making coffee in "his pot." Each day he added coffee and water. Then he boiled the coffee on the fireplace stove. Nobody else drank from "his pot." When the coffee grounds filled the pot to the top, he dumped it out and started over. To fill it completely took about a week.

Tom and Mary got up and started fixing the "regular" coffee pot. She had some biscuits left over from the night before but nothing else—no meat—no eggs. She didn't see Lizzie when she came down from the loft, but Mary heard her voice. "Them chickens should have laid some eggs this morning. You can go gather them if you are of a mind." That was Mary's indication that Lizzie *could not* gather the eggs—and that R.L. *would not*.

She never counted the hens roaming around the backyard but found over a dozen eggs—some in out-of-the way places. Didn't matter—they would still scramble. And, if there were enough chickens, dinner might be taken care of. Then she remembered, she and R.L. were going to town for groceries. Mary Stone was actually going into town with her father-in-law. A real father-in-law.

This whole thing seemed surreal but she didn't mind the "newness" of it all. She had family again. She had family to care for. She had family to love.

She scrambled the eggs and served the biscuits. She felt badly that they did not have any meat or potatoes for breakfast [the big meal of the day] but she couldn't change that. They had enough for now. Besides, it was a hot meal and neither she nor Tom knew how long it might have been since his mother and father had eaten a hot meal. She was pretty sure they couldn't have fixed it by themselves. She thought back to the letter they had gotten some weeks before: "R.L. and Lizzie were in pretty bad shape." Apparently, nobody had been doing much of anything to help them. She wondered why. It just did not seem right.

Since Mary was the only one that could drive, she would go into town with R.L. She knew what they needed for the time being—including baking powder, flour, coffee, bacon, some beans, and some meat [pork]. There were "potato hills" in the garden. Tommy Bob could dig those. She was also going to get some bar soap. She had plans.

Carbondale only had one store so that was not a choice that had to be made. Mary went into the store and Bob Lee said he would meet her back at the car. He may have had something to tend to. He likely did not want to be seen being driven by a woman—women didn't drive cars—nor did women haul men around.

R.L. actually met Mary in the store. He got dipping snuff for his wife and both chewing and smoking tobacco for himself. He told Mary to "git what you need. I'll pay for it. . . Better get a little candy for them kids—they'll *need* that." She got all the things they needed for the next few days. R.L. waited at the front of the store as though he was looking for somebody. When she was finished, he paid for everything. After what little she'd heard about him, he did not "seem so bad." He was a bit gruff but anybody who would buy "candy for them kids" had to "have some good in him." Besides, her mind was on getting groceries and getting back to the house.

Back at the "home place" there was plenty of work to be done both inside and out. And she finally had a house where she could do the kind of work she loved to do—cook and clean. Mary felt good about the decision to come to Georgia.

165

While Mary and R.L. were in Carbondale, Tom took the kids outside and "showed them around." He still remembered most everything. He showed them the corn crib and the barn. He showed them the outhouse and the pit where they used to fatten up hogs. The day they arrived, he had noticed the mules were gone—he never asked his Dad about them but found out later they had been sold—with the money most likely going to Tom's brother, Paul. The kids saw the hills where their Dad had spent hundreds of hours picking huckleberries for shipment north. He didn't think much about it, and all of this probably meant very little to them.

Tom found some wood that he would use for shingles to fix the holes in the roof later that day. He and Bob started gathering and stacking wood outside on the porch. They built another pile that would need to be cut and split. The axe was in the shed and it looked like somebody had used it recently—it was fairly sharp with not a bit of rust. The old axe brought back many memories.

He looked at the garden more closely. There were some tomato plants but they had pretty much dried up from lack of rain or watering. He saw several hills of "Irish" potatoes and dug a few up with his boot—there seemed to be lots of "yaller taters" [sweet potatoes]. He saw some stems from a large patch of onions that had not been pulled and had dried up. There were quite a few squash [green and yellow] both in the blooming and ready-to-pick stages. It looked like somebody had tended the garden within the last month or so.

Bob took wood inside and Tom "banked" up the main fireplace for cooking. He had Bob start moving some of the wood they had gathered over near the fireplace where his mother usually sat. It wasn't winter, but she liked the warmth any time of the year.

R.L. and Mary got back from town. You could tell he was not comfortable riding in a car—likely because a woman was doing the driving. Mary brought the groceries in. There was enough so it took two trips. "Grandpa" got the candy out of one of the boxes and gave some to each of the kids. Tom thought to himself: "This is a man I never knew."

Mary was ready to fix some dinner [their noon meal]. She didn't ask what anybody wanted but R.L. mentioned he would sure like some more "of them high-top biscuits." She assured him she'd bake some more. She fried some ham and white potatoes and set that on the table along with the biscuits and some squash and onions mixed together. She made some gravy [redeye] with the ham drippings and flour. Tom and his parents put it on their biscuits. Some of the vegetables were left over after dinner. Mary did not like leftovers—for some that meant waste—but Nigger was there for lunch as well. He may not have liked it, but he ate it when Mary poured some of the ham drippings on it—and threw in a couple of fried potatoes.

While she didn't think much about it at the time, this was surprisingly the nicest kitchen she'd had in 10 years—the same for the house. It had a roof [leaking but soon to be fixed], windows and doors and a solid wood floor. It was pretty dirty but she would soon start taking care of that. She was actually looking forward to cleaning—for her entire family--both old and new.

After the noon meal, Mary started cleaning in the kitchen. She didn't ask either Lizzie or R.L. for "permission" and figured if they didn't want her to do so, they would say something. They didn't say anything at all. Mary was going to clean some in the downstairs and then do some laundry from the trip. She was also pretty sure Tom's folks could use some clean "things." One thing about Mary Stone, she was not shy.

Tom went outside. R.L. and Bob went with him. Tom told R.L. that he was going to fix the roof. R.L. said he thought the roof was alright. Tom asked for a hammer and some nails. R.L. got them from the shed. Tom had no idea how he was going to get up on the roof—maybe he'd have to build a ladder first. But, R.L. had a ladder in the barn that was used to get up into the hayloft. He told Tom about it and Tom and Bob carried it to the side of the house. With hammer and nails [carried in the back pockets of his overalls] Tom carried the shingles and climbed the roof. The pitch of the roof was not bad and he had the holes "covered" in less than an hour. R.L. and Bob watched from down below. Tom finished and put the ladder back in the barn.

The next project was to fix the chicken coop. The leg that had been "broken" off was lying near the coop. After Tom propped up the coop with some unsplit firewood, he "reset" the leg and nailed it back on. "Good as new," the two "advisors " heard him declare.

Inside, Mary was cleaning the downstairs. She had heated some water and put it in a mop bucket. She had fashioned a mop from some "rags" that she found in the shed outside and tied them onto a makeshift handle--always the Mary Stone who could "make do with what she had." Lizzie sat quietly in her chair near a small, but warm fire that her "new" grandson had built for her. She seemed content.

Mary mopped the floor as best she could and started to gather all the things she considered laundry—including their own from the trip. It was quite a batch even before she looked upstairs. With all this space downstairs, the two girls had plenty of "running room." They did. None of their antics seemed to bother their grandmother and that was a relief to Mary.

While there was a "washtub" on the back stoop, Mary could not find any rinse tub—so she emptied the mop bucket to rinse the laundered clothes—a few at a time. Tom told Bob to get "your Mother the water she needs." He did. This was, in a way, almost fun. Mary brought a cup of hot coffee to Lizzie—it was likely that nobody had ever waited on her before. Mary felt Lizzie's gratitude. She always said "thank you."

Things were starting to settle down. Meals were served on a regular schedule, R.L. and Lizzie had coffee [and high-top biscuits] all day long if they wanted them. Mary was enjoying just helping them. She could see them even start to "perk up" some.

Near the end of the week, R.L. started showing Tom around the "place." They walked through the barn, looked in the shed and then walked down the "road" about a half-mile. R.L. pointed to the sides of the hills that surrounded the homeplace. He gestured to the barn and the main house—even pointing at the old wagon. He told Tom that if they stayed, all of this would be his.

All things considered, this didn't impress Tom much. Things were in bad shape. Every one of the buildings needed work. There were no animals except the few chickens and the berries hadn't been picked for at least three years. The brush was so thick on the hillside it would take a month or more just to clean that out on one side so you could even get pickers in there.

For the first time, Tom noticed that his Dad had aged. While he should have expected that, he had never really thought about it. Now he saw it first-hand. He was surprised. His Dad had mellowed quite a bit as well—that surprised Tom even more. Though it was likely that Tom had never thought of his Dad changing—if he had, he likely would *never* have *imagined what he was now seeing and hearing.*

It was time for dinner. Mary had the laundry hung out on three lines she had drawn from the house to the shed. The hooks were already there so it must have been used for clotheslines before.

While they did not have running water or electricity, R.L. and Lizzie had a bathtub! Wonder of wonders. And, while using the tub would mean hauling and heating water, it would be worth it. Bob and Tom hauled water. Mary heated it on the ever-burning fire place and they filled the tub about half full. Mary draped a couple of blankets around the tub [for privacy] and announced to Lizzie that it was time to take a bath.

It became immediately apparent that Mary Elizabeth Harper Stone thought taking a bath was a very private matter. "I'm going to be right here to give you all the help you need. You sit on this chair and get ready [Mary did not say undressed] to take a nice warm bath."

There was some hesitation but Lizzie moved to the straight chair near the tub. Mary waited a couple minutes and then moved to help her into the tub. Lizzie probably didn't weigh 95 pounds and Mary Stone was young and strong—she had helped lift sheep almost that heavy during lambing. And Mary Stone was resolved that Lizzie Stone was going get a bath. She gave Lizzie the multi-use bar of soap [used for laundry instead of lye and bathing as well]. As Mary unfurled Lizzie's hair to wash it, she noticed a bit of a grin on her mother-in-law's face. This <u>was</u> good—really good. Who knows how long it had been since she had been able to take a hot bath. . . . just imagine.

The third day of "discovery" led Mary to uncover a large object downstairs in the far corner of the house—it was an upright Baldwin piano. Exciting! Mary played. Lizzie had played. R.L. regularly used the bench to hide his .45 caliber handgun—and it was loaded. Mary just looked and wisely said nothing. R.L. took the gun and put it in the hip pocket of his overalls.

Mary spent the next two weeks cleaning in and around the house [the porch, the outside windows]. She washed the curtains and planned to make some new ones but Lizzie had no sewing machine—that project could wait. Mary cleaned the piano as best she could. She sat on a small kitchen stool and played some things from memory. Everybody seemed to love it even though they likely could not identify Claire de lune.

It was only a matter of time until "company" came by. Tom had several first cousins in the area and around Dalton. And R.L. and Lizzie had three more kids who lived fairly close. Paul, their youngest child lived just a couple miles away as did Fred, their oldest. Jessie, their youngest daughter had just moved back to the area from Chattanooga. She had a new husband—again. Mary wanted to meet everyone. Tom "just as soon" they stayed away. He would remind Mary later that he "knew what they was like."

In the middle of the fourth week Paul, his wife and two of his kids came by. They just appeared—almost out of nowhere. If they had a car, they must have parked it out near the main fence. Not much was said even after Mary tried to get the conversation going. She offered to make some coffee—nobody indicated they wanted any. It was uncomfortable. The silence shouted ill at ease.

Neither Paul's kids nor his wife said word one. Tom said he "figgered Paul had told them to hush up." They didn't stay long. Paul asked R.L. to walk outside with him so they could talk. At the time, that didn't mean much. Later on, Tom figured he was asking R.L. for money—that may have been the only reason Paul even came to visit. It was pretty apparent he had not been doing anything around the home place to help them.

Neither Fred nor Lillie came by. None of the rest of the still rather large family stopped to see the "returning son." Tom did see his favorite cousin Doc in Resaca one day. They had been friends since elementary school [all three partial years]. They had been very close. Doc was still very mild in his manner. He assured Tom of two things:

> They don't like you cuz' you were the one who left em'. They figger you think you're bettern' them. And now, they think you come back to get everything that R.L.'s got. They ain't a one of em' that's done a thing to help your mother and father. It wouldn't surprise me none to hear that someone found them dead in that old house one day. They ain't in good shape—I guess you see that.

Tom didn't say anything right away. He was pretty sure Doc knew why he left over 15 years before. Tom reminded his cousin:

> Sooner or later he'd a killed me. I wasn't gonna stay here and do all that work at home when Fred, the laziest sonofabitch in the world just sat around. And Paul. . . Mother never made him do a thing either. all he did was take money from Dad and raise hell in town. I just wasn't gonna be part of that!

The private conversation continued between the two cousins who had been closer than brothers all their lives. They thought alike and felt the same way about the rest of the family.

> "Well, Tom, they ain't neither one of em' changed. Fred still don't do a lick a' work and Paul is with a differnt woman every month. He's never held a job more

than 6 months at a time—and those are jobs that R.L. got him" Doc said supportively.

Tom concurred. He added:

> "They ain't any of em' worth the powder to blow em' to hell," Tom concluded. "I don't want nuthin' to do with none of em.'"

> "Are you plannin' on stayin' on. What are you gonna' do about R.L. and your mother?" Doc asked. "They can't stay by themselves . . .and you can see there ain't nobody around here that helps em'" Doc reminded Tom.

"Mother would just as soon stay. She don't mind takin' care of em.' She's already talkin' about finding a school for Bob and Phyl. It's always been important to her that those kids go to school. That's her only interest right now," Tom added.

Doc tried to ease Tom's "concern" by noting that "there's a school buildin' lessn' a mile from here. They ain't got no teacher anymore and I don't know if anybody around here is tryin' to get one."

That was actually good news for Tom. In his mind finding a teacher wasn't a problem—he figgered "damned near anybody can teach." While that may have been true in his school days, they had a good deal of trouble even finding that "anybody."

Doc and Tom agreed to meet again. Tom knew where Doc lived and it wasn't far. This was likely the only friend Tom Stone had in the valley. At least it was the one person who knew Tom the best—and Tom trusted Doc. He was the *only* one Tom trusted.

It was the fall of 1938. Things had been going fairly well, Tom had gotten the home place ready for winter as best he could. He had fixed two of the windows downstairs in the main house and put the door back on the shed. He and Bob had gathered and stacked enough wood to make it at least 3 months and put that in the shed. Tom didn't do any work on the barn because R.L. no longer had any animals to keep there. Tom remembered the days when R.L. had 4 mules around and at least 2 hogs all the time. Now and then he had a cow but that required someone to milk her and there was nobody to do that. "We need to get that ole woman's garden cleaned up so she can plant this spring," R.L. advised. Tom nodded.

The boys had always taken care of their Mother's garden. They tilled, helped her plant and hoed weeds for her. She was "in charge" but R.L. saw that the boys [actually Tom and sometimes Fred] did everything she needed out there. For some reason, she was very protective of Paul and he did very little work around the place.

While Tom and Mary lived there and took care of both R.L. and Lizzie, R.L. paid for all the *household* expenses. Neither Tom nor Mary had any idea where he got his money but he did have two stills "running" so may have been selling some whiskey. He had been in that business for years—making "only good whiskey" he always said. "I run mine through twict."

For personal things for themselves and the kids [such as clothes] Tom and Mary spent their own money. With no source of income, that cache was dwindling. Tom was too proud to ask his Dad for money but Mary broached the subject at supper one night when she said:

> "We're going to have to think about moving into town and getting some work." Nobody said a word. She continued: "The little bit of money that we brought is running out and there are things we have to get for ourselves and the kids

It was a fact. Tom knew it. Mary knew it. Neither Lizzie nor R.L. had even given it a thought. When Mary made the announcement, she hadn't considered *what* they might do. She didn't know the towns around there and had no idea if there were any jobs to be had or not—it was at the end of the most serious depression the United

States had ever seen. There weren't many businesses operating and the type[s] of jobs that she and Tom were used to doing, [herding sheep—or even cattle in a pinch] weren't available here. She started to think that maybe they had "pulled up" too fast and came down to Georgia with no plan—and no assurances.

Tom still knew some folks in the valley. He hadn't thought to ask Doc if there was any work in the area—Tom would do most anything to earn even a minimum income at this time. For right now, they didn't need a lot of money coming in. Mary knew that she couldn't leave the kids to work outside the home place, and both Lizzie and R.L. had gotten somewhat dependent on her being there to cook and clean—and generally take care of their basic needs. She didn't mind doing that but "reality was calling."

Uncle John and Aunt Mat[ilda] lived not far from R.L.'s home place. John was R.L.'s brother but they didn't have much to do with each other—family "stuff." Uncle John and Aunt Mat never had any kids of their own and lived a quiet life on their small but quite productive farm. They would soon "turn it over" to some government program and retire from farming. Since Tom had always gotten along well with his Uncle John, he thought he would give them a visit and see if they knew of any work—maybe even on their place.

For the first time, both Tom and Mary thought about going back home. They "knew" home. They knew they could find work there. They felt good about helping Tom's mother and father but had to face the "facts of life." You needed money to live. They even thought R.L. might offer to pay them for the work they did at the home place. He didn't.

Tom reminded Mary that his Dad had said if they stayed "all this" would be his. But "all this" didn't produce *any income*. And, Tom soon learned there would be annual taxes to pay. That bill was not his yet, but if it was in the future, he didn't see how the "farm" could make even enough to even pay the taxes—he "sure as hell wasn't gonna' sell his Dad's whiskey." That sounded like it could result in big trouble down the road. The times had changed.

Two days later, Tom visited his Uncle John and Aunt Mat. They had "signed" with the Federal Government to put their place in some kind of "bank" and get paid for it. That seemed to working well for them. They could stay in the house as long as they wanted to but didn't have to do any farming or produce any crops. They got to keep their garden and a "decent-sized" government check came to the mailbox every month from "the President." He also "paid their taxes."

Uncle John had never worked anyplace but his farm [that had been given to him by his father, James Joel Stone]. He said he had no idea where there might be work for Tom but they both wished him well "in his lookin'." He did not ask about either R.L. or Lizzie—and Tom didn't volunteer anything. Tom did ask about his brother Fred. His Uncle said Fred was living in the same place he had been given by R.L. but never had done much work—even on the house. Tom didn't ask but his Uncle told him to "watch out for Paul. He's around and he'll be trouble." Tom thanked him and said he'd see both of them in a month or so.

The next time Mary went to town, she and R.L. went to Resaca. She had seen Carbondale and figured out there were no obvious places of employment there. If not Carbondale or Resaca, there was only Dalton and that was over 30 miles up the road.

Once they started talking about it, neither Tom nor Mary wanted to work in "a town." Quite frankly, they had no idea what they would do for some kind of work in "town." Going "back home" got some more thought that night. It didn't feel like a good option—but it was starting to look like it might be *the only option*.

They didn't say anything to R.L or Lizzie—or the kids about their money concerns or their thoughts of returning to South Dakota. There was still some time and it was late fall—early winter in South Dakota. It was no time to go back there. This was going to take some planning and those plans would include "how' they would get through the winter here in Georgia.

Bob didn't have a place to go to school. The school never found a teacher. That bothered Mary a lot. She was so busy taking care of all those at home, she had not made much of a fuss about it. Along with their shortage of money, it mounted up as another argument for leaving. At least in South Dakota the schools worked to find a teacher for the kids part of the year. Somehow her children were going to go to school. Tom did not disagree with her. She had been right by his side in both South Dakota and now in Georgia—he was going to support her now.

While Lizzie didn't get close to the girls, R.L. had taken a "special liking" to Tommy Bob as he called him. The name, he felt, would differentiate him from his Dad and from his Grandfather [who was called Bob Lee by many who knew him. Others addressed him as R.L.]. The liking R.L. had for his grandson was mutual though "Tommy Bob" was a bit hesitant to get too attached. Still, he followed his Grandfather wherever he went. One can only imagine what the 11-year old learned.

It was the fall. Birthdays came and went—there wasn't much money for gifts. But, they had cake. Mary got some little baby dolls with clothes for Sissy and Jody in December and January, and a new belt for Bob in May. They skipped their own birthdays in May and July. R.L.'s birthday was in October and Lizzie's was in February. R.L. got some smoking tobacco and Mary gave Lizzie a hand-made handkerchief she had crocheted some years before. Not much fuss for birthdays.

The responsibility for keeping gas in the car [frequent trips town] and buying the growing kids a few new clothes [Sissy actually took Jody's "hand-me-ups" as Jody was growing much faster and taller] was taking a toll on the finances. Bob was growing straight up as well. His boots were tight and he needed some jeans that were longer In the legs--his waist stayed the same. And Mary now had to buy shirts as she had no sewing machine to make anything. The funds were getting depleted--and there was no way to replenish them down here as there was still no sign of work.

Mary mentioned that perhaps they could ask R.L. for some money since she and Tom spent all their time taking care of he and Lizzie. In that sense, it was "a job." Tom responded as you might expect. "No way in hell I'm gonna ask him for anything!"

The fall also brought thoughts of what was going on back home. They thought about shearing time at home—and the Stones missed that very much. It had been their life for so long. They missed their friend Lew Thurber and the "absolute stability" and relative security they found on the prairie with their sheep and their dependable job--and income. They thought about the coming of Christmas and wondered how they might get some gifts—at least for the kids.

The fall came gradually. It rained quite a bit but that was fairly normal. The road to town was a bit tough to navigate but Mary had seen much worse. She made her regular trips to town to get perishable things like milk—and their "staple": coffee. If you wanted groceries, you had to come to the one store in town—and most everybody did at least twice a month.

Late in the fall, Mary was "shopping" [R.L. had given her the money this time and did not come into town] for what basics they needed. In the store, a woman directly approached her and calmly stated:

"You're staying out at the R.L. Stone place?" It wasn't really a question. She knew who Mary was and where she and her family were staying. But it was a conversation "opener" that said "I know who you are and what you're doing." While some may have considered the entire encounter a bit impolite and pushy, Mary was interested in perhaps making a new "friend" outside "that house."

"My name is Mary Brown. I was Mary Stone before I was married. Tom Stone is my brother. I guess that makes us kin," she added for the seeming sake of some common identity. Mary, needless to say, was a bit taken aback. She had never met Tom's older sister and had heard very little about her—most of that was not good. Many years before, R.L. had "disclaimed" her and "thrown" her out of the house. She had not been back since.

She was a few years older than Tom but looked like she had lived a reasonably good life. Mary had a child but that child [the "catchcolt"] had been raised by R.L. and Lizzie. Nobody really knew her husband—Bill Brown. Tom always just commented "he was a sailor," which meant he was not around much—surely not this far inland. Mary had *heard* how Tom's sister "made her living" but wasn't concerned about that now.

> "Yes, I'm Mary Stone—Tom's wife. We're visiting his folks at the home place. I'm just in town getting groceries. *I drove my car* into town." That blunt statement was important.

Mary Stone instinctively held out her hand to shake the hand of her newly-found sister-in-law.

> "I'm just here picking up a few things and have to get back. Can you come by to see us while we're here so you can see our kids. I'm sure Tom would like to see you," Mary asked.

> "I really don't go out to the old house anymore. I've see *him* in town from time to time. I haven't seen my mother for over 15 years. Is she still alive? Guess I'd have heard about if she'd died. . . . " Mary Brown replied.

Mary assured her that both her parents were doing OK. She reiterated that she "was sure they would like to have you come and see them." She had no idea how wrong she was. "And, I know Tom would like to see you too." Wrong again. Mary Stone did not know much about the circumstances of Mary Brown's "departure" from the home place—it wasn't something R.L. or Lizzie talked about. What she had done seemed to be a "dark spot" on their good name.

Mary Stone had to get back. Mary Brown had found out all she needed to. They would never see each other again. From all accounts, nobody in the Stone family ever saw Mary Brown again.

When Mary got back home, she was excited to tell Tom who she had met in the store. He didn't share her enthusiasm. He made it clear that "she" was one of the people they didn't talk about—ever. Mary knew very little about "dysfunctional families," but as the days went by, she would learn more—much more than she ever wanted to know. How you could not want to see your own sister was beyond her comprehension. It was clear she didn't know "the full story."

Mary continued to cook and clean and take care of Lizzie. R.L. seemed to be getting some of his strength back [he was 70 years old now], and he spent some time up in the hills behind the home place by himself—Mary didn't let Bob go with him whenever she had a chance to stop him. But, it was the only Grandfather he was ever going to have. While she didn't always think it was OK to learn from his Grandfather, that seemed inevitable when they all lived together in such close quarters. Besides, what kind of things would a Grandfather teach his grandson that would be that bad? Great question! Make no mistake—they weren't as close as most grandfathers and grandsons. They just spent a great deal of time together. Quite likely her Bob was bored because he had no friends out there and he did get to "explore" with his Grandfather. It is worth noting that 75 years later, Bob still remembered the time he spent on the home place and the excursions with R.L. His memories of "that old man" were not all positive and endearing.

R.L.'s birthday came and Mary baked him a huckleberry pie.

She "splurged" and bought him some pipe tobacco from her own money—she was very unselfish. He had likely never gotten a birthday gift before and saying "thank you" made him noticeably uncomfortable. Expressing gratitude was something he had probably done very little of as well.

December 1st was Grandma's birthday. Though nobody else seemed to know about her "special day," Mary had been crocheting an afghan for her upstairs with yarn she had gotten a little bit at a time with grocery money. Mary never felt guilty about spending that little bit of grocery money on something for her mother-in-law. Birthday gifts for Lizzie had likely been few and far between.

The practice of not "celebrating" was a part of their way of life. And, it was *more* than birthdays. They just didn't celebrate much of anything—holidays, birthdays, anniversaries. Well, it was coming up On Christmas. "We are going to have Christmas!" Mary asserted.

Christmas came. R.L. gave Mary $20 to buy presents for everyone. Since she had not been able to sew, she got some badly needed clothes [socks and underwear] for the kids and a new pair of [striped] bib overalls for Tom. She got R.L. a new pair of long underwear [after doing the laundry, she knew he needed them]. And, she got Lizzie two nice lace handkerchiefs and two sets of undergarments.

These may not have been gifts Grandma would ever have chosen, but she loved them. She held the handkerchiefs next to her cheek as though there was a special potion inside. She was learning to love Mary. There was no doubt, her daughter-in-law treated her much better than her own kids.

While that distinction was *not* particularly important to Mary, it was critical that these two "old people" were well taken care of. They were family.

There was enough money left to get each of the kids a special gift—and two sticks of candy for each of them as well. Mary would have preferred getting them some more clothes to wear but also realized that neither the children nor R.L. would have supported that decision.

She found two new little, all-rubber "baby dolls" for the girls—she could hand-stitch the dolls some clothes from the cloth scraps she'd found at the house. She bought Tommy Bob a toy gun and holster— that would likely please both he and his Grandfather. They *weren't practical gifts* at a time when practicality was becoming increasingly more important. But it was Christmas.

Mary bought nothing for herself. Nobody noticed that.

The long, rainy winter was interrupted by very few things. Mary had to make "her trip" to town every two weeks and Paul came by at least once a month. He and his Dad went out on the porch to talk as this youngest son rarely even acknowledged his mother, who sat quietly by the warm fire much of the time. In most cases, she would sit there all day and into early evening. Mary regularly brought her coffee [Grandma didn't like tea—and they had none anyway] with a saucer. Mary believed "ladies drank from cups and used a saucer on which to set their cup." She treated Lizzie like a lady.

Lizzie Stone was now 68, but the years had not been kind to her—having seven children and a husband who was less than gentle or considerate. And, after leaving the Harper household over near "Ugly Girls Holler," she rarely had a chance to get out of her new home place. Women of her day worked long and hard hours. They stayed home. They took care of kids, the cooking and cleaning, and their husbands. They did not complain. Lizzie Stone was, in a phrase, worn out. She would live only a short time longer.

Winter seemed long. Maybe it was the weather in the damp confines of north Georgia. Maybe it was being "cooped up" in the home place after being used to the open country of home. Maybe it was sitting around doing the same drudging chores every day—and with little thanks from anyone. New Year's Day arrived—it was 1938.

Paul still came by regularly. You could often smell that he had been drinking—and he only talked with his father. While nobody really knew what they talked about, you could be fairly sure it was about getting money from his father. He came by on a Friday morning in early January for what seemed to be a typical "visit." But it was not.

R.L. did not volunteer to go out on the porch to talk. Paul moved toward the door and motioned for his Dad to follow him. R.L. voiced his unwillingness to do so. You could sense this "time" was different—you could sense something was wrong.

Well, it was "bad wrong." Paul grabbed his father by the front of his overalls and told him to "Come on outside. I need to talk to you."

"I ain't goin' outside. And, I ain't got nothin' to say to you," R.L. positioned himself resolutely.

Paul still had a hold of the strap of his overalls. "Yer gonna' come outside if I have to drag you. Now what's it gonna be?"

Tom was getting uneasy. Mary moved the kids over near her on the other side of the main room. Lizzie rocked in her chair by the fire. Very likely, she had seen this before. Besides, this was her favorite child. R.L. and he would "work it out."

Tom got up and tried to get in between them—to get Paul to let go of his father. It all happened fast. The next thing they knew, Paul had a gun in his hand. He wasn't "waving" it around, he was pointing it right at his father.

The three of them grappled for the gun and Mary joined the fray in an effort to "hold Tom back." But, before Tom could get the gun, it went off. Paul turned and ran out of the house. R.L. reached to his back pocket and got his .45 caliber pistol, pulled the sock off it and headed out the door after Paul. As soon as he got to the porch, he started shooting in the direction Paul had run down the road.

The next sound was Mary screaming—"My God Dad, you've been shot—you're bleeding—oh my God!"

While in between Paul and his father, Paul's gun had gotten pointed downward. Paul pulled the trigger and a bullet went into the middle of Tom's left leg—about 8 inches above his knee. It was bleeding badly. Mary had seen gunshot wounds. She knew they had to get pressure on it to stop the bleeding. She had Tom sit down first and then lie down flat on the floor.

R.L. came back in. "He's gone—and it's a damned good thing cuz' I'd a shot him sure as hell. Comin' in here and threaten' me with a gun. . . . Who the hell does he think he is?" Everyone knew "who he was." He was the youngest of the Stone children who had been babied since birth. He was the one who never seemed to have to work around the house or farm. He was the one who got all the money he wanted to do whatever he wanted to do. Yes, they all "knew who he was."

"What happened to you," R.L. asked as he saw Tom on the floor with Mary holding a dishtowel over the middle part of his leg. "That fool shot him," Mary answered—in tears but angry as she could be. The strange caution came back to her: "You don't know what them people is like down there." It rang hollow but loudly. "Why did we ever come to this Godforsaken place?" she muttered.

"It's gonna' be alright Mother," Tom said in a strong and direct manner. "Did you shoot that son-of-a-bitch. . . because he sure as hell shot me," Tom said while choosing not to even look up at his father.

Lizzie got out of her chair and came to where Tom lay on the floor. "I don't think Paul meant to do that," she said trying to make a case for an accident.

"He came in here with a gun and didn't waste any time using it," Mary countered. "He would have killed Grandpa if Tom had not stepped in. Grandma, that was no accident."

"Well, when he comes back to the house, we'll clear this all up—we'll straighten it out. It'll be all right. He didn't mean to hurt anybody—least of all his family."

"Mother, *he* ain't no family of mine and he damned well better not come back when I'm here. He's always been mean and lazy and worthless and you know it. We ain't family with him," Tom argued.

"We've got to get the doctor," Mary said. "I'm going to town for the doctor. Bob, you watch over your Dad. You keep this towel pressed on his leg. I'll be right back." Sissy and Jody just stood there—they finally started crying. They knew their Daddy was hurt. They knew their Momma was leaving. They were just plain scared. Bob moved over to his Dad and held the towel in place--pressing as hard as he could but the blood keep coming--further soaking up the towel.

Mary drove to Resaca. She had no idea if there was a doctor there or not—she had forgotten to ask R.L. in her haste. She stopped at the store—where they knew her. She asked for a doctor and told them it was an emergency. They told her Dr. McCrory lived between Resaca and Carbondale. His sign was posted on the highway that went by his house—it was about 7 miles away.

It would be pure luck to find him at home—but he was. He grabbed his bag after hearing "my husband's been shot" and told Mary to drive ahead and he'd follow her in his car. He was all business and seemed not to get excited—he had likely been in such situations before. It was nearly twenty miles back to the main house. She doesn't know how fast she drove but Dr. McCrory stayed right behind her—she checked her side mirror every few seconds. She knew she could not come back without him.

Dr. McCrory drove down the old road right behind Mary's car. He'd likely seen "roads" like this many times in this back country where he had chosen to practice medicine—quite a change from his former job on staff at Emory University Medical School.

The house was quiet. Mary thought the worse. When they got inside, everything seemed as she had left it. Tom was on the floor, Bob was still holding the now blood-soaked towel over the wound--his 11 year-old hands and arms drenched with his Dad's blood. The girls were sitting quietly near a window—so were R.L. and Lizzie. Quite frankly, there wasn't much anybody except Dr. McCrory could do at this point.

Dr. McCrory took the towel away and glanced at the wound. "Let's get him up on the table." Bob, Mary and R.L. all pitched in to help the Dr. lift him—Dr. McCrory managed the side with the injured limb.

Mary had already torn a hole in his overalls and underwear to expose the wound. After looking at the wound again, Dr. McCrory cut the pants leg and the underwear leg all the way to the groin area. Mary was already heating water and getting what she could for much--needed bandages—anything clean and white. The Dr. cleaned around the wound as best he could with gauze and an antiseptic from his bag. The bleeding continued.

The doctor did not talk. He was still all business—there would be time for talking later. He looked for an exit wound—to see where the bullet had gone through. He found it. Digging out a slug was one task that had been eliminated—now stop the bleeding.

The bullet had hit the femoral artery, about eight inches above the knee. It was difficult to see how badly it had damaged this major artery, but the amount of blood indicated serious trouble. In a very methodical manner, the skilled hands used a scalpel to open the wound further. While that bothered Mary, Dr. McCrory had to get to the artery to repair [close] it.

Ellet McCrory didn't waste time talking or telling anybody what he was about to do—he just exercised his skill. He found the spot where the artery had been hit "going in" and hoped that no more damage had been done as the bullet exited. Amidst what seemed like a huge pool of blood, he placed several sutures in the spot of the internal wound.

The next step was to "suction" [mop up] the blood in the wound area to see if the sutures were holding—and the bleeding had been stopped. After an "hour-long minute," Dr. McCrory concluded that the bleeding had stopped. The artery was repaired although he knew it was far from *healed*. He continued to clean around the wound, both inside and out, making sure nothing "foreign" was left inside the incision area.

Satisfied, he again wiped the external portion of the leg with antiseptic and immediately began suturing a 6-7 inch slit in Tom Stone's leg. Remarkably, Tom had not lost consciousness during the surgery. He was sweating profusely and sick to his stomach, but he "hung in there" and had said nothing—typical Tom Stone.

Dr. McCrory had Mary watch while he wrapped the leg.

> "You're going to have to change this dressing every day. If it [the wound] starts to bleed again, you come get me right away. If I'm not at home, my wife will know where you can find me. Don't wait if this starts to bleed—you come get me."

Not surprisingly, Ellet McCrory talked only to Mary. She was the only one, he concluded, that could/would do what needed to be done. It was obvious that he knew both R.L. and LIzzie Stone. He didn't even acknowledge that they were in the room. Dr. McCrory finally looked straight at the kids--"Your Daddy's going to be all right," he assured them. That had to help. Mary heard the words and wanted to believe him, but she was still in shock over this whole episode--and still very angry.

Things had calmed down some. The doctor had told them to leave Tom on the table.

> "Don't move him. He will need to eat but not much early on—nothing very heavy. He should drink a lot so you'll have to figure out how he can pee without getting up. I know you can do that. Regardless, I'll be back in two days unless you come get me."

Mary felt reassured. She could do what he told her. She could change the dressing, watch for bleeding, feed her husband as the Dr. had said and take care of his urinating.

Mary Stone had decided: her husband was not going to die. She knew how strong Tom was—together they would get him "back on his feet." She thought about Paul for a moment and then decided it was best to save her energy to take care of her family.

Mary Stone thanked God Tom was alive.

She talked with the girls and Bob and told them a simple story about the accident and that their Daddy had gotten hurt—but she assured them that he was going to be OK. They both listened but just stood and clutched their "little rubber baby dolls."

In the morning of the second day, as she was changing the dressing, Mary noticed some slight darkening of the skin around the entry wound. While she was relieved that it was not bleeding, she was concerned about the discoloration. She cleaned the incision, rewrapped it and told Tom that "it looked good." She did not want to alarm him but knew she was not telling her husband the full truth. At this stage, any change in the appearance of the wound concerned her. She had

seen gunshot wounds before and knew some of the terrible developments that were possible even after stopping the bleeding and dressing the wound.

Dr. McCrory had assured her that he would be by "to check" in
the afternoon of the second day after he had "patched" Tom up. Mary
did not want to wait until later in the day—she was not willing to take
any kind of chance. This new development may be life-threatening.
Within minutes, she decided to go bring the doctor back to "look in
on her husband." Although Tom was wide awake, he did not sense
anything was wrong as he could not see his leg.

She took Bob and the girls with her. She told R.L. and Lizzie she
was taking them to "see" town. She told Tom she would be right
back—he assured he would be alright. "You go on mother. I'll wait
right here," he answered as he tried to calm her by joking. "I'll be
right back," Mary repeated.

She got the kids in the car. Nobody said anything.

It was a fairly quick trip. Mary didn't make any stops along the
way as she remembered exactly where Dr. McCrory lived. His car
was not at the house when she pulled up but Mrs. McCrory said he
had gone "out to the Stone's place." Mary assumed she meant the
home place—she hoped so. She did not stop on the way back and
was relieved when she saw Dr. McCrory's car in the front yard. Somehow, she thought things were going to be OK now that Dr. McCrory
was there.

Mary hurriedly got the kids out of the car and took them inside.
Dr. McCrory was standing over Tom. He had removed the new dressing and was looking at the wound. It seemed obvious he had seen the
darkening skin as well. He observed that

> it closed up nicely and we can be quite sure there is
> no bleeding. I'm a bit concerned about this patch of
> darkening skin—could be a small blood clot. We'll
> need to watch it very carefully. I've got some other calls
> to make but I'll be back tomorrow morning—before

noon.

"I'll see you in the morning Tom. . . you rest easy. It looks like you're healing up pretty good," he said reassuringly. Miss Lizzie, always nice to see you. R.L., haven't seen you in town lately," he added, trying to include everybody, unlike his earlier visit.

He went over to where the children were sitting. He reassured them just as he had on his first visit: "Kids, your Daddy is going to be fine," he said in a calming tone. He sounded like a good family man.

Mary walked him to the door and out on the porch. As they walked to his car, she pointedly asked:

> "Is he really going to be OK? Should we be worried about that spot on his leg? What else can I do for him?"

The Dr. responded in both a professional and guarded tone.

> "The wound closed up nicely. The bleeding has stopped. Those are the big things. Now, if that spot on his leg gets any bigger, we'll talk some more about it. Right now, just change the dressing twice a day as you have been, and keep an eye on him. Keep him eating at least twice a day. Mary, you're doing a good job. And, try not to worry too much. He's a strong man."

His words both comforted and concerned Mary Stone. Her husband had been shot. He bled badly. He was lying on a table with an unnatural black spot on his leg. Even though the discoloration area was small, Mary was concerned—justifiably so. Tom Stone was her rock. Her husband. The father of those three little kids. He was the anchor in her life. And, right now, he and the 3 kids were the ONLY people she considered her family. And she was the only one "on her feet" that could hold all this together.

She thought: "I'm the one who insisted we come down here. Dad never did want to come. This is all my fault!"

Mary was up early the next day—she had a family of 6 others to take care of—fixing meals and tending to her increasingly ill husband. The first thing she did was remove the bandage. The dark spot had grown—she didn't need to measure. She thought about going after Dr. McCrory but she remembered him saying he would come by in the morning—she had already learned to trust and rely on him.

She cleaned the wound with some antiseptic the Dr. had left for her and she proceeded to fix breakfast—constantly looking back at Tom and wishing she could do more. Bob dutifully brought in some firewood for the fireplace/stove. The kids ate at a little table on the porch and R.L. and Lizzie ate at the main table. Mary had no idea what she had fixed for them.

Tom sat up a bit and had some coffee. He said he wasn't hungry [which was strange for a man whose biggest meal of the day was breakfast] but would have some dinner [at noon]. Mary did her best to keep busy anticipating Dr. McCrory's arrival. It was almost 9 o'clock when he drove into the yard. He had wanted to get there early—he was obviously concerned too.

He thanked Mary for the offer of coffee but said he had two cups at home. Methodically, he went to work. He unwrapped the dressing. He "prodded" around the incision which seemed to holding very well. Mary watched closely as he then "touched" the darkened skin around the wound. It was solid—it did not seem to "give." His touches, though obviously soft, did not leave any kind of impression around the injured portion of Tom's leg. While Mary saw this, it didn't mean much to her until later.

Dr. McCrory asked Mary to carefully lift Tom's leg by raising it from the foot—so he did not bend at the knee. He cleaned the exit wound but said nothing about what he observed there.

Her hand was on Tom's bare shoulder. She was looking from his face to that of Dr. McCrory—waiting for his declaration that "everything was still OK." He didn't say that. Instead he looked at both of them and matter-of-factly "laid it out."

> This looks like gangrene.[77] I've seen plenty of cases
> and I must tell you this is serious. There's some kind
> of infection in there. I don't know from what—maybe
> the bullet. We will try to treat it with sulfanilamide
> right now. That's the best we've got.[78]

Dr. McCrory continued in a very calm tone and detailed what would be done. "I'll be here to look at this every day. We're going to take it just that way—day to day. Mary, you just make sure he's getting plenty to eat and drink. One encouraging thing is that Tom doesn't smoke much and doesn't have a sugar [diabetes] problem. We're just going to have to watch this carefully," he said in a cautious tone.

Neither Tom or Mary knew exactly what to think. "Was this leg going to get better? Was Tom going to be 'stove up'" for life? They were afraid to ask. Not knowing was heart-wrenching. "Knowing" may have been even worse.

Dr. McCrory said his typical, brief goodbyes—especially to the kids—and left. Mary was very appreciative that he spent time on each visit talking with the kids. [Months later Mary would comment on how badly she felt for the kids because she had not spent much time talking with them about their Dad]. He sat in his car for a few minutes and made some notes in a small black notebook. Mary felt they were in good hands with Dr. McCrory but now admitted that the progression of the darkening areas on both sides of his leg was not a

---

77 Gangrene is a type of necrosis caused by a critically insufficient blood supply—generally to extremities. Such reduced blood supply to affected tissues results in cell death. It is potentially life-threatening and often occurs after an injury or infection.

78 While there were several "treatments" for gangrene, including amputation, repeated operations to remove infected dead tissue, operations to improve blood supply to the impacted area, antibiotics [i.e., *sulfanilamide, which was released onto the pharmaceutical market in 1936]* as well as an x-ray technique designed to "kill" infectious organisms. Benzylpenicillin, *the first penicillin,* was *not available* until 1942.

good sign. They had faced some tough times in their nearly 14 years together—this was going to be the toughest.

For the first time since the "accident," Mary sat down to "take stock" of their predicament. Actually, the shooting shouldn't have surprised any of them. Most every man in this part of the country carried a gun—and used them on occasion. Paul always carried a small handgun while R.L always carried a loaded .45 in his back pocket. Local law enforcement knew there were some shootings in Whitfield County but spent more of their time working with the Federal "reve- nooers" busting up [illegal] local stills than they did policing "domes- tic disturbances" like this one.

Such internal family matters were very common and left up to the family to settle. To "the law," in Whitfield County, Georgia, that's what it was—a domestic disturbance—a matter for the family to deal with. No formal charges were filed. Within a couple of weeks, Paul Stone would be free to return to the home place. In their minds, and in their hearts, Tom and Mary Stone both "filed charges." Tom Stone's intense disdain for the "way they did things down there" was reinforced. Mary Stone was learning some things about family that she never could have imagined. She saw "blood relatives" not only threatening each other but carrying out those threats. "Paul was actually going to shoot his own father," she realized. "And he could have killed my husband."

Mary Stone was beside herself. She was in a place she didn't re- ally want to be any longer, with a family whose values she did not understand and certainly did not share. She had three little kids and a husband, her only real friend in this "whole mess" had been shot and now might lose a leg.

She looked first at their kids and then at her husband. Tom was tough, so even shot and flat on his back, he was "mad as hell." Mary, not given to prayer, prayed "hard" for her husband and their young family.

R.L. and Lizzie just seemed to go about their daily business as though nothing unusual had happened—displaying a lifelong "hardness" as a way of dealing with situations such as this one. The days went by. Dr. McCrory came every day—even Sundays. The only changes were that the leg got worse. Tom ran a temperature all the time. Things couldn't have been more dire.

After 11 days of trying to heal the infection and stop its spread, Dr. McCrory had reached a decision that his efforts had failed. While as a human being he was an optimist—as a doctor, he was a realist. He faced the inevitable: amputation.

He asked Mary to join him on the porch early that afternoon and told her of his decision. She was devastated and noticeably shaken. She put her head in her hands for a moment and asked if that was the only option.

> "Yes." Dr. McCrory replied in an almost apologetic tone. "We have good medicines but not one that will cure something like this. I'll be back tomorrow morning and we'll do the surgery. We do not want to move him off the table.
>
> I'll do the surgery right there. I'm going to need you to help me—and Tom will need you too. You're going to have to be just as strong as your husband."

Mary heard the words of this experienced physician. She was still in denial about everything—from the shooting nearly two weeks before to an operation that—at best—would leave her husband with only one leg.

> "What am I going to tell him—my husband? How am I going to tell you you're going to cut his leg off? My God, what am I going to say? None of this is his fault! He tried to do the right thing and now he'll pay for the rest of his life. Dr., this will kill him," Mary lamented.

Dr. McCrory had been "here" before. Amputations were extremely traumatic—before, during and after. The shock, both physical and emotional was unbearable for some—he knew that. He didn't try to convince her this would be easy. He spoke as both a man and a doctor with years of experience.

> "Mary, you'd be surprised how people face such things as this. Tom is physically strong—he's also emotionally tough. And, he's got you and the kids to help him get through this. I can't tell you how much that will mean. I know you can do this."

Thinking back later, Mary remembered his words. She did not know if he really "knew she could do this or not." How could he—even she didn't think she could do it.

> "Mary, I'm going in to talk with Tom. I don't think it's the right time to tell the kids just yet so do that after I leave. You can tell R.L. and Miss Lizzie at the same time. They don't need any details. I'll take care of that in the morning. Tonight, everybody, especially you and Tom, just need to rest. That will be best medicine for what we are doing tomorrow."

Dr. McCrory went back inside to share his decision with his patient. He was, as always, kind, but matter-of-fact. He did not go into any details or talk about "post-operative" plans—Tom only had one question: "No other way?" Dr. McCrory answered: "No other way, Tom. We all need to keep you alive. This is the only way we can do that."

You might wish someone would have added something like "this is the only way *short of a miracle*," but nobody did.

Dr. McCrory administered one more injection of *sulfanilamide*, and headed toward the door. "This is all going to work out just fine," he encouraged everyone as he closed the door. "I'll see ya'll first thing in the morning." Again, Mary thought, he was a good man.

It's likely some can explain what happened that night. It's likely some would dispute such explanations. There is one thing that nobody can argue, however. When Dr. McCrory removed the new bandage the next morning, he was noticeably taken aback. He announced loudly enough for all to hear: "This wound is healing. The discoloration has receded by half. *Some things* are working just the way they should. Tom, I think you're going to be OK. Mary, I think you've nursed your husband back. . . . Kids, we think your Dad is going to be just fine."

While the "report" was "glowing" in contrast to what they all had expected, Tom was still not "out of the woods." Dr. McCrory knew they had to continue cleaning and dressing the wound twice a day. He knew he needed to continue administering *sulfanilamide* just as he had been. He knew Mary had to keep feeding Tom all he wanted to eat—with plenty of coffee. He knew that *whatever anyone and everyone had been doing, they needed to keep doing it!*

The next three days showed marked improvement in the continued recession of the discoloration. Tom was eating well, sleeping well and he had no fever—night or day.

Miracle? Think what you want. The gangrene wasn't even halfway gone but it was going. Dr. McCrory had read about this happening but had only seen pictures of it in medical journals. Still, he knew what he saw—a dramatic decrease in the discoloration and a significant softening of the tissue [skin] around both the entry and the exit wounds. Tom's spirits were up and his temperature was down. Tom Stone was not only going to live, he was not going to lose one of his legs.

It was nearing springtime and it was beautiful!

Tom Stone had made his decision. He had not thought long about it but had thought hard about it. He and his family were going to pack up and go back home. There would be no discussion and there would be no argument. He did not need any "permissions" or "blessings."

So, shortly after Dr. McCrory's visit on the fifth day after the cancelled surgery, Tom directed Mary to "load the car with the kids and the dog, put that gun on the seat between us and if anybody tries to stop us, shoot. We're going to get the hell out of here."

Mary had no argument with leaving. She did have some big concerns about leaving this soon—she thought it was too early. And she surely wanted to talk with Dr. McCrory before they "loaded up" and left. He had pulled them through this. In Mary's mind, his opinion on traveling was the only one they would listen to.

She also had some concerns about the "gun." She had never fired a handgun before—and for sure never at another human being. But there was no question in her mind that if anyone did try to stop them, *she would shoot.* "I told you we should never have come down here. . . I told you what these people was like," Tom would remind her. He was getting back to his old self.

Mary was only too willing to do most of the things her husband said. And though she knew her husband was still not totally healed, she wanted to go almost as much as he did. Still, she would not leave until she had talked with the doctor.

Dr. McCrory was there the next day—a bit later than usual but in an obviously optimistic mood. They exchanged pleasantries as he removed the dressing and examine the "patient." "You're doing well, Tom. I can see marked improvement every day. You should be on your feet in a day or two—not doing much, but at least on your feet."

"On your feet" was not enough for Tom Stone. He wanted to be "on his feet," in the car and heading up the road. He knew he was indebted to the man who had saved his leg—perhaps even his life. He respected that. He didn't want to push.

"How soon do you think I can travel?" Tom queried.

"Where you planning on going?" Dr. McCrory inquired—halfway knowing the answer.

"Home," was Tom's resolute reply. We're going back to South Dakota. This ain't home," Tom was clear.

"Well, you certainly can't drive, but I guess Mary can handle that. Something else. . . you can't sit in one position very long—a blood clot is always a concern. I want you to stay here, resting, for at least another week," he added, hoping for at least 5 days.

"Dad, he got us through this in one piece. The least we can do is listen to him. He knows what he's talking about." Mary wanted to go "yesterday" but was *not* willing to take a chance on some additional trouble. Dr. McCrory cautioned them:

"You should also know that both ends of this wound could open up again. I surely don't expect that would happen, but too much jostling around in a car could do that. I want you to stay at least 5 more days—then we'll talk about travel . . . Please. . . . "

They both listened to him—they knew he was right. And, it was reasonable to assume he "knew" what had happened with the shooting—he'd practiced medicine in this valley for over 30 years. Ellet McCrory *knew* the people of this valley because at one time or another, he'd treated most every one of them.

In three days, Tom was up from his "table bed" and got dressed. Mary had fixed his overalls although all the blood didn't "come out in the wash." In some ways, it would stay there as a reminder for some time. Again, he was "ready to pack up and go." He made that very clear to everybody in the house. R.L. and Lizzie didn't say anything to their son about his intentions although it was clear they wanted and needed both Tom and Mary to stay at the home place and take care of them.

Still, they weren't going to say as much—at least not yet. It may have been that in some ways they felt responsible for the "accident." After all, Paul was their son too. Did they really know what he was like? Were they willing to admit that one of their children would actually *threaten to shoot his father*—and almost kill his brother? Or maybe what had happened was just a part of "a way of life" for them. One thing for sure, Tom and Mary Stone didn't care—they were going to leave just as soon as they reasonably could.

Dr. McCrory came by the next morning. He again asked them to reconsider staying for a few more days. Neither Mary nor Tom responded.

"You need to pay him Mother," Tom said in a matter-of-fact tone.

"How much do we owe you Dr. McCrory?" Mary asked.

"$62.00," Dr. McCrory replied after some figuring. Mary got her purse from upstairs and counted out $62.00 in cash. She thanked Dr. McCrory for all he had done. He nodded a "welcome."

Everything seemed matter-of-fact. There was no emotion.

The Dr. made one more request for them to stay just a couple more days—"Just so we can be sure those holes close up good and there is no infection." He knew by the look on their faces his request was not an option. They were "going home."

It was very early in the spring of 1939—Tom and Mary both knew it was nearing lambing time back home. They missed "home."

Early the next morning, they loaded the kids and the dog in the car. Tom laid a pistol on the seat between them and told Mary if anybody tried to stop them, use it. She likely would have. She was probably more angry than her husband.

They waited until the sun came up. RL and Lizzie both came to the front porch. They both half-waved and they wept. Neither R.L. nor Lizzie were very well. They were both diabetic and in the early stages of lung cancer. They knew the only people who ever really cared about them were driving away.[79] Both couples knew they would never see the other again.

> Nobody said "I'm glad we got to see you."
> Nobody said "I'm sorry this happened."
> Nobody said "Have a safe trip."
> Nobody said "We'll see you again."
> Nobody said "We'll miss you."
> Nobody said "We love you."
> Nobody said anything.
> Everybody knew it was "time to go."

In their own ways, both Tom and Mary Stone had vowed to "never come back to this hell-forsaken place again."

---

79 Tom and Mary Stone actually did return to Georgia [Dalton] in 1973. A year earlier, on a professional trip to Miami, John had made a stop in Dalton on the chance he might locate some "family." He found only his Aunt Jessie at that time but determined there were other family members in the area. Returning to graduate school at Penn State, he called his father and mother [living in Phoenix, AZ]. At first, the proposal to visit Dalton was meant with a blunt "no." John persisted and convinced them it was "right" to at least visit. He flew them back to meet him and they made a trip to Dalton [GA] to "reunite." While Tom consistently objected, he went along. John, Linda, Tom and Mary all traveled in John's camper and stopped along the way at parks and campgrounds. Visiting was memorable. Tom was happy to see his brother, who had shot him, was dead and buried. All paused at the graves of grandparents and parents. Tom was pleased to see his mother and father now had gravestones [John had researched the dates and had them made in Auburn [AL] where he now taught.] Tom's cousin Doc knew right where their graves were and placed them at the spots in the Swamp Creek Methodist Cemetery. While Jessie, Tom's younger sister, was overjoyed to see him, he held his feelings in reserve—cautioning all of us that "you can't trust a one of em'. They're lower than snakes." Some wounds just don't seem to heal.

CHAPTER 13

Heading Home: Back to South Dakota

THE STONES HAD decided follow the same route going home they had used in coming from South Dakota to Georgia as it had worked well on the way down. Mary had checked her purse—she had 57 dollars and 90 cents. It would have to be enough.

With the exception of the few clothes Mary had bought for the kids and their Christmas gifts, they took nothing they had not brought with them. She had packed their blankets and two large jugs of water. All their "cooking gear" was still in the car. They took no food from the house. It was important to know that nobody would accuse them of taking something that was *not theirs*.

They did not look back as they drove away. Nobody talked until they arrived north near Dalton—except the kids and their chatter. There was not much to say—Tom and Mary were both relieved. They had not afforded themselves the luxury of worrying about "what ifs." There would be plenty of time for that later. Now it was time to just get away.

The first day they made it to a good camping area just south of Manchester [TN]. They had stopped once for gas and gotten some bread, some bacon, some beans, some coffee and some milk—even though the milk wouldn't last long on the road, she thought it was important for the kids. And, there were still some roadside stands along the way where they could buy some fresh vegetables and fruit. And, even though Tom and Mary slept on the ground that night, it was one of the best night's sleep they had gotten for several months. They felt unusually safe. They were back on their own—where they needed to be.

She checked Tom's dressing every couple of hours—even though he insisted he was fine and she needed to just "keep goin'." Each morning and each night she changed the dressing and carefully looked at both of the wounds [exit and entry]. She was relieved to see there was no bleeding, no swelling, no sign of clots and virtually all the bad "gangrenous" color was gone from the "wound areas." Mary had gotten very specific instructions from Dr. McCrory—and was afraid Tom would not say anything even if there was an issue. She knew, more than anything else, just like her, he just wanted to "git away from all of em'."

"It won't be too long and we'll be home," Mary repeated at least once a day—both to assure the kids and herself. In reality, she knew it was a long way and they didn't have much money. She also knew *they would make it!* She just had to hope they didn't have any trouble with Tom's "wounds" and the car would hold up. They deserved some good luck for a change. The travel, which would have been a tedious prospect under other circumstances, was "almost" a pleasure.

The second day they drove a bit slower—again, Mary felt good about their progress. They neared Nashville [TN] and were headed in the northwesterly direction of St. Louis [MO]. To them, these were just places on their homemade map. They weren't places to stop or stay—just places that meant they were getting closer to home.

The three kids did well. This was their second "car trip" and they were interested in seeing other cars and a number of farms along the road. For them, the most exciting sight was seeing the towns along the way—it was fascinating as they had no idea the world had so many people--and such big buildings.

Mary stopped regularly so they could go to the bathroom and run a bit. Although still "pretty stove up," Tom Stone traveled well, too. He was tough and still a young man.

His *physical wounds* were healing fast. The "others" never did.

Staying on the main roads most of the time, they had no trouble finding filling stations where they could use the bathrooms and get a fresh cup of coffee—and pop for the kids--on occasion. This was *not* a vacation but it certainly was a relief.

They headed west at St. Louis for Kansas City—stopping as they needed to. While they never thought about being in a hurry, they wasted no time in their travels. Their money was short and they weren't exactly sure what they would find once they got back "home." Being the "survivors" they had become, nothing could be worse than what they had gotten out of. And, like so many other times in their lives, they *knew they could deal with whatever faced them* as long as they were all together and could just get "home."

Two more days and they crossed into South Dakota. It felt like they had rediscovered their "world." A few hours and they would be in White Lake and then they could stop for a night, eat a good meal and sleep inside. They drove through Mitchell and knew it was less than an hour to White Lake.

Of course, Louie did not expect them. They had not been in touch with each other since they left for Georgia. He and Eva welcomed them and the kids into the house and started to make plans for supper—and where everybody could sleep. Mary felt good to be with her family.

That night they talked quite a bit about their Georgia "experiences," although not every detail. Eva was very concerned about "the shooting" though Louie, who had lived a life that was a bit more "reckless," took it in stride. The kids were understandably worn out and went to bed early in makeshift beds on the floor. Tom and Mary were given the bed in the boys' room. They agreed on getting an early start the next morning.

They got back to White Lake with $13.25 in Mary's purse. No place to live. No job. No prospects. But they were happy to be "home."

The next morning everybody got up early as planned. Eva and Mary fixed breakfast and they packed the car. Tom said that he wanted to take a few of the things that Louie had been "storing" for them—just a couple small pieces of furniture and some of the kids' toys.

This was not going to be a good time!

"Sis," Louie said addressing Mary [and not even looking at Tom] "I never thought you'd be coming back. I needed the space where that stuff was stored and I sold all of it."

Silence.

"You did what?" Mary asked as though she had not heard what he said.

"I sold that little bit of stuff that was here," he repeated.

"That 'little bit of stuff' was all we had!" Mary responded in an angry voice. Downtrodden, she repeated, "It was all we had."

Tom Stone said nothing. It was better that he didn't. He and Mary would talk about it later. He and Louie would never talk about it.

They loaded the car. Eva made them a good-sized box of food and drinks—along with cookies and milk for the kids. Louie filled the car with gas and checked the oil and tires. Tom got in the car without speaking. Mary talked with her brother for a moment and he almost apologetically handed her a twenty-dollar bill.

The Stones headed west. They would be in Wasta before suppertime. The loss of their "little bit of stuff" was not the end of the world but it hurt to know that your own family would sell those things you trusted him with. Tom muttered, "I will be damned. He even sold the kids' toys. If that don't beat all. . . "

No time for worrying. They still had 10 hours of driving. But everything was going to be all right. They both truly believed that. They both *had to believe* that—just keep going.

They stopped four or five times along the road so they could eat the great food Eva had packed—and for bathroom breaks. They stopped once for gas in Murdo and Mary continued to check on Tom's rapidly-healing wounds and was satisfied he was doing really well. Nothing more was said about what Mary's brother had done with their stored belongings. As was often the case, "what's done is done." Tom and Mary weren't *fatalists* but they were *realists*.

They got to Wasta by suppertime. While Percy and Lee Collier had no idea the Stones were coming back, they greeted them "with open arms." Neither of the Colliers asked any questions about what had happened—they were true friends and knew when either Tom or Mary wanted to talk about their ventures, they would.

Lee "adjusted" supper and they all sat down to eat. And even though neither Tom nor Mary had much of an idea what would happen "tomorrow," it was good to be "home. Here they *knew* the people. Here they could rely on people to have the same set of values they did. Here, with hard work, they could make it.

"We're gonna' be all right Mother," Tom said just before they went to bed. Bless him. . . he knew she needed that.

"I know we will Dad," Mary responded. Neither one of them had reason to be as sure as they tried to sound but they had learned to lean hard on each other when times got tough—they had the scars to prove it and they had made it through some truly bad days.

The next morning Tom and Mary drove into Wasta. They stopped at the feed store to ask if anyone knew Lew Thurber and if he had any herds in the area. The feed store owner didn't know the name but told them to go to a sheep farm just at the edge of town.

> "If anybody knows about sheep in this area, it'd be
> Ray Purvich. Talk to him."

They found the Purvich place with the familiar site of lots of woolies grazing in the fields as they drove up. Mrs. Purvich was in the house. She came out and told them her husband was out with the sheep. She sent one of her boys out to "get their Dad and bring him to the house. There's some folks here want to see him."

She offered them some welcome coffee—Tom and Mary graciously accepted her hospitality. Making small talk, Mary told Mrs. Purvich that they had herded not far from Wasta just a year and-a-half before and had spent three full summers in the Badlands, which was straight south of Wasta. Mary mentioned their friend Lew Thurber but Mrs. Purvich said the name "didn't ring a bell."

> "If he's been around here with sheep, Ray will know him. The sheep men in this area get along pretty good— they have to with more and more fence going up."

Tom and Mary could tell by *what* she said and the *tone* of her voice she was a "sheep person" and she had a good sense of what was happening to sheep country. Most sheep herders didn't talk about it much—they didn't have to. They knew that as more and more cows came into this country, more and more fence would go up—and "fences would choke off" their way of life. Eventually, the herder's life would *change as they knew it--or disappear*. This was an inevitability but one that herder's didn't talk much about.

Long-range planning had never been a priority with Tom and Mary Stone. They needed a job now and Lew Thurber was the first person they "knew" could help them. All they had to do was talk with Lew. . . .

The Stones and Velda Purvich talked a bit about "the weather" and specifically about the "good winter" they had just gone through. In this country, weather dictated much of the lifestyle of the inhabitants and how farmers and ranchers conducted their business—and made their living. It was always a concern. And, for all the country people in this area, it was a topic of interest virtually any time of the year.

Within 30 minutes, Ray Purvich rode up to the house in a buckboard. The back end of the wagon was loaded with supplies that Tom and Mary immediately recognized as the "tools of their trade."

Ray and Velda Purvich had lived outside Wasta all their married life. Ray had been in the "sheep business" for over 40 years and had learned the trade from his uncles and his father. While sheepherders owed their first loyalty to their own herds, they felt a kinship with other herders as well. Ray Purvich was only too happy to talk with Tom and Mary and help them if he could.

"Did you know a sheepman name Lew Thurber? He was from Montana but had herds in this area as late as last year. We ran his herds here and down into the Badlands," Tom explained.

While he told them that he did not personally know Lew Thurber, Purvich knew *of him* and his spread that had been located in the Wasta area until a year or so ago. That "spread" was the one that had been managed by Tom Stone before he and Mary left for their fateful trip to Georgia.

> "I knew Thurber's herd. It was not far west of here during the spring and then back again in the fall. They didn't winter here in '38 and '39 though. They must have moved on someplace else."

> "Have any idea where they might have moved," Tom asked.

> "Wouldn't have been east. Not much grass there for sheep and that's mostly country for cows and some horses. Heard they haven't fenced it much yet—but that will be comin' soon enough," Purvich added.

Tom and Mary thanked the Purvichs for their help and headed back to Lee and Percy's house in town. While they had not gotten very favorable information, what they found out dictated their next "move." They had to keep heading west and north.

At least they knew the country and had transportation. Mary still had just over $17.00 from the $20.00 that her brother had given her when they left White Lake. This would buy gas and some food. It was not very good weather for camping, but they would make do. Luckily they could stay with Lee and Percy one more night but were anxious to head west and figure a way to get settled.

Getting "settled" meant *getting a job*. They needed to find Lew Thurber and that meant heading toward Montana.

They got into New Underwood within their first hour on the road and stopped to ask around about Thurber or his herds. Nothing. There was no sense going to Rapid City so they headed north. The plan was to go up to Sturgis, then to Newell and eventually to Belle Fourche. Surely they would locate their friend by then. Surely.

Their stop in Sturgis provided no information. This should not have surprised them. Townspeople often knew little about what was going on outside town—especially when it came to herds of sheep and their "nomadic" herders who rarely came into a town.

Straight north of Sturgis lay the town of Newell. This small town was, and still is to this day, a "sheep town." If anybody knew, the people around Newell knew what was going in the sheep business in the western plains of South Dakota as well as eastern Wyoming and Montana. Several people in Newell had known Lew personally. Tom and Mary stopped at the hotel. They were sent around the corner to the café that had been a landmark for years.

Tom and Mary unloaded the kids and went to the café. The owner knew who Lew was and sent them over to the stockyards and wool market—just down the block. Tom went to the main corral and talked with two of the men looking over a small "bunch" of sheep.

"I'm lookin' for Lew Thurber from over in Montana. I used to work for him," Tom said. "My name is Tom Stone."

The men glanced at each other and then one looked right at Tom and gave him some bad news. "Lew Thurber died this last winter. I know because we bought a large herd of his that was down around Wasta. Sorry to have to give you that kinda' news," the man said with sincerity.

Tom said nothing for a moment. The two men leaning on the rails of the corral waited quietly for him to speak.

"He was a friend of mine—a damned good friend," Tom finally responded as he was trying to process the loss of his friend and the best hope he and his young family had for getting "back on their feet." This was not good news--at a time when they most needed some.

"You know who bought his sheep?" Tom asked.

"Yeah, two bunches went together and bought all he had. I got their names in the office. I'll get em' for you if you want. I'm pretty sure they've got a big herd not far up the river from here," one of the men volunteered.

"Preciate it," Tom told him. It was a typical "short" comment but you knew Tom Stone meant it sincerely.

The three men walked the short distance to the office. Tom thought about his next "step" in finding work and how he was going to tell Mary of the loss of their friend.

They got to the office and Tom was told that Lew's herds had been bought by two ranchers named Cranston and Enberg who both lived between Ekalaka and Alzada. Tom didn't recognize either of the names. Still, their purchasing of Lew's herds seemed to fit. Living where they did, they would have known Lew and a good deal about his sheep business since he had been there for years.

Tom asked about the herd mentioned earlier to be located "not far up the river from here." Tom wanted to verify that they meant the Belle Fourche River.

"Yeah, that's right. They can't be any more n' 10 to 12 miles up on the north side of the river. I ain't seen em' but was told they would be in with a couple hunnerd head for sale and some wool this fall."

Tom was still thinking about Lew. He thanked them again and headed back to the car. Tom Stone did not "mince" words. From his upbringing it was pretty evident that he said what was "on his mind" straight out. Tact was not part of his nature—even when it came to his wife. He got back to the car and told her without hesitation "Lew died while we was gone. His herds all been sold to somebody over near Alzada." Tom wanted it to be closer to Alzada than Ekalaka because he didn't want to go back near Gib Nims.

Mary was saddened. But after what she had been through the last 6 months, it was hard to "dent her" emotionally. "Well, Dad, we'll talk to them about a job. Do you know who they are?"

"That fella in there told me their names. Nobody I ever heard of."

"We'll just head up that way," Mary suggested. "We know the 'land' and lots of the people—we'll find something. . . ." That's the way survivors think--and talk. That's the way the Stones had to think and talk. There comes a time when you just "push ahead" and believe that something good will happen. Tom and Mary Stone were at that *very time* in their lives—again.

It would have been *closer* to go back to Wasta and spend a day or two. It would likely have been much *easier* to go back to Wasta and get a good night's sleep and start for Montana early in the morning. It would have been. . . . but Tom and Mary didn't. They headed west for Alzada, Montana.

An hour out of Newell they saw a large herd of sheep. The kids were first ones to notice. This must have been what the men at the stockyards were talking about. No way to tell where the base camp was but Tom spotted a dog and knew the herder couldn't be too far away. At least if it had been Nigger he wouldn't have been too far away from his base camp.

They drove less than a mile up the road and spotted a sheep wagon. "There's the wagon, Mother. He has to be fairly close by." He was. While no two herders are alike, Tom Stone knew this was the man in charge of this herd. Mary drove the car slowly through the pasture so as not to spook the herd—it seemed that none of the sheep even noticed them.

Tom and Mary could hear the sheep. They could smell them. They could see them. They wanted to go to work. They hadn't talked with anybody. They didn't really know whose herd this was, but in their own minds, both Tom and Mary felt they were closer to some kind of home.

Mary stopped the car and Tom got out as the herder and his dogs approached them. "Evenin," the herder called out. "Evenin," Tom responded.

"I'm lookin' for Lew Thurber's old herd. I understand they been sold to a couple fellas name a' Cranston and Enberg," Tom told the herder.

"My name's Cranston. My brother and his partner own this herd. They bought all of Lew's stock when he died. Didn't buy Lew's home place—they had all the buildings they needed. You kin' to Lew?"

"No kin. I worked for Lew Thurber for right at 12 years. My family and I been down south on family business. We're back and we need work," Tom responded. That was all the information he was going to give right now.

"You must be the one that used to run Lew's herds down in this part of the country—even down in the Badlands. We heard about you."

"I did," Tom replied.

"Can't tell you when either my brother or Val Engberg will be down here. They mostly stay around their home places out between Ekalaka and Alzada. I guess you know that country," the herder offered.

Tom didn't have to talk with Mary as she had heard their conversation. And, they knew the country alright. "I reckon we'll head on up there and see if there's some work. You have any idea if they're puttin' on men?" Tom asked.

"They're always lookin' for good herders. I know I'd sure like to have somebody take over this bunch so I could get back to my family. My wife and kids are all up north of Ekalaka. I ain't been home for near three months. It's pretty late. Why don't you and your family stay here tonight and get an early morning start. I ain't got sleepin' room but got plenty to eat and lots of hot coffee. You're welcome to join me. I'd like the company."

Mary didn't wait for Tom to respond. "That's very kind of you. The kids would love to stop for the night and we would all like something to eat and something hot to drink. We'll sure take you up on your offer."

"That's settled then. Let's get those young ones some supper and sit around the fire a bit," Cranston offered. No question—for Tom and Mary, this was "home." Good to see some dogs again. . .

"Camp stew" and cornbread never tasted so good. The boiled coffee was strong and hot—just like it was supposed to be. The Stone's laid out their bedrolls under the wagon and fell asleep right away. The kids were worn out. Tom and Mary still did not know what "tomorrow would bring" but they were together, the kids were good and they were "home" and that meant "everything is going to be all right."

Everybody was up early—even the sheep. Cranston fixed the coffee [Mary didn't want to "mess" in his wagon] and everybody had at least one hot biscuit. Tom was anxious to head up the road. If there was work to be had, he would find it.

"Which one do you think I should talk to—Cranston or Enberg—who does the hirin'?" Tom asked.

"I'll tell you what—they're cousins and they think just alike. You can talk with either one of em' and it's just like they was both there. I'd go to my brother's place since it's closer from here. He lives about 3 miles south of Ekalaka. There's a road but it ain't much. . .well you been there, you know."

"We'll get there," Tom said deliberately.

"His name is Charles Cranston and he goes by Charles. He doesn't talk much but means what he says when he does talk. I think you and him will get on just fine knowin' you worked for Lew for all those years—that will set good with Charles."

The herder was very encouraging. He gave them some final directions and had packed a bag for the kids. Mary said they hoped to see him soon and they were on the road—headed for Ekalaka.

For the first time since they got back, Tom and Mary really looked at the land. Western South Dakota was faithful. It had not changed while they were away. It was almost like *this land of small rolling hills and waving fields of high grass knew they would be back—and patiently waited for them.*

They were excited to see Belle Fourche and spent $1.50 on gas there. They didn't really have money for anything else but that "knowing herder" near Newell had graciously packed some biscuits and bacon strips for them—and they had plenty of water.

They passed over Owl Creek and in just over 2 hours after leaving Cranston's base camp, they were in Montana. They headed north for Ekalaka knowing they probably had another 3 to 3 ½ hours to go. Mary stopped about 30 miles in so the kids could go to the bathroom.

The "road" was rough but at least it was passable. This was one of those times you were happy there was no rain. If there had been rain, the "gumbo trail" would not have let them through.

They stopped a cowboy on horseback near the road and asked him if he could guide them to Charles Cranston's place. "Sure can," he answered. "I'm workin' for him." They had passed the turnoff to the Cranston place but only by three-quarters of a mile. So, back they went, made their turn and in 5 minutes saw the ranch they figured must have been Cranston's place. It was.

They pulled into the yard—which was full of kids, dogs and chickens—plenty of each. Mrs. Cranston heard them drive up and came out to greet them. You didn't see much company in these parts and there would be months when you didn't even see a car. She seemed to be a very outgoing woman—large and friendly.

"Hello there," she shouted as the Stones drove in. "This is the Cranston place. Who are ya lookin' for?"

"Charles Cranston," Tom said as he got out of the car. "Is he here? We just came from his herd just outside Newell. . .wanted to talk with him about some work. This is my wife and kids. My name is Tom Stone. We used to live up here and we worked for Lew Thurber for about 12 years," Tom volunteered. He was careful not to mention their Ekalaka "connection."

"Charles has been gone all morning but it's about noon so he'll be back here for dinner [the noon meal in this country as well] shortly. Come on up and sit on the porch and we can talk til' he gets here. Can I get you a cup of coffee?"

"We'd love some coffee," Mary offered thankfully.

"My name is Jessica Cranston. You can imagine most folks call me Jess. We been livin' here going on 30 years. We knew Lew pretty well and are sorry to see him pass. When Lew died, Charles and his cousin Val bought his spread—all but the buildings—we didn't need any more buildings. But, we bought all his sheep."

"How many head do you have?" Mary asked trying to show interest and be a part of the conversation.

"Can't tell you for sure—but it's close to 8 thousand head. I don't do much with em' cause I've got this herd of my own—these 7 kids keep me plenty busy. I used to help with lambin' and shearin' but my back finally gave out. You say you're lookin' for work? That's somethin' you'll have to talk with Charles about. I can hear his old truck comin' up the road now. He'll be here in a minute or two."

Charles pulled into the front yard in a black Ford straight truck. There was a saddle and two bags of feed [or seed] in the bed of the truck. He got out of the truck and hollered hello to the kids as he headed for the porch. "Hello Jess—did ya' miss me?" he said in a teasing manner.

Charles Cranston was a big man. He wore a large white Stetson hat, jeans and beat-up cowboy boots—that looked like they had seen the inside of some corrals. He was a Montana cowboy.

"Afternoon folks," he said to Tom and Mary as he came up onto the wide, covered porch. "My name is Charles Cranston. Me and Jess and the kids live here and run some cows and some sheep. What are you folks doing in this country?" He seemed quite affable, but got down to business pretty fast.

Tom Stone was not much for words. "I need work. I herded for Lew Thurber for about 12 years and worked for A.E. Blackford for eight years before that. Before we went to Georgia to look after family near two years ago, I took care of Lew's herd down between Wasta and Newell in South Dakota."

"That's good to know. Lew was a good sheepman and a good neighbor for many years. Don't know if you knew that my cousin and I bought Lew's herd when he passed—not the buildings but all his sheep. My brother takes care of that bunch down around Newell now."

"We just talked with him yesterday and spent the night at the basecamp. He gave us directions about how to get up to your place and was very helpful," Mary chimed in.

"We just got back from a long trip to Georgia to see my Dad and Mother. But this is home. We need some work—pretty bad. We wondered if you could use a good hand," Tom openly admitted.

It was quiet—even a little uncomfortable.

"Well, I can always use a good hand. We got a lot of cows and a lot more sheep—how many head of sheep would you say Jess?" Charles asked of his wife.

"I told the Stones that after we bought Lew Thurber's herds, we must have at least 7 to 8 thousand head of sheep—and they're all over the place," Jess Cranston answered. "And as you folks know, you just don't settle sheep in one place very long anyway," Charles concluded.

"We're willing to live wherever you have a herd. We're used to taking care of a large bunch as long as we've got a couple of dogs and some good horses—we'll go anywhere," Mary volunteered.

"Well Tom, if you liked that country down around Newell, my brother would just as soon get out of there and come home. Any interest in going back down there where you were? I think we could sure work that out," Charles said in an encouraging manner.

"We appreciate the offer and we'll take it," Tom said with finality. He and Mary couldn't have asked for anything more. While it would *not* be like nothing had happened in the last year, getting back to work meant everything right now.

"We've got a good cook wagon and a team down there at the base camp. That should work for you. We'll find you a dog or two at Val's place—he's got at least a dozen—you'll need to pick them out for yourself Tom. I'll drive my truck down to the basecamp when you go to the herd and bring your supplies—I don't know what my brother has there. We'll get you plenty," Charles said in a most accommodating manner.

It was going to be "just like old times" Mary thought. Although Thomas Wolfe had observed "You Can't Go Home Again [1940]," Mary Stone would have argued his premise *this* time

"Charles, they're going to need another wagon for sleeping. They got three younguns' with them. We've got another wagon out here that we can fix up with beds. It's a good wagon and we just put a new set of canvas on it—for winter. It's got a good stove and good wheels. I think it will work fine," Jess added as she thought about some of the things a "mother" would think of. It wasn't all just about sheep.

"We'll head back down there in the morning. We'll be at the base-camp by the time the sun goes down tomorrow, Tom said assuredly.

"You can take one of my 30-30s until you get settled--and a box or two of shells. There's still some winter left—you'll need them—you can be pretty damned sure those coyotes will be comin' down to make regular visits. Tom mused silently: "That's one thing that ain't changed."

It was obvious that Charles Cranston had spent some time with sheep. "I'll provide your wagons, your supplies, and your horses. Since you have family, I'll pay you $50 dollars a month. Will that be all right?" Charles asked, almost knowing what the answer would be. Mrs. Cranston stood approvingly near his side. This was her husband's business—she apparently trusted him to make good decisions when it came to the sheep business.

"That'll be fine," Tom answered in a genuinely sincere and appreciative tone. "That'll be fine," Tom repeated for good measure.

"Well, let's take a look at that other wagon out in the barn and see what it needs for sleepin.' You said you think it will work all right Jess? Let's go take a look Tom. Jess, these folks are most likely pretty hungry. We want to invite you to stay and have supper with us. We've got an extra bedroom that we'll squeeze all of you in for tonight and you can get an early start in the morning to get down with that herd," Charles added.

"You folks don't have to do that. We will be alright for tonight and be in camp tomorrow," Mary said half hoping the Cranstons would *insist* they stay. They did.

"Won't hear it," Jess chimed back. "You and the kids will eat here tonight and sleep in a bed tonight. Lord knows you may not see a real mattress for months to come. Mary, would you mind helping me in the kitchen. We've got over a dozen hungry folks to feed," Mrs. Cranston added.

Mary was only too happy to oblige. A hot meal for her family and a real mattress. "We are truly blessed," she thought. Things could not have worked out better.

Dinner was good—beef steak [he was a cattleman as well as a sheepman] and potatoes--and plenty of biscuits. The Stones were all ready for bed—and excited to get up early and get down the road to their new job. Nigger had stayed in Wasta. He would join them as soon as they could drive down to pick him up and put him back on duty. They were back "home" and back to work—doing what they knew and living the *way* they knew best.

CHAPTER 14

Familiar Surroundings: Open Range

EARLY THE NEXT morning Jess Cranston had fixed some biscuits, coffee, pork tenderloin and scrambled eggs. It was good to sit at a real table and eat off glass plates and have silverware to use again. The kids each drank at least two glasses of milk.

Just to say thanks to the Cranstons seemed not enough. This eastern Montana family had "saved their lives." In addition, they had been so very kind in the process.

Jess extended her hand to Mary and told her to "take care of them young'uns. They'll be a handful in a couple of years—but this is a good place to raise 'em. It's been good for ours."

Mary took her hand and shook it gently. "Thanks for all you have done for us. We will not forget your kindness," Mary said in a most appreciative manner. "Thanks to you too, Mr. Cranston," she added.

"Just 'Charles,' and you're welcome. I needed a good sheepman down with that Newell bunch and I think you and Tom will be just the ticket. I know you want to get down there so we'll say goodbye and I'll see you soon. I'll be bringing your other wagon and your provisions down tomorrow. Tell my brother what we settled on. He'll be more than agreeable with that," Charles Cranston concluded.

"Tom, Let's pull your car over to the gas tank and get her filled up. There's not a lotta places you can get gasoline around here." Mary drove the car over near the shed by the large tank and Charles filled their gas tank. Truly thoughtful--and practical--and necessary.

Tom held out his hand to Charles. They cemented their deal the way people did in that country. Then, he gathered up the kids and put them in the back seat, thinking: "Old Ford, you been good to us." Jess Cranston had packed them a big tote-bag full of food for the trip and their first night in camp—in case Val was short on supplies. "These are just real thoughtful people," Mary said to herself.

Off the Stones headed down the dirt road back to western South Dakota—it was a new adventure but in a familiar setting. It would take time to "heal" from Georgia, but if there was anywhere to do just that, this was the place.

They arrived at the basecamp and were greeted by Val Cranston and his dog. "I figgered you'd be back. Charles is a good judge of men. If he thought there was work someplace, just seemed right that he'd hire you. . . . Where you gonna be located?

"Looks like right here. Hope that's OK with you," Tom said almost apologetically for *taking* Val's job.

"Don't bother me a bit. My family's all up north of Ekalaka and I been anxious to get back up there. 'Sides, we got plenty of sheep and cows to take care of all over this country. I won't get lonely. You folks take the wagon for tonight and I'll be ridin' out in the morning. Let's have some supper and we'll talk about this herd and what supplies you've got while we eat."

Mary chimed in with an offer to fix supper and Val was glad to accept her offer. It didn't take her long to get a good meal ready on the stove in the [cook]wagon and the coffee pot was already on the campfire—and over half full.

"It's good to be back in camp," Mary said. Her voice was direct and solid—there was no question how strongly she felt about what she said.
It was starting to "sink In." Things really were "going to work out."

After supper, Mary put the kids to bed in the cookwagon. It was still just warm enough for the adults to sleep outside so long as you had as much under you as you did on top. The ground was cold and by morning would be damp. Val and Tom would take turns circling the herd and talking about the specific area of this basecamp—where other herds might be [both sheep and cattle], where the water was and what sign there was of coyote packs.

"Tom," Val Cranston said, "this dog might just want to stay with you. He was with the herd when I first came down here and he 'knows' this bunch pretty good. We'll see what he wants to do when I leave. If he wants to stay, he'll be a big help right away."

"I've got one dog down in Wasta with some friends and I'll be bringing him up. But if this one will stay, that'll be good if they can get along. Your brother will be bringing a couple of horses down tomorrow along with a sleep wagon. We'll be all set up by the time the sun goes down tomorrow. I appreciate all you and Charles have done. We needed the work," Tom added.

"Glad to have you and the Missus with us," Val responded. "Good sheepmen ain't as easy to find as they used to be. Some things like that have changed up here," he added.

Tom wasn't sure about the "changes" Val referred to. After all, the Stones had been gone for over a year and would not have seen any immediate differences. More important, in his own way, Tom Stone didn't think about change—he didn't want to think about any changes in the country, his job, and, most important, his life. Looking too far ahead was *not* something he wanted to do right now.

As a matter of necessity, Tom and Mary easily "assumed" control of the herd the next morning as Val headed out for Ekalaka. As Val had mentioned, the dog "chose" to stay with the herd. To Tom, this was almost like having someone with them that "knew" this bunch of sheep and this country—in its own way, it gave both Tom and Mary a little more assurance in what they had taken on in the last 48 hours.

Tom saddled one of the horses. He missed his own saddle but knew it would not be long until he could get all his own tack. Tom decided he would let "his new dog" show him around the herd and the basecamp. Almost as second nature, the veteran sheep dog took over and conducted "a tour." They were gone about two hours and Mary got the kids somewhat oriented to their new surroundings. All three kids seemed happy to be "home" as well. It was early spring and the weather was beautiful on the northern plains of western South Dakota.

When Tom and the dog got back from their "tour," Mary and Tom sat and had some coffee. Tom gave Mary a brief account of what he had seen looking at the herd and what he was able to tell about the area surrounding the basecamp. Tom estimated that there were about 1800 head in the herd—apparently, they had shipped a bunch in the fall.

"They been eatin' good," he told Mary. "I don't see no sign of any other herds close—and me and the dog went 4 or 5 miles each way." For Tom, this was just as well. . . he didn't need or want anybody close. Instinctively, Tom wondered if the dog had a name.

He and the dog had traveled a little under 5 miles each way. Although Tom had been in this area before, it was important to get his "bearings" [water, grass, other herds, any ranches, sign of coyote packs]. This looked like a good spot-- for both spring and summer. Tom wasn't anxious to make any decisions about the herd until he met with Charles later that day.

About the middle of the afternoon, Charles Cranston arrived in his truck with supplies. Charles had brought a second saddle for them [since he knew Mary rode as well] and he would leave both the horses with the wagon once his hired hand got there with it. By the end of the day, the Stones had plenty of provisions to get them well into the fall. And they had three horses.

"You plannin' to move this herd any place this spring or summer?" Tom asked Charles.

"We'll talk about that later when you get your bearings, Tom," Charles answered. He added, "You know this country pretty well. I'll want to know what you think about moving them. We'll talk about it in a couple weeks after you folks get settled."

As Tom and Charles unloaded the supplies, you could tell that Jess

Cranston had "loaded" a few things with Mary and the kids in mind.

"We're gonna' have to go down to Wasta to pick up the rest of our stuff and get my dog. He's prob'ly wonderin' what the hell happened to us," Tom mused.

It was important to get his own dog back with him to be sure the two would get along—that was something you never really knew. Tom knew that Nigger was a dog that "needed to be in charge." If the "new dog" went along with that, everything would be OK. He'd thought about it before, because "ya just never knew."

On Thursday, Mary loaded the kids in the car and they headed down toward Wasta to get Nigger and the several things they had left at Lee and Percy Collier's place. They started late as they planned to stay the night with the Colliers—even though it was just a little under a three-hour drive. Mary understood this time of year, travel could be limited—even short distances in this country as weather would "come up" all of a sudden. Luckily, this winter had been unusually mild by South Dakota standards. Tom would be more than fine at the camp by himself—a "spot" he'd been in many times and truly enjoyed for short periods. Mary hoped he wouldn't overdo with his leg.

Just before she left, Tom asked Mary to take a bridle to Wasta to get fixed before it came apart even further—it was wise to keep a backup in good repair and he didn't know when he would get to see a saddlemaker any time soon to get it fixed.

Though it had only been a few days, Lee was happy to see Mary and the kids. They had an early supper so the kids could get to bed. Mary explained to Lee and Percy all the things that had happened the past week. Lee was happy for Mary, Tom and the kids. And, even though Lee Collier wouldn't have dreamed of that kind of life for *her family*, she knew Tom and Mary would be doing just what they wanted to do. "I'm happy for you and Tom and the kids, Mary. Just remember, you folks are always welcome here with Percy and me—always," Lee added.

Mary appreciated that. She often said that "Lee Collier was one of the very few friends *I had time to make* during those early years—we never settled anyplace for long." Even when the Stones moved into Pierre [SD] some years later, the Colliers would visit on occasion [the Stone's did not have a car for travel during their early years in Pierre as it was a small town so you could walk most places and Tom still didn't drive].

After breakfast the next morning, Mary loaded the few things they had left at Collier's, got the kids settled in the car and got Nigger "on board." They said their goodbyes, knowing they were less than 3 hours away but in this country—and at this time of the year—that could be a long way. Right now, she needed to get back with her husband and the herd. It was time to get "resettled,"

That spring was normal—that was a welcome relief. Charles sent men down from the main ranch to help with spring lambing. With new lambs all over the place, even the noise and the chaos seemed a welcome reality. Summer was right on schedule. Tom and Charles agreed they would keep the close to where they were for the summer and get ready for fall shipping since they were close to the Newell railhead.

In all, the spring and summer--and even fall--just dashed by. It may have been that Tom and Mary were so happy to be "home" and out of "that damned Georgia mess" that they didn't give the seasons a thought. And so, Mother Nature move through her normal patterns and the Stones adapted--as always.

Charles and Val brought their own ram herd down to Tom's base-camp and the 40 or so males did their jobs. It all went very smoothly. Both Tom and Mary kept thinking: "What a change from last year!"

Winter did show signs of coming early as the first snow [light] came the last week of September—not unheard of but early. Tom was ready. He had moved the herd a bit closer to the low hills near the Belle Fourche River just east of Vale. The dogs helped. Nigger was "in charge" and the "new dog" took his role in stride—he followed Nigger's lead.

After a menacing start, the winter of 1939-40 graduated into what most would have considered "normal." There was plenty of very "wet" snow so everyone knew the rivers and creeks would be full—and the grass would be plentiful. This also meant there would be lots of lambs to deliver—that was a very positive thought but also had some downsides. For sure, they would need a lot of help with lambing.

As 1940 approached, things were fairly typical for western South Dakota this time of year. There were some bone-chilling cold days but very few below zero nights—some frozen creeks and coyote packs—one stray mountain lion who hung around for a couple of days but did little damage. In all, the winter was nothing new to Tom—he had dealt with much worse in his years on the plains of western South Dakota

"I guess the Cranston's know what this means for spring. We'll need lotsa' help," Tom cautioned in advance. "There'll be lotsa' grass and plenty a' lambs. We're gonna need some extra hands. I just hope they know that." He should not have worried. The Cranstons would take care of their investments and their herders.

Even though the winter "started early," it *didn't get worse*. The temperatures were "decent" with some sunshine nearly every day. There was a good amount of snowfall but no "bad" blizzards which could easily take its toll on any herd—even those well taken care of with the proper shelter and movement[s].

It was hard to believe that through all this relative turmoil, the kids were growing up to be pretty normal youngsters. They fought some, played hard and asked "why" countless times every day. Of course, this life was pretty much all they knew. They had rarely been around other people [especially children]. Very rarely. Their environment was limited—but it was nearly all they had ever seen. Most of the Georgia "experience" was forgotten. The Vale school was open and Mary got Bob, Sissy and Jody there at least 3 days a week. As a Mom, she felt very good about that.

News! Mary was going to have a baby in the winter. For Mary, it brought back memories of Dorothy Jean. In itself, those were mixed emotions at best. Tom, on the other hand, looked forward to a new baby in camp as a sign they were "rebuilding" their life in South

Dakota. Bob, Sissy and Jody just weren't sure--the girls would come around after the baby was born.

Spring of 1940 was good. Tom and Mary didn't think much about the winter—they were just living day to day. They were thankful they had 3 healthy kids, a good job and a reasonable income. Still, something ate at their insides. Their hearts still hurt: It was some Dorothy Jean and some of that "damned Georgia mess."

The summer of 1940 brought plenty of high, green grass and abundant water from the winter snows. It was good that the winter snows had been plentiful as there were few spring rains. That was quite unusual. From melting snow, the larger creeks and the Belle Fourche River were full but the countryside started to get dry from lack of rain. The small creeks started to dry up and the grass started to lose its green much earlier than usual.

After spending shearing and lambing time at the basecamp, Tom had moved Mary and the kids back into Wasta into a cabin court. There was a small kitchen and a separate bedroom. By the end of July, Mary was "settled" there. She was close to her friend Lee and Bob, Sissy and Jody could go to school with Larry Collier, Lee and Percy's son, in Wasta. Bob Stone was nearly 13 years old and Sissy, though small in stature was ready for 5th grade—Jody was in 2nd.

That summer on the prairie, there was little rain which made it easier to manage the sheep as they could move without the restrictions of swollen creeks. On the negative side, the shortage of water means a shortage of grass. These are the two things sheep need the most. So, even in late summer, Tom was thinking about moving the sheep to decent [stable] winter grazing. At the time, his plan was to move nearer to Wasta. While it was not an ideal place to winter the herd, it would be close to Mary and the kids. Such a move would mean that Tom could come to Wasta every couple of days to see how she was doing and help some with their growing family. Mary's friend Lee was there and was a great help. She checked on Mary virtually every day.

Tom took care of the herd though his heart was with his kids and his wife in Wasta. They got through shearing, thanks to the men that Charles had hired and Tom decided not to move anywhere for the winter—right where they were was going to *have to be fine.*

The last winter had been unusually mild. The chances of having two in a row was unlikely--Tom knew that. The buck herd came down and got the breeding completed. The herd had grown by over 200 ewes and Tom, Nigger and the other "dog" were now in charge of over 2000 head.

They wintered well. They had typical trouble with coyotes and the occasional mountain cat [and a suspected wolf or two] but Bob could now take a full turn at riding herd and he had his own 30-30. And he was very skilled in using it. The four of them [Tom, Bob and the dogs] kept the herd as safe as could be expected.

Spring came and it looked like time to move—but they made no plans to do so. Charles didn't come down so Tom knew whatever he decided was OK. Spring brought a freshness—good grass and clean water in the creeks all over the prairies. Everything looked bright and fresh.

While the job with the Cranston's seemed permanent, it just did not seem to "fit." Quite likely, it wasn't the job but the place and the times. It was here that their 4th child had been born. It was right *here* that Tom and Mary Stone had lost their newest baby. It was *here* that Dorothy Jean had failed to thrive. It was *here* they had to bury her under the ground. Mary kept thinking, "no baby belongs under the cold hard ground." Their baby was forever gone from their sight and they now knew they would not be able to touch her soft little being. That was "here." And that feeling about "here" was bad.

Nobody, not even the kids, talked about Dorothy Jean.

Things just didn't feel right. The job was fine. The salary was good. Charles Cranston kept them well-provisioned. They had made it through the winter of 1939-40 but didn't seem to even remember it. In some ways, the loss of their baby made them somewhat oblivious to the outside world. Still, no talk of their loss.

Tom and Mary both felt some indebtedness to Charles Cranston.

After all, when they were as far "down" as they had ever been, he gave them a job. For all they knew, it was a job that would last "as long as they wanted to stay." That may have been the major issue: How long did they want to stay—they had experienced some good times here. Even great times. Logical? Illogical? This was not a time to classify their "manner of thinking--of making decisions."

So, they stayed. They stayed with the pain. They stayed with the memories—knowing that their lost baby was just a few miles away— but a lifetime gone. They stayed but they did not forget. They had to plan for the future. Their four kids were growing fast. They needed a more stable life than "living on the plains in sheep wagons" and being able to go to school if one was available--and they weren't always.

Summer was good—plenty of new lambs. They actually had a "bumper crop." Charles and his brother brought a crew down to help them with lambing and assured Tom they would be back in the early fall for shearing and getting the herd ready for shipping from the rail head near Newell. While Charles and Tom did not talk about it, Charles knew Tom and Mary were very distraught about the loss of their daughter. Charles and Jess had lost two infants in their early days in Montana. Charles remembered *his* pain. He also knew enough *not* to tell Tom he "understood exactly how he felt."

Making *no decision* is actually making *a decision*. That's what Tom and Mary Stone did—or didn't do. They went along day to day— doing all the things that *needed* to be done. Tom and Mary did not think about going back to Badlands for the summer of 1940 even though they were sure Charles would have supported the idea. They moved around Meade County and found plenty of good grassland.

And, they noticed more and more barbed wire being strung and more cattle grazing on land that was once "dedicated" to the roving sheep herds. There was no trouble with cattle ranchers *yet*, but you could see that it was just a matter of time. Importantly, for anyone who "liked things just the way they were," the signs "on the horizon" were not very promising. Things just kept on changing. Deep down, Tom Stone probably never liked *change*—at all. These changes would soon force him to alter his entire way of life.

Fall of 1940 just happened. They sheared. Charles and some hands from the main ranch came down and they drove nearly 500 head to be shipped to market. Charles brought in his own "ram herd" for breeding. Everything went like clockwork. Tom was pleased with "the way things stood." He had done and continued to do his job as one of the most accomplished herders in the area.

Mary mentioned that Charles and Jess had given the Stone family a Christmas gift--$100 [a great deal of money in these times] in addition to their monthly salary and some special "Christmas provisions" along with gifts for the kids. Jess Cranston was a very considerate person. And though she likely knew about the loss of the baby, neither she nor Charles ever mentioned it. In sum, "there was not much anybody could say that would make things better." Let time pass. Let hearts heal. But know the memories won't ever go away. "She was such a pretty little thing."

They hadn't talked much about the baby that was coming. She was understandably excited. He had mixed feelings. He loved his children [in his own way] but worried about complications similar to that with Dorothy Jean. After all, they were living in the same part of the country—within 30 miles of where they had lost her. The due date for the expected baby would be about the same time as the month they lost Dorothy Jean—it didn't feel good to Tom.

The pregnancy went well. Mary had regained her physical strength some time before and the excitement of a new baby helped her to rekindle her emotional base. Mary sensed Tom's concern.

"It will be alright Dad," she would comment several times a week—reassuring him as much as convincing herself. The difference was, Mary Stone firmly believed "it *would* be alright."

And Tom would respond, "Well, you know what we went through last time. . . . " She knew. He knew. Neither wanted to go through that again.

Rosalie Luverne Stone was born on December 4, 1940. Everybody, even the three older kids were happy. It was an easy delivery and Rosalie was a pretty, dark-haired girl. She was full-term, healthy and a happy baby from day one. The other kids had likely erased the memory of Dorothy Jean and they welcomed their new sister with glee.

Sissy and Jody "took to her" right away. They wanted to hold her and play with her. Mary, even more excited than they were, let them name the new little girl. Her two older sisters somehow came up with the name Rosaline Luverne. [3 weeks later they would want to change her name and she grew up with the new name: Lindy Lou].

At the time of the new arrival, Bob was a "teenager" and Sissy was 11. Jody would be 8 in a couple of months so they had some ideas about their new baby sister in addition to changing her name. They decided what she would wear, what she would eat and which one of them their new sister "liked the best."

None of the Stone kids looked alike. Bob was tall and lanky with lots of brown, wavy hair. Sissy was small and a bit chunky with short curly blond hair. Jody was and tall and slim with long auburn hair. This new young lady didn't look like any of the other kids either. None of the Stone kids looked much like their Mom or Dad either. That was fine. They were healthy and got along fairly well with each other.

"Linda Lou is her name," they declared. There was no real indication where either of the names had come from but for many years Mary referred to Rosalie as "Lindy Lou." And, she said it in a way that showed a Mother's special endearment. She wasn't meant to be a replacement for their loss but she helped mend hearts that had been severely damaged.

In time, Mary stopped asking the "why" questions with regard to the loss of her baby. While she never did get angry about losing Dorothy Jean, she was learning to accept her painful passing as something that was "meant to be." In some sense, she was reaching a degree of closure—but would surely never forget.

Rosalie was a full-fledged member of the family from the day of her birth. The older girls [Bob didn't care much] doted on her and wanted to carry her around. And while they were still a bit small for toting her, Mary did let them take turns holding her once they got "set down" in a stable chair.

Tom Stone was relieved. His fears of losing another child had been without foundation. His family seemed "intact" again and he started getting back into "the swing" of being the herder that he had always been. This meant planning some moves. And, as to the west and north of him, things were getting "crowded," he decided to look toward the east—past Wasta and even Wall—past both the towns of Cottonwood and Quinn.

After that, Tom moved the herd a bit closer to the Black Hills—almost a matter of habit. And yet, it was almost like his "heart wasn't in it." Mary and Tom still liked their work and their life on the prairies but a big chunk had been taken out of their collective hearts—and the hole remained—it resonated constantly.

The winter of 1940-41 started out very mild with some early snow near the end of October that didn't stay long. The herd acted like they didn't even notice—they just kept grazing. Tom stayed close to the base camp with Mary and the kids until near Thanksgiving and then Mary and the kids went into Wasta to be with Lee and Percy. Tom planned to join them after he got the herd settled just south of Elk Creek. He rode over to Wasta and spent Thanksgiving with his family and the Colliers.

This "allocation of his attention" was new. For perhaps the first time, the herd was starting to take a "back seat" to the family. While Tom may not have been *aware* of *his changing* values, his priorities were different. Long after the loss of Dorothy Jean, both Mary and Tom would experience "lost" days and months—for over two years. The "outside" things got done—they had to be done. The "inside" things were there but neither Tom nor Mary knew how to deal with *them*.

The spring of 1941 was here. The weather cleared in late March and the winter snow had provided the country with the rich, green grass for which these sheep lands were known. The streams all seemed to be full and as the ice cleared along the banks, they were all accessible. It was good "sheep time."

In late April and early May it became obvious that both the ram herd and Mother Nature had done their jobs. Lambs! New lambs provided a "shot of adrenaline" to the herder. It was like a new lease on life. And when the lamb crop was good [and this one was outstanding] it was an even greater lift. New lambs were like a "contract extension." Marketing nearly 500 head and still increasing the size of his herd with new lambs was very rewarding news for their economic bottom line—and Charles and Val Cranston were in the sheep [and cattle] business to make a profit.

Tom kept the herd in the same general area [with limited movement] for nearly 3 months—this was pretty unusual considering his propensity to move to "new ground." Deep down, it almost seemed they wanted to stay close to their lost baby. In some way, *leaving this area would be no different than leaving her.* And, at least on Mary's part, there was *still* a feeling they had "let her down."

And so, the Stones stayed around Wasta and the Colliers. At the same time, they stayed fairly close to Dorothy Jean's resting place. It seemed the ability to cope with losing her never developed. Still, nobody talked about the loss or the pain—but the pain persisted. It's one of those "things" that would not go away.

It was time to move. While he had not been there before, Tom got ready to go further east. Where he was located was good sheep land, but he still wanted to move. Perhaps it was the "nomad" in him--perhaps it was merely instinctual. Besides that, this sheepman could see "more cows and more fences all the time."

For Tom, this was somewhat unknown territory. He knew little about the "lay of the land," how much grass there was and what his water sources would be. He talked with Charles about it and his boss was not in favor of what appeared to be a somewhat major move—a venture Charles could not see any real need for. After all, things were fine where they were. Lamb production was high, they were shipping an average of nearly 400 head a year from this herd and the wool production was very profitable. Why move? Especially that far.

Charles didn't argue long. He had his men deliver a newly-built sleep wagon for Tom and Mary and their growing family. The new wagon looked to be over the normal 12x7 [84 square feet] dimensions of the standard sheep wagon. It had *glass windows* on *each side* and on the *front door* and a brand-new double canvas top supported by shiny steel joists. It was a very nice wagon. Charles looked at it as an *earned bonus*. Tom and Mary truly appreciated it.

In this new country, Philip and Milesville were the closest towns to Tom's herd. After the first trip to deliver provisions, Charles determined that it was at least twice as far from the home place as the former basecamp[s] had been. He began to question the advisability of the move again.

Although Tom did not talk with Charles directly about the latter's concerns, the men that delivered provisions were instructed to make it clear that "the boss" thinks this is a bit too far from home. In one way, Charles argument made sense—it was a long way. Come breeding time, shearing time and marketing time, it would be an extra chore to travel so far—and, Charles thought, needless travel. Besides, if there was trouble with Tom or the herd, getting word to the home-place would be a real problem.

The winter of 1941 was tough. It didn't snow much more, but the snow seemed to stay on the ground longer. The temperature wasn't much lower but it just seemed colder. The wind blew like it always had and there were fewer hills for shelter and no trees to slow it down. And, after a few years in that country, you start to get worn down.

For Tom, Charles' lack of support for the move, challenged his independent nature. He felt his decision-making authority being questioned a little bit. In this case, Charles was right—with little doubt. Would resolution of this issue cost him the best herder he had? It was the spring of 1941 [World War II had begun] and hired men were hard to find. Charles knew that. Still, business is first of all, business. He needed to talk face-to-face with Tom. He would come down to the Stone's base camp for lambing--and stay for shearing if need be.

Charles Cranston came down for spring lambing and shearing and spent some time talking with both Tom and Mary. Charles' made the case that it was much better to be closer to the homeplace as well as the railhead for shipping. Being closer would make it much easier to bring men in to help with spring lambing, docking and shearing. In the fall, it would be much easier to cut out those headed for the market and get them to the railhead. In addition, Charles did most of his wool business in Newell and moving back near there would truly simplify things.

Tom actually *liked* being "on his own." Charles' position was one a businessman would make—and it was the most viable position. Charles was not going to "order" Tom Stone to do anything. He had made his case. Tom had made his. At the close of the exchange, Tom said he would "like to spend one more season" in the area north of Philip. Charles agreed to "one more season." It was not what he had wanted but he was a businessman and knew that if he weighed having a highly qualified herder with this large herd, his investment would more than balance the additional expense of having them located so far away from the home place.

Still, Tom knew Charles meant "one more season."

The summer of 1942 was "quiet." That meant no real issues except a seeming rise in the coyote population. Again, with two good dogs and Bob being an excellent shot, they dealt with the predators. They knew if the coyotes were bad in the summer, they would be even worse when cold weather came and food became more scarce. And even when you're on alert, a *hungry* predator will take more chances to feed themselves and their little ones. It's natural.

Fall came early. Winter would not be far behind. Charles brought the ram herd in and they finished within 6 days. Neither of the Cranston brothers came down during breeding but both Charles and Tom remembered "one more season."

Tom was right—it was the worst year he'd ever had with coyotes. He and Bob spelled off most nights and did not leave the sheep alone much. Still, their losses were heavy in contrast to what he had experienced in the past. The snow was heavy—but not wet. It was cold and the wind blew across the plains. Tom was now in his early forties and this life was beginning to take a toll. Mary saw it more this winter than she had ever seen it before. But, this was their life. They didn't know anything else. And, they weren't going to "give up" on anything.

The spring of 1942 came late. The shearing crews, who kept close track of the weather, arrived late. The lambs came when they were ready—even if the weather didn't cooperate. Bad weather during lambing can be a major issue if there is too much snow on the ground or if it is too cold for the young ones. Such timing was under the control of Mother Nature—and hers alone.[80] Herders did what they could but even with extra help [and a place to keep the new lambs—which was rare], the loss of lambs was high.

This weather was right on the border of being a disaster. Luckily, Tom had his herd in good bedding grounds with plenty of feed—although the water was a bit of an issue until real melting started. Maybe it was the colder than normal winter or the late arrival of decent weather, but the lamb "crop" was not as good as it normally was. And still, the coyotes. They went after the docile ewes and the helpless lambs as well. "Keeping herd" was an overtime job. Even with increased attention to the ever-present predators, losses were high.

The shearers came in and completed their work in less than two weeks. And, even though production was down, the price, because of the military needs for wool, raised the prices to more than cover lower production. The end of "one more season" was getting close. Normally, the "season" would end in the fall with shipping older ewes and lambs to market *and* moving the herd to winter ground. Tom knew this. Charles knew this. Decision time was fast approaching. "One more season" echoed.

Tom Stone always had the confidence that his wife would go

---

80   It was difficult to provide any protection from the cold for new lambs—who had little covering on their pink skin. Extremely cold weather and snow was also a problem for ewes in delivery even with some assistance from the herder.

along with anything he wanted to do that was reasonable—through "thick and thin" she and the kids would be by his side. He also knew she wanted the kids to go to school. The kids could all ride a reasonable distance to school and the Stone's both knew it was going to require them to go back near Wasta or move closer to Philip. Moving back toward Wasta would keep Charles satisfied with their agreement. In essence, a move back toward Wasta would satisfy the "one more season" stipulation. On the other hand, moving toward Philip would likely cost Tom and Mary their job.

Tom made his decision. He was going to move the herd east and stay a ways north of Philip and just south of Milesville. While the grass was OK, the major water sources were quite a ways to the south [Bad River] and Plum Creek to the north and east of Milesville. But, after good [and late] winter snows, the creeks would be full. That was always a good sign this time of year—heavy snow meant plenty of clean water for the sheep.

He didn't think much about what might be going through Charles' mind. If he had, he might have guessed that his boss, although *hoping* Tom would move the herd back west, *suspected* that Tom would move further east—"Damned if I know why. . . " Charles would query. Still, Charles Cranston trusted Tom Stone.

Tom didn't think about how far he was from the homeplace either—likely close to a hundred miles. When it came to getting provisions delivered or help during lambing or shearing, he would likely be on his own. Neither of these situations was good. If they didn't get help with supplies, they could buy their own. And, if the weather held, they could get through lambing all right. Shearing was another matter. They could not get the shearing done and get the wool to market by themselves.

Tom was forced to conclude: "This move east had to be temporary." Tom would rationalize it as "summer grazing." He had found some good new land for the herds, but they were too far away to be "serviced" by the homeplace.

After two months, Tom started moving his herd south, toward

Philip and then headed them back west to a spot north of Wasta. Somehow, Charles knew where Tom was. Within a week of arriving north of Wasta, Charles' "crews" met the herd. It was well over a month past shearing time and most of the lambs that were going to be delivered were already there. Charles sent no word. Instead, along with the shearing crew, he sent more than ample provisions and Tom's pay. Tom halfway expected to be fired. But, he didn't ask about that--and nobody said a word.

From time to time, Tom's thoughts drifted back to his Dad and Mother in Georgia. He wondered how they were. He wondered if anyone had stepped up to help care for them. He did not wonder if he and Mary had made a mistake leaving when they did. He had no answers to any of his questions. He quit asking . . . . for now.

While Tom and the crew from the homeplace all talked daily, nobody passed on any word from Charles. If they did know anything about how he felt, nobody said anything. It was as though the "trip east" had never taken place—although both Tom and Charles knew it had.

After 9 days, the shearing crew left with the wool. They also cut out about 450 head to take back to the market in Newell. It was early to take sheep to market but they obviously had orders from Charles to do just that. If there was any issue with where Tom was and the "condition" of the herd, the lamb production and the great results from shearing it was the distance the hands had to travel to and from the Newell markets.

It was quiet in camp after the crews left and they had taken a good part of the herd. Still, Tom didn't sleep in the next morning. The herd was still his to care for and he had Increased its size even though nearly 450 ewes and lambs went to Newell.

Typically, Nigger was up before him and ready to go to work. This morning, he was laying under the wagon--very unusual. When Tom told him it was "time to go to work," he slowly raised his head. As well as he knew this dog, Tom sensed something was wrong. He knelt beside his "herding partner" and started to examine him. "No sign of swelling around his face--that's good." Swelling often meant he had been bitten by something--usually a rattlesnake. Tom checked his legs to see if there was any sign of being broken. There was none and NIgger didn't flinch at all when his "partner" checked him over. "Maybe you just need a day off," Tom remarked. He knew that was not so. Something was wrong with "his dog" of nearly 15 years. Maybe something bad.

Tom had some coffee, saddled up and went out around the herd--all the time thinking about his main "helper" and his closest friend next to Mary. He turned around early and went back to camp. His dog was still under the wagon--and very still. Tom knelt to talk with him but this time there was no response. He lifted Nigger's head but the dog did not move at all. He talked softly to him but there was no sign of life--his once-sharp eyes were shut. His long-time, four-legged partner had "given up herding."

Tom carefully picked his dog up, took a shovel from the side of the cook wagon and got on his horse--carefully cradling his "friend" in his arms. He slowly rode to a spot not far from camp close to a small stream where several small trees stood. He was sure Nigger would like it here.

He talked about this dog often. "He was the best dog I ever had. He was smartern' any herder I ever knew. He stayed with ya' and knew how to take care of them sheep." Tom would likely never forget him.

It was early in the fall of 1942. For some reason, Tom was heading back toward Philip and planned to winter near there. He knew they would be on their own for winter provisions although Charles had sent a good supply of everything from beans to cartridges. He had sent them plenty of staples—as though he didn't expect to be in touch with them again until the following spring.

Tom was concerned about breeding the ewes in this herd as he had no ready access to rams. Such ram herds were available for rent— if you had the cash to pay for such services. Paying for such services was obviously *not* an option for Tom Stone.

Still, as a seasoned herder, Tom Stone knew the breeding needed to completed on time. And he knew that if it was not done soon, the lamb crop for the spring of 1943 would just *not* happen. Unthinkable! No lamb crop would cost Charles thousands of dollars in the long run.

It was *not* a miracle. Miracles often have no logical explanation. The appearance of the ram herd was clearly explainable. Charles Cranston had secured [hired] the rams to "service" his herd. It was the middle of the day—a beautiful day made even nicer by the sound of a full and "eager" ram herd. They immediately began mixing with the ewes—as though they needed no "introductions." Their work would be done in a few days.

Initially, Tom was surprised. The man in charge of the ram herd greeted Tom Stone by name even though *Tom did not know* any of the ram herders. They told Tom they had been paid—but not who had paid them. What they *did not say* spoke volumes. Tom was pretty sure what had happened. And even though the breeding was a bit late, the coming spring would hopefully bring plenty of new lambs.

It started out as a mild winter. No snow in October or even into the early part of November. Tom had time to go into Philip every couple of weeks. He was hedging his bets. He had pushed his luck pretty far with Charles Cranston. And, he thought it was just a matter of time until they went their separate ways. So, Tom was looking for future employment.

While in town, he talked with others about "work." Folks said things around this entire town were centered on livestock [mostly cows and hogs]. And much of *that* focus was around the local sale barn. Tom went to the sale ring and watched--and learned. Some options?

By middle November, Mary shared some family news with her husband. She was going to have a baby in the spring—likely sometime in May. Their new addition was "scheduled" to arrive during the normal lambing, docking and shearing season. This was not a concern for Tom or Mary at *this* time—they never had planned their family around herd "seasons."

John Danley Stone was born on May 18, 1943—right in the middle of lambing, docking and shearing. It was, as always, a very busy time for everyone in "camp." And even though close to delivery, Mary Stone worked as hard as she was able, cooking for the "crews" that were there to help. Always doing "all she could do."

John was named after his great-uncle John [from Georgia] while his middle name was Mary's "maiden" name. Mary would often remember that "John looked like a tired, little old man" since she had worked so hard right up until the time he was born. He was full-term and over 11 pounds [many people believed at that time that it was a sign of a healthy baby to be this heavy].

That summer on the prairie, there was little rain which made it easier to manage the sheep as they could move without the interruptions of thunderstorms and the accompanying lightning as well as the mud. The downside was finding enough fresh water for the herd. Plenty of drinking water was not an option but an absolute necessity. Weather, Tom was again reminded, was not something he could control.

Not surprisingly, this new baby was just one more nagging reminder that the Stone's needed to move much closer to a regular school—a school where the kids could attend year-round. Could the family move into town while Tom stayed "on the prairie?" Would this only work if he moved into town with them? How would he be able to continue working as a full-time herder if he did not "live on the open range with the herd?" Could they keep Charles' herd this far east?

Tom Stone didn't like the questions. Moreover, *he didn't have any answers* to them. He did not want to give up his life as a herder. He did not want to move into *any town*—no matter how big or how small. He *did* want to do what was best for his family—most especially for the kids, remembering *how he had been raised*. One thing was certain: this was not familiar "territory." He seemed to be losing some of the control he had almost always felt over his life and that of his growing family. It was very uncomfortable. It would get even more uncomfortable as these days went by.

CHAPTER **15**

Leaving the Sheep

THE STONES MADE it through the summer and fall of 1944. They cut out the lambs and ewes that were to go to market. Tom settled the herd just northwest of Philip—staying purposely close enough to the Haakon County seat to make it easy to "go into town" on a regular basis—he had reasons for doing so.

It was a good winter except that Bob had made it clear that he was not going to spend another year on "the prairie." Bob had already told his mother about his plans to leave sheepherding. But, he had heard enough "Stone history" to know not to tell his father that "he was leaving." Bob remembered: "You don't leave the family." Afraid of his father's reaction—perhaps? He just knew, no matter the consequences, he could not stay. If Bob left, it would make taking care of any herd much more difficult since Mary could help very little since she now had 2 smaller children to care for.

Tom and Mary both knew it was decision time. Things were changing in their family. Bob was going to the service [he would join the U.S. Air Force in Philip—he "misled" the recruiters on his age]. The other kids all needed a more stable environment [regular school]. Tom was nearing the point [although he didn't want to admit it] where the cold winters and boiling hot summers on the prairie were exacting a heavier toll. In addition, hours in the saddle were not as tolerable as they once had been. He was comforted in knowing that Mary, his ever loyal, constantly supportive, and never [almost] questioning partner . . . was there. She was there—with him and for him—whatever he decided.

Tom and Mary went into Philip and rented a small cabin in the west part of town--it was within walking distance to the stockyards. That was for good reason--at least for the time being.

He got word to Charles Cranston that he needed to talk with him. Charles had been not only good enough to give him a job when Tom had been "down" but had tolerated some of Tom's more "selfish" moves with Charles' herds. Tom knew he owed Charles.

When Charles got word from Tom, he knew what was coming. He knew the life that herder's lived and was, in some ways, surprised that Tom had stayed on as long as he had with his growing family while being forced to live a herder's lifestyle.

Tom liked Charles. Charles liked Tom.

Tom respected Charles. Charles respected Tom.

Within two days, Charles came down to the base camp. It was quite a distance. He brought Tom's wages and some wrapped gifts for the kids [likely from Jess Cranston]. They didn't say much. They didn't need to. Tom made sure Charles knew he appreciated all Charles had done for them. Charles acknowledged that and assured Tom the feeling was mutual. They shook hands. Charles helped Tom load his two saddles and his rifles into the car where Mary was waiting. [Sissy and Jody had Rosalie at the "cabin" and John was in the car with his Mother]. Charles saw her tears. He did not think for a minute that her tears were a sign of weakness. Charles knew how strong this sheep-herder's wife had to have been. Tom and Mary Stone drove away. They didn't look back.

One thing was sure. Tom Stone had to have a full-time job. He had to work. Where? Doing what? A life of herding no longer seemed a viable option. So, Tom's thoughts more frequently began consider-ing "work alternatives." There weren't many choices. He was looking not just for a new venue but likely a whole new "type" of work.

Tom Stone could not read. He could not write. He could not drive a car or a truck or a tractor. *But he could work.* He had a very strong sense of responsibility, was totally honest and could figure things out when problems arose. And he *never* gave up.

The Stones moved east to get away from some very bad memories. It was time to get out of the sheep business, out of sheep wagons [no place to raise a family on the prairies] and into some kind of house "with a roof and some walls." This meant Tom would have to find a different line of work. This meant the Stone family would have to "build" a different kind of life.

Tom Stone knew two things at the outset: he was going to get out of the sheepherding business and he would likely have to move closer to some sort of "town." The "biggest" town near the base camp was Philip. This was a logical place to start. His new "choices" didn't appeal to him very much. He was truly in a comfort zone herding sheep because he was away from people and was his own boss. Second thing, he "didn't care much for town."

During his early days in Montana, Tom had learned a few things about cattle. And while he had immediately chosen to work with sheep, he understood the fundamentals of *herding* cows. Working with cattle was different from working with sheep. As animals, cows and sheep have somewhat different needs and very different habits. Some of this he understood. So, he asked, where could he find cattle to work with? The logical place was on a cattle ranch.

Tom Stone had no trouble "finding his way" around this small South Dakota town of just over 800 people [the population in 1945]. He didn't much care for towns, but his need to find "something" truly outweighed his dislike of "town life." If Philip had something to offer, he was going to do his best to find it.

Leif [pronounced Lafe] Hanson had moved to Philip in 1945 and "operated" the Hanson Hardware and Implement Co. Looking at the larger areas of Haakon, Stanley, Jones and Ziebach counties, Hanson saw a future in livestock *auctions* [buying and selling]. This would include all kinds of cows and hogs. So, Leif built the Philip Livestock Auction the same year [1945]. Hanson ran the Philip Livestock

Auction until 1953 when he opened the Ft. Pierre Livestock Auction.

Tom had no trouble finding the sale barn in Philip. What he was seeing here was a completely different side of the "cattle business" than herding. What he was witnessing was the buying and selling of cattle—and it seemed to move very fast. While he thought he had learned a few things about the *cattle business* in Montana, he soon figured out that he did not know much of anything about *this part of the cattle business*. This part was a business that moved in large numbers. It was a business that involved looking at stock and making decisions in the moment. It was the livestock business but nothing like he had seen. *It was the business side of the business.* In Montana he had learned about different types of cows—and bulls. Now he was learning some things about how cows and bulls and hogs and calves and yearlings loaded up, were brought to a sale barn to be priced, auctioned and sold. It all moved very rapidly.

He had learned some things about raising cows and calves as well. But, this business was about *buying and selling* cows and calves and hogs and bulls *that allowed these "dealers" to produce revenue.* So, he admitted, "this is a helluva of a lot different from raising sheep." In actuality, it would be *an entirely different life.*

While Tom did not imagine *he* would ever be able to actually buy or sell livestock, those who did, obviously needed help—help to round up, ship and handle what they marketed. Someplace in this "mix" there must be options for him he concluded—there must be some work for someone who would do "almost anything." Tom was "moving toward moving." He knew he could fit in somehow. He had to!

It was at the sale barn in Philip that Tom Stone first met Leif Hanson. Leif Hanson was a *dealer* in livestock. He bought them, he "readied" them in feedlots and he sold them at a number of different sales barns in towns such as Philip and Ft. Pierre.

Leif was a businessman in every sense of the word. He made major decisions "on-the-spot." Hanson dressed in tan work clothes, with ill-fitting trousers and a shirttail often out. He wore a large [usually black] Stetson-type hat in virtually all situations—inside and out. He nearly always carried a large business-type checkbook under his arm to assure anyone that he was very serious about the decisions he made—to buy or sell "right now." He was described as a man with "lots of vision and lots of faith" and had a reputation as a good man who would always help someone who was in need. Having grown up in a large family in hard times himself, "he came to believe that someone in need was someone who had to be taken care of." [sdex-cellence.org/LeifHanson_1988].

Hansen drove a large 4-door sedan. He would just as likely have someone in his car that he had just hired as he would a newborn or abandoned calf that he was "claiming." He was "open" and "fair," yet quite blunt in his personal interactions with others. He was considered "up front." In that sense, "what you saw was what you got."

At this time in his life, Tom Stone was just as blunt. Quite likely, that was his only course of action. Tom approached Leif Hanson: "I need work," Tom said with conviction. "I buy and sell livestock," Hanson answered in a conclusive sense—as though that would be a satisfactory response to Stone's request.

Tom repeated himself: "I need a job. I can do any kinda work you got. I got a wife and 4 kids. We ain't got much." Tom didn't beg but you could tell he was not leaving without some kind of work. Maybe Leif Hanson sensed Tom's anxiety. Perhaps he recognized in Tom Stone the potential for hard work and dedication to a task. Maybe he felt sorry for the "unemployed" father of 4 [Bob was gone to the Air Force]. Leif made a quick decision to give this man a job—at least a chance.

"Go see Thorson in the big corral out back. Tell him I've put you on. Tell him your family needs a place to live and you need some way to feed those kids."

Tom said nothing. He headed for the "big corral" at the back of the sales barn to look for somebody named Thorson. This was no time for any second-guessing. Truth be told, things were close to being desperate.

Tom saw a tall man with a large cowboy hat leaning against the corral fence holding a large clipboard. "I'm lookin' for Thorson," Tom said directly. "That's me," the man said in a matter-of-fact manner. "What can I do for ya?"

"Leif Hanson just told me you'd put me to work. I've already got a place for my family to stay." Tom paused, then added, "I appreciate any help you can give me." He wanted Thorson to know he was serious—not begging, but insistent.

Tol Thorson was much more affable than his boss but was still one of few words. "That's good. I need some help right here. Take your wife and those kids upstairs to the café and get them something good to eat. Just tell them up there you work for Leif. You go ahead and eat with them and then come back here. I'll be right here in this main corral."

"I'll send my wife and kids up there to eat but I'll be right back so I can get to work." It was the middle of the afternoon. Tom had not eaten since the day before. But, it was time to show this new outfit he could do what they needed done.

"You better go get yourself something to eat too—we'll be here til' midnight. My wife will be up there to talk with your missus. She can help her kinda get settled." Thorson reassured Tom. "I'll talk to her later this afternoon. It'll work out alright."

So the Stone's had both food and housing, even though it was just for "a day or two" That was more than they had when they drove into town. Tom was *willing to take whatever he could get* at this stage.

While Tom was living in a scenario that seemed even shorter than day-to-day, starting work with Leif Hansen signaled a major departure from the life he and Mary had been living for the last 20-plus years.

He was no longer "his own boss." He was no longer able to get up at the break of dawn in familiar surroundings and go to bed under the stars knowing that tomorrow would be pretty much the same as the day before had been. That was comfort. This would not be the same.

Still, in a real sense, this was *again* about *survival*. Tom Stone was doing what he had to do to provide for his wife and kids. He was

243

doing what he had to do to feel worth something. While he likely never thought about in such terms, Tom Stone was trying to find some meaningful purpose in his life—purpose that had almost slipped away.

Anybody familiar with South Dakota knows that there are some significant differences between east river and west river [Missouri River] people. These differences exist in their thinking, their behaviors, their lifestyles—even the way they dress, walk and talk. But the largest differences between east and west river people is the manner in which they feel about their very existence. The farms/ranches in eastern and western South Dakota are different as well. For, much of East river is structured country. It is fenced. East river has organized farms. In east river they grow crops in very organized patterns. West river is different with a good deal of unfenced grazing land. It feels *endless*. West river, even to this day to some degree, is "open" country—it smacks not of control or structure but of a sense of *freedom*. Leif Hansen was west river.

Leif Hanson's approach to livestock was very direct: he bought stock wherever he could--whether "in a barn," a corral, a feedlot, or from a herd in the field. He paid for it on the spot and moved his "purchases" immediately to feedlots or sales barns. His purchases were often large quantities of stock that required a sizable work force to manage both the movement, feeding and transfer to sales barns. There were plenty of areas for Tom Stone to work. He was genuinely relieved that he had found something.

Tom worked the rest of the day in the corral "sorting" cows mostly by what he "figgered" they weighed. All calves and bulls [and there were a few], had already been moved to different corrals. The larger steers would be moved right to the sale ring. The smaller stock would be transferred to a feedlot—three of those lots were within a mile of the sales barn. Tom's work would take him to all three of those feedlots within the next week.

Not surprisingly, Tom didn't think much about the work he was doing—the important thing—the most important thing—was that *he was working*. He had no idea what his salary would be. But, he did know that Mary and the kids would have a "roof over their heads" and would get enough to eat. *He was providing for his family.*

Tom's new boss moved the Stone family from their "cabin" to a small house in town not far from the sale barn. And, though it was over a mile from 2 of the three feedlots, Tom did not mind walking to *work.* And, though Philip was *town,* it was a small town and he felt relatively comfortable there. But, he was not going to be "in town" for long as Leif Hansen's business was mobile—and it was rapidly expanding. Tom remembered: his new boss bought and *sold* livestock. That meant there would be constant turnover. So, as stock was sold, "new" stock had to be located and purchased. That took money, transportation and manpower.

Most of the stock came from nearby ranches as far north as Milesville, south to the area around Kadoka and east around Midland and Hayes. Though Tom did not drive, he went on most of the trips to pick up the stock Leif had purchased. Often, Leif actually led the caravan of two large semis [stock trucks] and made deals, wrote the checks and loaded the stock on the same day. He wasted no time. It was good work and Leif Hanson paid top wages.

Mary and the kids seemed happy. For the first time, they had a "permanent" residence. They lived in a town, in a house with separate rooms—and a kitchen! The "good old days" were gone again. Mary's sewing machine was gone; her Maytag was gone and the milling sheep were gone. But they had walls and a roof and plenty to eat. For Sissy and Jody, Rosalie and John, there were a few other children around. Mary dared to dream about sending her kids to a real school in the fall.

Their time in Philip, however, was not to be very permanent. Leif Hansen was hell-bent on expanding his business. He was not opposed to having a sale barn in Haakon County but wanted to spread out. He looked north but there was little there until you went all the way to Mobridge. He looked south and considered Kadoka—even Presho, Vivian and all the way to Chamberlain. Leif knew the way to more and larger sales meant opening up another barn and sales ring.

He looked at Pierre and then at Ft. Pierre.

Either one would give him a larger town in which to operate and provide him a base to expand further east—that meant east river. It also would mean more ranches and farms from which he could buy stock. A "new" sales ring was "in the cards."

Leif Hansen never asked his men to do anything he wouldn't do himself. From wading through a corral of fresh cow manure to getting up in the middle of the night to drive 100 miles to pick up a load of stock for an upcoming sale. The work was doable. However, there were times when Tom had to be away from his family for up to 2-3 days at a time—something he was trying to avoid. And, while both he and Mary knew they needed the work—and were happy to have it—they didn't like the time apart. Tom started thinking about something more "stable." He and Mary talked about a job where he could be home every night—to be with her and the kids. Part of Mary's concern had been addressed. They were in town, close to school. Still, this issue of being away from home for days at a time began to loom a bit larger.

As Leif moved his operations further east, his men were expected to move as well—or at least be able to get to work every day in different parts of central SD. This would rapidly change as well since Leif looked as far away as the farms and ranches near Chamberlain, Winner and even Mitchell for stock.

It was spring. Mary was going to have another baby in the fall. Because Tom felt his employment depended on his ability to move "at the drop of Leif's hat," the decision was made to move Mary and the kids to be near her brother Louie and his wife Eva in White Lake. This was a painful but necessary decision. Looking back some years later, Tom and Mary both thought it was an unwise move. But, they still did just that. Leif moved them and their few belongings in one of his straight trucks.

Mary Kathleen Stone born November 9, 1946 in Mitchell, South Dakota [a short distance from White Lake and Louie's place]. She was the last child Tom and Mary would have and the first to actually be born in a "real" hospital. She was petite and blonde and for virtually all her life was the "apple of her Daddy's eye." He constantly referred to her adoringly as the "Little Kid." And, in their later years, she was the one who faithfully and lovingly cared for them without reservation.

Still, working for Leif Hanson actually provided *less* stability in the sense of being grounded. Tom thought again: "The pay's good and the hours ain't bad. But I can't be away from Mother and them kids so damned much. If they needed me, I wouldn't be there." And so, Tom Stone was looking again—for something much more permanent, solid, stable—regular.

Tom had met Dick Williams in Philip. Dick was A.J. Williams' son and together with Dick's brother Pierre [Ole], they ran a sizable ranch near Hayes. Their "operation" [nearly all cattle] was large enough so that they needed fulltime ranch hands. These "extra hands" and their families lived in houses near the main ranch. Right now, the Williams' ranch needed more hands at the home place. This meant steady work, a place for the family to live and decent wages. *And it meant being home every night.*

While Tom very much appreciated the work he had gotten with Leif Hanson [the income and the housing had literally saved the Stone family in time of near disaster], Tom and Mary felt they both wanted and needed more stability for them and their kids. It was another "move," but they were used to moving. Tom took a job with Dick Williams.

It was while living at the Williams' ranch near Hayes that Tom and Mary Stone first saw Pierre, SD. Every two weeks, on Friday night, Mary and Tom would drive [she drove] to Pierre [about 34 miles each way] in a "rag-top" Jeep [loaned to them by their boss] to get groceries. While Mary shopped at the Red Owl grocery store, Tom stayed in the Jeep and watched people. Rosalie and John stayed with their Mom or Dad and, on rare occasions, were given money to go to "the show" at the Grand Theater. The movie house was just a block-and-a-half from the Red Owl where the Stone's parked the Jeep. They looked at Pierre--another move?

CHAPTER **16**

Moving to Pierre: A New Life

IN THE LATE spring of 1949, the Stone family moved into Pierre [SD]. They rented a small duplex in an alley behind the Grand Theater. 110R West Pleasant Drive would be their next "permanent home." The duplex only had 3 rooms and no indoor bathroom, but the family had all "been *there*" before. Again, they had a roof over their heads, solid walls, and, for the first time, a real "street address."

In the fall of 1949, Rosalie and John started school at Lincoln Elementary School, just 3 blocks from where they lived. Looking at other kids, seeing how they dressed and visiting their houses, the kids realized, for the first time, how poor they truly were. That was a feeling *never to be forgotten* by either Rosalie or John.

Sissy had gotten married for a second time [her first was to a man named Richard Morgan—there were no children]. Her second marriage was to a man named Richard [Dick] Wilsbacher. He had a very productive farm just west of Milesville, SD [45 minutes north of Philip]. Sissy and he had three boys: Richard Leo [Dickie], Dennis Lee [Dennie], and Steven Mark [Stevie].

Dick Wilsbacher was a hard worker and a good farmer—and when he was not working hard, he was drinking hard. Sadly, he was what people often called a "mean drunk." His personality changed and he was not very social at any time. He did not show love to others—that we ever saw. He shared what he had [often to a fault when

248

Tom and Mary Stone at their first rental home [duplex] in Pierre, SD. It was in an alley at 112 Rear West Pleasant Drive. They had no hot water nor an indoor bathroom.

he was drinking]. Though he did not abuse his children, the same could not be said for Sissy, his wife. The "marks" [both physical and psychological] were apparent. They split—got back together—then split again—eventually divorcing some years later. The boys always stayed with their mother.

Although she did not finish high school, Jody started nurse's training in Pierre but stayed only a short time in her studies. She began waitressing in Pierre and seriously dated a man named Oscar "from Oklahoma" [all we knew]. She eventually married a man named James [Jack] Crellin. Jody waited tables for his mother [Dell Crandell] at the Sunset Café on Pleasant Drive in Pierre for a short time as they would have two children [Elizabeth Lynn and James] and move to Igloo, SD [a military ordinance depot in southwest South Dakota]. Jack's job was steady and the salary [including benefits] though minimal, were regular [Department of Defense].

Jack worked hard, was quite reliable on the job and very likable. He made several attempts to improve his job by moving up from general maintenance to a "guard" [variation of an MP] but was never able to "pass the exams" required for such a position.

Jody was a "stay-at-home" mom and kept a spotless house while sewing virtually all the clothes [except jeans] that the entire family wore. She tactfully managed what money they had and kept the entire family on a reasonable/level plane.

Their marriage seemed relatively secure—not unlike many "younger marriages," money became an issue. Since Jack worked full-time, his only additional income came from his service in the Army National Guard [he had served a 4-year stint in the U.S. Navy before he and Jody were married]. That additional income wasn't much and their "quarters" [a six-plex on the base at Igloo] was barely enough. The biggest issue was that there appeared to be no signs of things getting any better.

Even though their children were not yet in school, Jody decided to hire a babysitter for them and take a job as a waitress in the nearby town of Edgemont [SD]. It wasn't long before Jody had found a new "friend" who worked in a Sinclair gas station near the restaurant where she waited tables. Maybe it was exciting. Maybe it was different-not the same old grind. Maybe it was. . . . . . Whatever it was, it wasn't meant to last long—just long enough to destroy what was left of their marriage. Jody and Jack divorced.

As is common in most divorce cases, the Mother kept the children. Jack went his own way. Jody moved to Pierre to be close to her parents.

Under the circumstances, that was what Mary wanted.

Sissy had done the same. Mary was very much in favor of that as well—Tom Stone, on the other hand, was very much opposed. "Coming back home" when you had trouble with your own marriage was not an option in Tom's mind. He consistently argued "you made your own bed and now you have to sleep in it." This was a sign of things to come.

Bob was in the Air Force and stayed stateside for a while [Texas] but came home infrequently. When he went overseas, he was stationed in Kwajalein-Atoll, Guam for a short time and in Alaska [near the Bering Straits] for a lengthy tour. He learned a very valuable skill in the service: how to operate and overhaul all types of heavy equipment. He mustered, and after a failed marriage [ending with him being shot] in North Carolina, he also returned to Pierre where he lived the remainder of his life. He married a fine lady name Gertrude Clark and had two children: Cheryl and Clark.

Pierre was not the "end of the story" for Tom and Mary Stone. It will, however, be the end of this story of "over two decades of trailin' sheep." Eventually, most of the Stones would move to Phoenix, Arizona. Tom, Mary, Mary Kay, Sissy, Jody and their families. Rosalie traveled with her second husband in the Air Force, Mary Kay married Jerry Sulkosky and they had two boys, Bob stayed in Pierre with his family and John attended college and graduate school, taking breaks to teach and earn money to return to his studies. He eventually earned his PhD at Penn State in 1973. He is married to Toni, has three grown children and 6 grandchildren in Virginia, North Carolina and Singapore.

Epilogue

YOU CAN'T SAY that Tom and Mary Stone had a "bad life." You can't say they had a "good life" either. One could justifiably conclude that Tom and Mary Stone had a life that, for the most part, they chose for themselves. Additionally, you can say is that they *survived* some of the most difficult times two people ever saw. As Tom Stone would so often say: "times was tough. . . and you got by becuz' you was just as tough ."

In some ways, Tom Stone was a prisoner of his environment. Unavoidably, he was victimized by society. It was not Tom Stone's fault. Nor was it the fault of the society or the environment. It was a matter of fact. Once he got away from his home in Georgia, he thought he was "in control." But, for much of his life, Tom Stone could not control his environment and he could surely not control the larger [even his smaller segment] of society. You took the kind of job you could get and the type of job you could do. You lived where you could afford to live. You didn't change things—things changed you.

Tom and Mary Stone found this was especially true when they moved "to town" Much to their dismay, there was a certain amount of "structure" you could not avoid. Major adjustments were *mandatory* if you were to survive—literally. Organized societies have rules and regulations—laws both written and unwritten. Mary had seen some of this before—not so with her husband. "Town" did not break Tom Stone's back but it did break his spirit.

Tom Stone was raised in an environment that shaped his values,

*Tom and Mary Stone on their 50th Wedding
Anniversary in Phoenix, AZ. Date: 1975*

his attitudes and, to a large degree, his behaviors. And while he "mellowed" in his later years, when you saw him at work or at home, talked with him on virtually any subject, you saw who he truly was. He was blunt, strong in his beliefs, opinionated and did not change much during his 77 years. He *liked* very few people though he did not *dislike* many either. He was a loner. He liked being by himself or with Mary and his dog. He enjoyed working alone and sitting in "his chair."

He could work harder and longer than any man I have ever known, but he did not like working *for someone else*. His life as a herder had been an independent one. In that life, he worked for and answered to himself—that was his "way." His short-term jobs in "town" were under direct supervision. None of them were successful or very long-term. Eventually, "running" his own café and doing yard maintenance as an "independent contractor" saved his very existence—it made him partially "whole" again.

Tom Stone's "line" for his children was stern. Looking back, he sounded very much like his father—in so many ways. He probably would not agree with that observation. Still, during their years in Pierre, most of his children came back home to live in an effort to escape from their often-dysfunctional lives. Mary welcomed them. Tom did not! He disagreed—strongly with this practice.

Dealing with their married/separated/divorced children would cause no end of dissension between Tom and Mary Stone. They strongly disagreed on how their offspring should deal with their familial relationships and to what extent they, as the parents of their "returning" children [and grandchildren] should get involved.

In such situations, and they were frequent, Tom Stone spoke his mind. In his presence, you always knew "where he stood" whether you liked what he said or not. Even when he was told his opinion upset someone else, he really "didn't give a damn." Tom Stone was truly one of a kind.

APPENDIX A

The Ekalaka Eagle

OFFICIAL NEWSPAPER OF CARTER COUNTY

EKALAKA, Carter County, MONTANA, FRIDAY, MARCH 27, 1925.

NUM

SPLENDID DANCE

given by Carter Post No. day night was largely attended. The most enjoyable evening by those in attendance. The decorated in green and the lors, with a scattering of about the walls. Music ed by a five-piece orchestra Legion' boys were much h the big turn-out, which oked for considering the , weather and bad roads.

FARM SALES

us a large attendance at sale held at the A. K. farm, 11 miles southwest Wednesday. Everything t a good price and the bidvely. Mr. and Mrs. Mcesday, April 1, there will t the Ed. Reichelt farm, thwest of Ekalaka. We armed what the future inMr. Reichelt will be in residence.

, April 3, A. H. Cross will at his farm eight miles alaka. Mr. Cross has deto southern California for of his health, upon the e Mayon.

day, April 4, A. D. Strain auction sale at his resiEkalaka. Mr. and Mrs. et to move to Buffalo, ake their future home.

SCHOOL ELECTION APRIL 4.

The annual school election for School District No. 15 will be held on Saturday afternoon, April 4, at which time one out trustee for the three year term will be elected. Up to date no candidates have come forward seeking the position, so it is highly portable that some public spirited person will be drafted for the job.

MOISTURE IS WELCOMED

All Set

A MATRIMONIAL TANGLE

Walter Scott tells us of things that happened on the day set for the wedding of "Fair Ellen of Netherby Hall" and Walter says: "Her mother did fret and her father did fume."

It was like that on the day set for the wedding of Fair Ellen of Ekalaka. It is an old saying that the course of true love never did run smooth. Tom Stone and Ellen Danley were married at early candle light on Sunday evening, at the residence of Mr. and Mrs. W. A. Hedrick, the nuptial knot being tied by Justice W. H. Peck. A charivari was staged, and the newlyweds with a number of their friends who had witnessed the marriage ceremony were loaded in a truck and taken to the Old Stand, and all entered in. Three rousing cheers were given in salute to the bridal party, the cheering being led by the chief of police, W. P. Flake, an old friend of the bride, tried and true. The groom set up Bobby Burns cigars to the house and all went merry as a marriage bell.

But hush, hark! What comes to disturb the general joy? The sheriff enters and says to the jocund groom: "I want you!" The bride has made her home with Mr. and Mrs. Gilbert Nims, Mrs. Nims being her sister and legal guardian. They said Ellen was not yet eighteen, and that she had not obtained the consent of her guardian in regard to her marriage, and that minors are required by law to obtain the consent of their parents or guardians before they can be called in question. They arrived on the scene in marrv.

A SUNDAY BLAZE

The clanging of the fire bell at about 4:20 on Sunday afternoon broke the Sabbath quiet of Ekalaka and startled her citizens. The fire was in a log house in the block west of the Fairview House. The building is owned by Bert Hall and was occupied by Miss Mary Belle Berry, central girl at the telephone office. The front part of the building was a mass of flames inside and out when the

Police Patrol

New Instit

Ekalaka is putting on mo every day, and in more w one is assuming metropolita The latest big city stuff that adopted is the use of a patro For the first time in history, tives woke up last Sunday and experienced the sight of wagon backing up to one of t ings and taking on a cargo s the "boosgcow". Sheriff Mc Marshal Fiske conducted the and with the aid of "Doc" his truck went through with gram with neatness and disp The round-up netted five for the jail and five witnesse day morning, the prisoner charged with taking on to "meat" cargo and hailed befor Judge Peck. On pleas of g Judge passed sentence as fol

Case No. 1.—$100 fine and in jail.

Case No. 2.—$100 fine and in jail.

Case No. 3.—$100 fine, ar days in jail.

Case No. 4.—$100 fine.

Case No. 5.—Bound over to court with the recommendat the defendant be sent to th school at Miles City until

eserve bank of Minneap-
City and vicinity for the
concluded his work and
Minneapolis. All the
were liquidated and con-
paper was turned back
clused banks, Mr. Crow
is to the future of Mon-
d:

s coming back in excel-
The fact that a number
nking institutions have
of their obligations to
Reserve would indicate
the time that I have
have realized upon a
f paper which a year or
d among the frozen as-
institutions. The good
year and the gradual re-
erity has been responsi-
edition. Montana has a
ahead. The man who is
ment cannot find a bet-
e country. Farm lands
e more productive than
fact that farmers have
d the value of diversifi-
that they are going to
ssfully. Hogs, corn and
ng to contribute lavishly
of Montana in future

TO HOSPITAL

uam went to Baker on
this week and expects
operation at the Lake-
Mr. Putnam has been

told that there was lots of grumbling
done in the year of our Lord 1915, the
year of the big crops. We have been
told that they have the best crops
here in the years when warm weather
is slow in arriving. You may grum-
ble all you wish about the weather and
but listen to what the Livingston
Enterprise has to say on the subject:

"Those who were disappointed because of a turn in the weather and
the fact that snow and cold appeared
to give March its usual reputation
have the pleasure of knowing that
such disappointment brought gladness
to the vast majority.

"It is an indisputable fact that in
order to assure good prospects for a
grain crop in Montana a certain
amount of winter moisture is necessary. Until the present generous
blanket of snow, this section of Montana, at least, has been without the
desired winter precipitation. Today
the prospects look much more flatter-
ing for the right kind of a spring
farming reception, an important item
with Montana's greatest industry, the
farm.

"The snowfall has been heavy, but
not too heavy. The weather, though
somewhat colder than since the advent
of the New Year, is of the variety
that insures better health. If you are
compelled to buy an extra load of
coal, buy it with a smile, for without
the success of the farmer the coal
bill next winter would have been
much more difficult to care for. The
March weather, and particularly the
March snowfall, is most welcome."

MAY SEARCH AUTOS

Prohibition enforcement agents can
lawfully stop and search an automo-
bile without a warrant, the supreme
court decided in a case from Michi-
gan. The decision which upheld the
ruling of the lower courts was an
appeal brought by George Carroll and
John Kiro.

WORST STORM COUNTRY HAS EVER KNOWN

The tornado which ravaged portions
of Indiana, southern Missouri and
southern Illinois on Wednesday of last

ical engine was on the job in less
than five minutes and held the flames
in check until the house cart arrived
and the water was turned on which
soon extinguished the fire. But the
blaze had such a start that almost
everything in the interior of the
building was destroyed, clothing,
books, furniture and all manner of
household articles. Mr. and Mrs.
Thos. F. Wilson occupied the house
for awhile last fall and part of the
furnishings belonged to them. Miss
Berry lost all of her clothing except
what she was wearing at the time.
She was at the telephone office when
the fire was discovered and as there
was no one in the house the fire was
under good headway before any alarm
was given. The loss is considerable
and there was no insurance. The
building was badly damaged but we
understand that Mr. Hall will repair
it. The value of a fire department
was again demonstrated beyond question. The fire was put out in short
order and the adjoining buildings
which were endangered escaped injury. It is not known whether the
fire started from the stove or flue,
or was started by small boys lighting
matches.

GOOD PROGRESS REPORTED

"Tolly" Hartwick, representing the
N. P. railroad, was here on Wednesday in the interests of the immigra-
tion campaign. He attended the Mc-
Quistan sale in the afternoon and
grave a few minutes talk to the farmers present. Mr. Hartwick reports
that the campaign is going over with
a bang and that the results so far
obtained are most encouraging. The
campaign in Carter county is pro-
gressing nicely and the people are re-
sponding to the call for names of
prospects, although in order for us to
complete our quota it will be necessary to do much more.

Let us again urge that you mail in
your cards as soon as possible. To
every person whose name is turned
in, will be sent truthful literature on
southeastern Montana, and a special
pamphlet telling of the resources of
this particular county. Be sure to

to her home. To this both bride and
groom most strenuously objected, but
Sheriff McLean told them it was best
to submit quietly for the time being.
He said the matter could be investi-
gated next day and the question of
title legally settled. He told the
groom he would not be placed under
arrest, and the weeping bride reluctantly went with her brother-in-
law.

This was not at all to the liking of
the crowd then and there assembled
—not to any one of them. A delega-
tion was sent to call upon Justice
Peck to get further instructions. The
justice expressed the opinion that the
couple were legally married and that
no man had a right to put them
asunder. Thereupon Marshal Fisk
and a few picked men went in quest
of the bride and brought her to Mr.
Peck's residence where she spent the
night.

The marriage problem was taken up
for solution the next day, but it seems
to be harder to solve than any cross-
word puzzle. It seems to be a question upon which the legal lights are
not in sweet accord and are not sure
of their ground. It appears to be a
matter of question as to whether the
girl's real name is Miss Ellen Danley
or Mrs. Tom Stone. They say that
she will be of legal age in three
months, and we have been informed
that attorneys consulted by Mr.
Stone advised him to sit pretty until
three months have elapsed and then
he can carry the war into Africa.
Baker or any other hostile seaport.

Mr. Stone is a young man who
came to Montana from Tennessee a
couple of years ago and has since
been in the employ of A. M. Blackford on his ranch on the upper Box
Elder. The young lady has been attending the Carter County High
school, being now a member of the
junior class, and it is the desire of
her relatives that she finish her
school work.

WORK ON EAGLE BUILDING GETS UNDER WAY

The work of laying the rock for the
new Eagle building was started Tues-

stified that unless the fines wer
aid they would be compelled to "lay
or out" in jail at the rate of one da
or every $2.00 of the fine, and tha
hey also be put to work for the town
Since the round-up, considerabl
scussion has been had pro and con
the subject of "moon" and drunk
nness in Ekalaka, and it seems to b
he concensus of opinion that the sen
ences given will tend to "put on th
brakes" on like cases in the future
Those in favor of law enforcement
ontend that the proper way to elim
inate this "wild life" is to give sen
ences that will show that the offi
cers mean business and that "raisin
the roof" in Ekalaka is a mighty ex
pensive proposition.

Up to date one fine has been pai

BUSINESS CHANGE

J. T. Buckingham has disposed o
his interests in the W. H. Peck Co
store, selling to Walter Peck an
Wm. Mowbray who will hereafter con
duct the business. It looks like ol
times to see "Billy" behind the coun
ter once more ready to greet all com
ers and goers. Mr. Buckingham ha
gone to farming on his place a fe
miles northeast of town on the Cam
Crook mail route. He has been en
gaged in the mercantile business her
for the past five years, confine
pretty closely, and thought he neede
a vacation and a more out-of-doo
life.

EQUINOCTIAL STORM

Born—To Mr. and Mrs. W. J. Cran
on Saturday morning, March 21, a son
Born—On Monday, March 23, t
Mr. and Mrs. Wm. M. Evans of Mi
Iron, a son. The child was born a
the home of Mrs. Vedell in Ekalaka
Born—To Mr. and Mrs. C. Enbur
of Ekalaka, on Monday, March 21,
daughter.
Born—To Mr. and Mrs. T. E. Nel
stead on Wednesday, March 25, a
8-pound boy. He bears the name
James Byron.

STOCK HAS NE..ER WINTERED BETT?!

th in Montana never came in

APPENDIX B

No. 157

MARRIAGE LICENSE

STATE OF MONTANA. } ss.

COUNTY OF CARTER.

To Any Person Authorized to Solemnize Marriages—GREETING:

You are hereby authorized to join in lawful wedlock and celebrate within this County the rites and ceremonies of Marriage between

Tom Stone a man whose color is white

whose residence is Piniele, Carter County Montana ; whose age is 34 years; born at

Tennessee on May 28, 1900 MSH yes

and who has not been previously married His father's Christian and Surname—is

R L Stone and Mary Ellen Brantley His mother's Christian and Maiden name was

Maggie Barbree a woman, whose color is white ; whose residence is Charleston Montana ; whose age is 15 years

born at Alathalam, Iowa April 1906 40 yes and whose Wastill to the end

Tom Stone and who has not been previously married. Her father's Christian

and Surname was George Barbree Her mother's

Christian and Maiden name was Edith Higgins

Both parties being legally competent to enter into such contract of marriage. And this shall be your good and sufficient warrant therefor.

Marriage License of Tom and Mary Stone March 22, 1925

259

MARRIAGE CERTIFICATE

STATE OF MONTANA, } ss.
COUNTY OF CARTER.

THIS IS TO CERTIFY, That the undersigned, a ...Justice of the Peace... did, on the twenty ninth day of ...March... A.D. 1925, at ...Ekalaka... in the said County of Carter and State of Montana, join in lawful wedlock ...Tom Stark... and ...Mary Ellen Hawley... with their mutual consent.

IN THE PRESENCE OF

Mrs. Ruth H. Wishart }
William D. Wishart } Witnesses.

Witness my hand this ...22nd... day of ...March... 19.25

W. E. Riel
Officiating.

Filed for Record this ...30th... day of ...March A.D. 19.25

N. R. Campbell
Clerk District Court.

IN WITNESS WHEREOF, I have hereunto set my hand and official seal this twenty ninth day of ...March... A.D. 19.25

N. R. Campbell
Clerk District Court.

By .... , Deputy

260

Works Consulted

"A Matrimonial Tangle," **The Ekalaka Eagle**, March 27, 1925, 1.

Aarstad, Rich, Ellie Arguimbau, Ellen Baumler, Charlene Porsild, and Brian Showers [2009]. **Montana Place Names: From Alzada to Zortman** [Helena, MT: Montana Historical Society].

Austin, Mary Hunter [1906]. **The Flock** [Boston, MA: Houghton Mifflin].

Barbash, Ilisa and Lucien Castaing-Taylor [2010]. "Sweetgrass" PBS Video.

Blair, Neal [April, 1976]. "The Sheepherder's Castle," **Wyoming Wildlife**, 17-22.

Baumler, Ellen [2010]. **Montana Moments: History on the Go** [Helena, Mt: Montana Historical Society].

Brown, Mark [1956]. **Before Barbed Wire** [New York, NY: Henry Holt and Co.].

Clark, Champ [1974]. **The Badlands** [Chicago, Il: Time-Life Books].

Doig, Ivan [1978]. **The House of Sky: Landscapes of a Western Mind** [San Diego, CA: Harcourt Brace and Jovanovich Publishers].

Dunn, Jerry Camarillo, Jr. [1989]. **The Smithsonian Guide to Historic America: Rocky Mountain States** [New York, NY: Workman Publishing].

Egan, Timothy [2006]. **The Worst Hard Time** [Boston, MA: Houghton Mifflin Company].

Ehrlich, Gretel [1985]. **The Solace of Open Spaces** [New York, NY: Penguin Press].

Elder, Dick [2002]. **Which Way is West** [Santa Fe: NM: Sunstone Press].

Fletcher, Robert S. [October, 1930]. "That Hard Winter in Montana:1886-1887," **Agricultural History, 4, 123.**

Fraser, George MacDonald [2008]. **The Steel Bonnets: The Story of the Anglo-Scottish Border Reivers** [New York, NY: Skyhorse Publishing].

Fritz, Harry W. "The Origins of Twenty-First Century Montana," **Montana: The Magazine of Western History**, 42 [Winter, 1992], 77-81.

-------------------, Mary Murphy and Robert R. Swartout, Jr., Eds. [2002]. **Montana Legacy: Essays on History, People and Places.**

Gilfillan, Archer B. [1929/1957]. **Sheep: Life on the South Dakota Range** [Minneapolis, MN: University of Minnesota Press]. See: Minnesota Historical Society Located in Libraries at Augustana College, SD and Radford University, VA.

Golden Anniversary 1910-1960 [1960]. Newell, SD: Newell Historical Society].

Griffith, T.D. and Dustin D. Floyd [July, 2009], 5th ed. **Insider's Guide to South Dakota's Black Hills and Badlands** [Barnes & Noble: Insider's Guide Series].

Harger, Charles Moreau [n.d.]. "Sheep and Shepherds of the West," **The Outlook**, LXXII, 689-693.

Hasselstrom, Linda [2001]. **Feels Like Far: A Rancher's Life on the Great Plains** [Boston, MA: Houghton Mifflin Company.

_____ [1994]. **Roadside History of South Dakota** [Missoula, MT: Mountain Press Publishing Company].

Heinert, Helen [1989]. **Butte County South Dakota** [Dallas, TX: Curtis Media Corporation].

Hennessey, Paul [November/December, 1996]. "A Sheep-Herder Named Gilfillan," **South Dakota Magazine**, 12, No. 4, 32-40.

Higbee, Paul [July/August 2006]. "Sturgis Sheep Dogs," **South Dakota Magazine**, 22, No. 2, 66-67.

Howard, Joseph Kinsey [1943]. **Montana: High, Wide and Handsome** [New Haven, CT: Yale University Press.

Hufstetler, Mark and Michael Beduau [Revised, December 2007]. "South Dakota's Railroads," [Pierre, SD: South Dakota State Historic Preservation Office].

Hunhoff, Bernie [September/October, 2004], "Autumn at Interior," **South Dakota Magazine**, 20, No. 3, 48-51.

_____ , ed. [2005] **South Dakota Photographed** [Yankton, SD: Middle Border Books].

_____ , [July/August, 2009] "Working Dogs," **South Dakota Magazine**, 25, No. 2, 80-84.

Hunkins, Ralph V. and John Clark Lindsey [1932]. **South Dakota: Its Past, Present and Future** [New York, NY: The Macmillan Company].

Huntsinger, Jami [1989]. "Pioneering Black Hills Sheepman: Myron John Smiley," in **South Dakota Leaders: From Pierre Choteau, Jr. to Oscar Howe**, eds. Herbert T. Hoover and Larry J. Zimmerman, [Vermillion, SD: University of South Dakota Press], 261-62, 266-67.

Kildare, Maurice [Fall, 1966]. "Some Men Need It Lonely," **Old West Magazine**, Vol. 3, 57, 73.

Malone, Michael P., Richard B. Roeder, and William Lang [1976]. **Montana: A History of Two Centuries** [Seattle, WA: University of Washington Press].

Mathers, Michael [1975]. **Sheepherders: Men Alone** [Boston, MA: Houghton Mifflin Company].

Mattison, Ray H. [October, 1951]. "The Hard Winter and the Range Cattle Business," **Montana Magazine of History**, Vol. 1.

McLaird, James D. [1989]. "From Bib Overalls to Cowboy Boots: East River/West River Differences in South Dakota," **South Dakota History,** 19, 454-91.

Michelson, Charles [n.d.] "The War for the Range," **Munsey's Magazine,** XXVIII, 380-82.

Mickelson, Connie J. [2007]. "What Factors Led to the Rise and Decline of the Western South Dakota Sheep Industry?" **Mountains of History** [U.S. Department of Education Grant: June Preszler, Project Manager, 1925 Plaza Blvd., Rapid City, SD, Ph. 605-394-1876]

Nelson, Paula M. [1996]. **The Prairie Winnow Out Its Own: The West River Country of South Dakota in the Years of Depression and Dust** [Iowa City, IA: University of Iowa Press].

Niland, John [1994]. **A History of Sheep Raising in the Great Divide Basin of Wyoming: Personal Reflections on the End of an Era** [Cheyenne, WY: Lagumo Corporation].

O'Neal, Bill [1989]. **Cattlemen vs. Sheepherders: Five Decades of Violence in the West, 1880-1920** [Austin,TX: Eakin Press].

Osgood, Ernest S. [1929]. **Day of the Cattleman** [Minneapolis, MN: University of Minnesota Press].

Parker, Ron [1983]. **The Sheep Book** [New York, NY: Ballantine Books].

Perry, Robert [1986]. **Sheep King: The Story of Robert Taylor** [Grand Island, NE: Prairie Pioneer Press].

"Ranchland Economics," [September/October, 2005]. **South Dakota Magazine**, 21, No. 3, 26.

Raymer, Robert G. [1930]. **Montana: The Land and the People**, 3 Vols. [Chicago, IL: The Lewis Publishing Company].

Rollins, George Watson [1979]. **The Struggle of the Cattleman, Sheepman and Settler for Control of Lands in Wyoming** [New York, NY: Arno Press]. [sdexcellence.org/LeifHanson_1988].

Schell, Herbert S. [2004]. **History of South Dakota**, 4th ed. [Pierre, SD: South Dakota State Historical Society Press].

Smiley, A.L. [1963]. "Smiley Sheep Outfit," **Central Meade County 1903-1963** [Stoneville Steadies Association].

Smith, Barbara [1983]. **Beginning Shepherd's Manual** [Ames, IA: Iowa State University Press].

Snow, E.P. [n.d.] "Sheepmen and Cattlemen," **The Outlook**, LXXIII, 839-840.

Spencer, Janet [2005]. **Montana Trivia** [Helena, MT: Riverbend Publishing].

Spritzer, Don [1999]. **Roadside History of Montana** [Missoula, MT: Mountain Press Publishing Company].

Straub, Patrick [2010]. **It Happened in South Dakota: Remarkable Events that Shaped History** [Guilford, CT: Morris Book Publishing, LLC].

Thane, Eric [December, 1953]. "Sheepherder: The West's Lonely Hero," **OutWest Magazine,** 17-22.

Toole, Ross K. [1959]. **Montana: An Uncommon Land** [Norman, OK: University of Oklahoma Press].

_____ and Merrill Burlingame, eds. [1957]. **History of Montana** [New York, NY: The Lewis Publishing Company], 3 vols.

Towne, Charles Wayland and Edward Norris [1945]. **Shepherd's Empire** [Norman, OK: University of Oklahoma Press].

Vestal, Stanley [1945]. **The Missouri** [New York, NY: Farrar and Rinehart].

Webb, Walter Prescott [1931]. **The Great Plains** [Boston, MA: Ginn and Company].

Weidel, Nancy [2001]. **Sheepwagon: Home on the Range** [Glendo, WY: High Plains Press].

Wilson, Gary A. [2003]. Outlaw **Tales of Montana**, 2nd ed. [Guilford, CT: TWODOT].